MAKE MENTORING WORK

SECOND EDITION

PETER WILSON

First edition published in 2012 by Major Street Publishing Pty Ltd
Contact: info@majorstreet.com.au or 0421 707 983
Second edition, fully revised and updated in 2015

National Library of Australia Cataloguing-in-Publication data:

Creator: Wilson, Peter S., author.
Title: Make mentoring work/Peter Wilson.
Edition: 2nd edition fully revised and updated
ISBN: 9780987542991 (paperback)
Notes: Includes bibliographical references and index.
Subjects: Mentoring--Handbooks, manuals, etc.
Mentoring in business--Handbooks, manuals, etc.
Employees--Coaching of--Handbooks, manuals, etc.
Dewey Number: 658.3124

Internal design by Production Works
Original cover design by Glen Edelstein, revised by Patrick John Aldana
patrickaldana.portfoliobox.me
Printed in Australia by Griffin Press

10 9 8 7 6 5 4 3 2 1

ISBN 978-0-9875429-9-1

Peter Wilson is available as consultant and keynote speaker on the subject of mentoring. For further information, visit www.makementoringwork.com.
Or you can contact Peter on peterswilson@gmail.com.

Praise for *Make Mentoring Work*

"Mentoring is an excellent way to give something back. Peter Wilson brings great qualifications to mentoring and his book, *Make Mentoring Work*, is a credible and comprehensive guide to a special skill."

The Hon. John Howard OM AC

"The mentors in my life have made inseparable differences in my professional success. *Make Mentoring Work* is a must-read for people who want to succeed."

Li Cunxin, Artistic Director, Queensland Ballet Company, and author of *Mao's Last Dancer*

"Everyone needs mentors, especially those from disadvantaged minorities and women trying to get ahead... Peter Wilson suggests approaches that work and those that don't. At stake is nothing less than the quality of future leaders in our community. So this is an important book for shaping our future."

The Hon. Michael Kirby, AC, CMG, Former Justice of the High Court of Australia

"I have never met a successful person who hasn't had mentors. Mentoring transfers wisdom, judgment, life's hard-won lessons. Peter Wilson's new book is a gem on this subject."

John Bertrand AM, Chairman, Sport Australia Hall of Fame; skipper of Australia II in 1983

"Peter Wilson, one of Australia's leading Human Resource practitioners, has written a most illuminating, experience-based analysis that fills a significant gap in the literature about leadership and its development through mentoring."

Professor Allan Fels AO, former Dean, The Australia and New Zealand School of Government (ANZSOG)

"It is a book that deserves the widest possible readership, particularly by those entering any level of management responsibility."

Major General Michael Jeffery, AC, AO(Mil), CVO, MC (Ret'd)
Governor-General Australia 2003-2008

"Peter Wilson has written a well-researched tome on mentoring, surveying various theories and writings on the subject while relating these to Australians from all walks of life."

Mike Fitzpatrick, Chairman, AFL

"The benefits that flow from a mentoring relationship that works are immense. *Make Mentoring Work* captures diversity and mentoring for a woman's career exceedingly well."

Catherine Burn, Deputy Commissioner, NSW Police

"Peter Wilson has filled a major gap in our literature with a quite distinctive and excellent contribution that not only defines best mentoring practice for those seeking to create and manage their own mentoring schemes, but also has major appeal for individuals who want some inspiring ideas on how to get the best out of their own mentoring relationships."

The Hon. Peter Reith Commonwealth Minister for Workplace Relations 1996-2001, and Minister for Defence, 2001-2003

"An excellent book on mentoring in a contemporary context. It includes good advice on how women can use mentors to assist them advance their careers."

Elizabeth Broderick, Sex Discrimination Commissioner

For two great children,
Emily and Alex, in whose future hopes,
my heart also beats.

About the Author

PETER WILSON AM is the National President (Chairman) of the Australian Human Resources Institute Limited (AHRI), Australia's leading professional HR association with 20,000 members. He was recently elected as Secretary-General of the World Federation of People Management Associations, the peak world body for the human resources practitioners covering 700,000 professionals in 95 countries.

Peter is also Chairman of Yarra Valley Water Ltd, a Director of the Vincent Fairfax Ethics in Leadership Foundation, and immediate past Chairman of Vision Super and now Chair of its Audit and Risk Committee. He directed the Business Council of Australia's mentoring program for senior executive women in ASX-listed companies during 2010 and 2011 and is the Mentor's Adviser in programs for Australia's Federal and Victorian Parliamentarians. He served as a member of the Advisory Council for the *Harvard Business Review* from 2012 to 2015.

From 2008 to 2010, Peter held a Research Fellowship role under the Prime Minister's Australia–China Climate Change Partnership and advised the Energy Research Institute of Beijing on reducing carbon emissions from the country's coal, power and gas industries.

In 2014, Peter Wilson delivered the 22nd annual Kingsley Laffer Memorial lecture at Sydney University, which is the principal national lecture on industrial relations in Australia, and followed earlier Kingsley Laffer Orations by Prime Ministers Bob Hawke and Julia Gillard, as well as High Court Judge, Michael Kirby.

Peter's executive career spanned 35 years of senior executive roles in the Commonwealth and Victorian Treasuries, Amcor and the ANZ Banking Group. He was CEO of one of Australia's largest private electricity and gas companies, Energy 21, during the 1990s. He was Chairman of Commonwealth Safety Rehabilitation and Compensation Commission; a Director and Chairman of the Melbourne Tigers Basketball Club; Director and Finance Committee Chairman of the 1997 World Basketball Championships; a Director of Dalgety Farmers Ltd and a Member of the Board of Commissioners at the State Electricity Commission of Victoria.

Peter's qualifications are B Comm (Hons), MA (Hons) University of Melbourne and he is a Fellow of the Certified Practicing Accountants (CPAs), the Australian Institute of Company Directors (Company Directors) and the AHRI. He is an alumni member of the Wharton Business School at the University of Pennsylvania and has completed senior executive programs in business strategy and leadership at the London Business School, the Ross School of Business at the University of Michigan, and at INSEAD in Fontainebleu, France.

In April 2003, Peter was awarded the Centenary Medal and in January 2005 he was made a Member of the Order of Australia (AM), for services to workplace safety and relations and community service.

He lives in Melbourne, with his two adult children somewhere nearby most of the time.

Contents

Foreword by Dave Ulrich

Mentoring Messages

Whenever, I mention "mentors" in a workshop, a few participants' eyes glaze over as they reflect on the important guides who shaped them. Most successful leaders owe at least some of their success to wise mentors who shepherded them through personal and professional mazes. Each mentor story captures the essence of nurturing relationships.

I was a young college student intent on law school. I was encouraged to take a course in a new subject called 'Organisational Behaviour' (OB) taught by Professor Bonner Ritchie whom I was told was a very innovative teacher. In only a few class sessions, Bonner captured my imagination. He had no formal assignments and told us to demonstrate to him what we learned about how organisations worked. His lectures taught us the impact of organisations in our lives and the methods to diagnose and upgrade organisations. He challenged us to explore deeply our organisation experiences. My first of a dozen papers for his class was "Beowulf: The Ideal Organisation Man". My English professor thought I was crazy and never understood the logic of this paper; but Bonner encouraged me. Bonner taught and prodded me that organisations can be a force for good and reminded me to do good as I go about my doing. Later that semester, when I told my parents I was changing my professional focus to OB they were excited I would become a doctor. Decades later, I am still seeking those organisation insights that change how people and organisations think and act. In the ensuing 30 years, Bonner has continued to be a true mentor. We don't meet all that often, but when we do, he inspires and challenges me. He asks me if I am doing the good in the world that I intended when we first met. He listens to what I am learning, shares my enthusiasm for new ideas, and pushes me to new insights. He shares what he is learning and asks my opinion. I have had the privilege of many mentors who have positively influenced me, but Bonner was probably the first and foremost.

While most of us have similar experiences, it is refreshing to know that these memorable people are not random. There are guidelines for the guides; mentor messages that mentors and mentees can master to better serve each other.

Peter Wilson's book captures both the emotion and formalisation of the mentoring process. He codifies what it means to be a mentor, how to choose a mentor, how to be mentored and how to institutionalise mentoring. Rather than remain an isolated act of personal goodwill, mentoring can be a systematic organisational process. As Peter points out, today's mentoring can be a significant contributor to tomorrow's leaders.

Make Mentoring Work answers some of the questions we often hear when we discuss mentoring.

1. How is mentoring different from coaching?

While mentoring has begun to emerge as a personal development tool, coaching has already become institutionalised. Both coaches and mentors encourage reflection to help individuals grow and change based on trusting relationships between two parties. So, how are they different? Let me offer some differences that may help coaching and mentoring better complement each other.

	Coaching	**Mentoring**
Time frame	Short term	Long term
Outcomes	Personal improvement on the job through behaviour change or delivering results	Personal insights about career choices and organisational settings

	Coaching	Mentoring
Key success factor	Diagnostic about specific behaviours that lead to results	Relationship based on shared values
Contribution	Problem solving	Personal advice
Metaphors	Sports	Parenting/teaching
Intervention	Directive intervention to correct weaknesses	Consensual intervention to nurture the person
Focus	Performance improvement	Individual growth
Conversations	About roles, responsibilities, and expectations	About what you have been thinking about

Mentoring matters in today's organisations because the wisdom of the elders can help the next generation navigate personal and professional choices that help them succeed quickly. With the pending exit of baby boomers from the work force, the organisational baton is passed on and without mentoring some of the lessons learned may have to be re-learned.

2. What does it take to be a good mentor?

As people age, they enter a stage where they begin to worry about guiding the next generation. As baby boomers accept the responsibilities and opportunities of becoming mentors, they work to pass on their insights to the next generation.

Peter does a marvellous job of laying out the qualities of a good mentor who becomes a combination parent, teacher and spiritual adviser. If someone opts to become a mentor, they need to learn to care passionately about those they mentor at a personal level, to share common values with them, to find their personal meaning in the progress of those they mentor, and to give of themselves. Mentors observe carefully and share concrete data very wisely. They probe outside-the-box ideas and behaviours. They both confront and cuddle when required. As one wise mentor said, “I must decrease so he can increase.” Mentors delight in the progress of those they mentor.

Peter’s work shows us mentors at work in business, government, education and professional organisations. These rich examples help those of us who yearn to mentor learn the skills of doing so.

3. How does one choose to be mentored?

In the past, mentoring was often a one-on-one relationship. In today’s complex world, network mentoring is much more likely to occur. I wrote of my relationship with Bonner Ritchie who has continued to advise me about thinking broadly. But, I also have been privileged to have other mentors who have helped me navigate organisations where I work and live. C.K. Prahalad, Ed Lawler, and Steve Kerr have shown me how to craft ideas with impact. Bill Ouchi and Wayne Brockbank taught me about working with clients and presenting ideas. Mike Volkema gave me insights on how to contribute as a board member. Thom Nielson, Byron Thomas and Helen Bauss helped me learn how to lead in a church setting. Les Woolsey took time to teach me how to invest in real estate. I am grateful for a network of mentors who took time to invest in my development.

Mentees who choose to be mentored need to examine the separate organisations where they work, to identify people who share their values and who have qualities they admire, to get to know these people, and to gently invite them to become part of their mentor network.

Mentors also realise that they can receive reverse-mentoring, where those who are younger introduce them to an increasingly distant and alien next generation world. My network of reverse-mentors includes students I have worked with who teach me as much as I teach them and a group of 16 year olds whom I teach weekly in Sunday School who are willing to teach me by sharing their hopes with me.

4. How can one be a good mentee?

Mentees need to be open to learning. They need to be willing to look outside themselves and their current environment for new opportunities. They need to take personal and professional risks and be resilient when things don't work. They need to run boldly into mistakes and humbly accept successes. They need to pay homage to their mentors to recognise the counsel they have received. They need to take personal ownership for adapting counsel to their situation.

Peter's insights on accepting mentorship will help those who want to learn and grow do so in a more structured way.

5. How can the mentoring process be scaled and institutionalised?

Throughout the book, Peter highlights the formalisation of informal mentoring. At times this means senior leaders attending to the next generation of leaders within the company. I have seen companies where high potential employees are matched (not assigned) to senior leaders not in their formal chain of command. These senior leaders mentor these key employees with monthly or quarterly interactions designed to support and inform. These organisation programs enable targeted employees to access at least two senior leaders (their hierarchical boss and their mentor) who can help them succeed in the company.

Formal mentoring may also occur across companies as professional groups or trade associations can facilitate peer mentoring. These networked groups offer social, emotional and intellectual support for budding professionals.

Formal mentoring may also occur with an aging workforce as retirees become mentors to their successors. A very public example is Lee Kuan Yew the first Prime Minister of Singapore for over 30 years. Upon his retirement as Minister, he formally held the title and cabinet role of "Minister Mentor" from 2004 to 2011. His challenge was to offer political and personal advice so that knowledge transferred across generations.

These are five questions to which I found answers in Peter's marvellous work. Others will find in this book better ways to institutionalise mentoring programs, to integrate mentoring with other HR practices, to become a leader-mentor and to adapt mentoring to others.

As Bonner continually asks me, "Are you doing the good you intended to do when you began your career?" I can share that Peter has done good works with his book.

Dave Ulrich
Professor of Business, Ross School of Business,
University of Michigan; Co-founder and partner, RBL Group

INTRODUCTION

"In Homer's 'Odyssey',
Odysseus had to leave home
for ten years to fight the Trojan Wars
and he needed someone very trustworthy
to look after his son Telemachus
and prepare him to be king.
He entrusted this most sensitive role
to his closest friend, Mentor."

Every generation thinks it's the hardest working in the history of mankind, and usually for good reason. The current generation, however, wins this prize hands down.

The latest evidence of workplace research – from hours worked to mental health statistics, to the nature and extent of relentless pressures on the job – shows the current working generation is working harder than any prior counterparts in history. Life at work has never been tougher. For many it is a continuously grinding 24 x 7 x 365 experience, where there is no convenient time to fall asleep, except when you have to or just do. Even then those happy little technological devices give you no peace, continuing to beep away impatiently under your pillow during the night.

With globalisation of business into the new millennium, world trade to domestic production and income ratios have never been higher. The strength of interconnections between national economies is now irreversible, notwithstanding the daily frustrations caused by all that to our political masters. Economic viruses like the 2007-08 global financial crisis, or the 2011-15 European credit risk syndrome can spread throughout the world faster than the speed of light, thanks to the power of communication and the huge economic bandwidths connecting world financial, product and service markets. Moreover, businesses and products now rise like the phoenix, and yet also fall back into the ashes, at breath-taking speed. As a 15-year-old company, Enron's share price was worth $90 in mid-2000. By October 2001 that price had fallen to $1, as $11 billion of Enron's shareholder value disappeared in a puff of smoke. This took the $63 billion company into bankruptcy the following year – the largest US corporate collapse in history. For comparison purposes, the Commonwealth Bank of Australia is a 100-year-old company worth about $ US100 billion in 2015. Facebook is an 11-year-old company that is estimated to be worth about twice as much. Mark Zuckerberg, a struggling Harvard student who dropped out in 2004, owns just less than 20% of it. When the late Steve Jobs took over as CEO of Apple in 1995, having been sacked from the same job a decade earlier, its share price was $5, and this company was smaller than the 150th largest company in Australia today. Early in 2015, and within six months of Jobs' death, the company was valued at over $600 billion, making it the world's largest corporation, passing ExxonMobil. The successful introductions of iMac, iPod, iTunes, iBooks, iPhone, iPad and iCloud had made their mark, as had Jobs' succession plans for leadership at Apple.

Something Old is New Again

Work patterns and behaviours have had to respond rapidly to the speed of global hyper-competition. So have the ways people learn about their job, what to do at work, and more importantly how to cope with the very high stress levels today. Most of us can now do our job 'anywhere, anytime, any WiFi'. Of almost counter-intuitive significance in this dramatically different set of paradigms for doing business, an old form of learning is being reinvented for its contemporary value. Something old is indeed new again. The importance and value of mentoring has been rediscovered. So has its relationship to how workers can manage this brave new iWorld of global business, with rapid transfers of information and economic shocks.

Although mentoring has existed for hundreds of years, recent research on workplace learning by Ulrich (2011) and Sweetman, Ulrich and Smallwood (2012) shows that in future 50% of a person's career learning will come from on the job experience; 30% from mentoring; with 20% coming didactically (from reading, downloads and personal study). Fewer than ten years earlier that figure for mentoring was assessed by the Center for Creative Leadership in the United States to be much less – 70% of learning came from 'doing' on the job; 20% from mentoring; and 10% didactically. The 70/20/10 of workplace learning had moved to 50/30/20, with mentoring firmly ensconced as number 2. The enormous growth of globalisation and the ease of accessing technical or factual information in this millennium, have together caused a sharp drop in our traditional reliance on 'learning by doing on the job'. Research underpinning the White Paper of the Australian Human Resources Institute (AHRI) on the Future of Work in 2020 demonstrated current generations, particularly younger adults, can and do learn many things by searching the web and downloading as needed (see Wilson 2010). Learning speed has now become a material differentiator of the economic 'quick and the dead'. Notwithstanding that, mentoring has become the great connector between the data available from online learning media and our knowledge gained from work practices.

As Homer described, and Odysseus well understood, mentoring

adds value because it has a core focus on developing a person's longer-term career potential. This 'old is new again' discipline and its applications have found an important new place within our lexicon of learning for a leadership career in business, government, professional sports and community organisations.

Mentoring vs Coaching

The skills for mentoring are subtle and unique. They are often confused with those of coaching, which is more about performance in one's current job. Pure coaching focuses on more directive interventions to correct perceived weaknesses or performance gaps at work today. Mentoring is not about that – it involves a total interest by the mentor to support and advise on the continued growth of the career and life of the mentee. Sometimes the personalities involved can confuse this distinction. For example, in professional sport, élite athletes will often cite their best mentor to have been a former coach – a person who played both roles for them. In politics and also business, however, the best mentors are usually identified as persons separated from the workplace. The reason for this is simple – there are often inherently conflicted interests between what a true mentor needs to be, and the complex and dynamic interpersonal relationships found at work, where peers are in heavy competition with each other for a limited number of career roles. In the police and armed services, true mentoring is usually hardwired within the internal leadership development philosophies, because the bonds of common experience are often necessary to defeat the common enemy. Nevertheless, having external mentors in these arenas can be highly valuable too. In this latter case, it's usually a mixture of both, not either.

Some confuse mentoring with having positive leadership role models. A role model is important to developing one's own leadership style, but by definition a mentor is someone who takes a direct personal interest in your growth as an individual, and also your career choices. It is someone with whom you have an intimate relationship based on deep personal trust, and not a leader admired from afar. Another point of confusion can be the relationship between mentoring and sponsorship. A sponsor is an influential person who can use his or her power to impact on a third-person's growth or career. This can be done by facilitating connections to other powerful figures, or opening up new opportunities not otherwise accessible. While mentors can be sponsors, that is not their prime role. Some mentees mistakenly believe that sponsorship will automatically flow from the relationship developed with a mentor.

The Foundations of Mentoring

True mentoring defines itself through an experienced professional or 'elder' from that business or profession taking the role of mentor (or confidential adviser) and engaging in conversations with an emerging professional known as the mentee (or protégé). Mentoring is more of a carefully-honed art and craft than it is a science and its essence is drawn from any or all of three underpinnings or rationales:

- Socratean philosophy
- Quasi-parental behaviour
- Spiritual connections.

The best mindset for any mentor to adopt comes from the first rationale, that the role of mentor is similar to that of a great philosopher – a teacher such as Socrates. Mentors meet informally with mentees in order to explore challenges, dilemmas and managing more complex business and peer relationships, through reviewing parallel experiences of a wiser and more experienced elder – the mentor.

A key for success as a mentor can also come from adopting the role of a parental surrogate who is perhaps dealing with a restive teenager. The mentee will be most responsive to positive suggestions of options they could use if they felt inspired to make changes for the better from within themselves.

For some people, mentoring will provide a spiritual connection between a belief in their God and a man's life. In these situations, a mentor is more like a disciple or a prophet who is seen to have a greater connection to God's ways than the protégé.

The Governor-General of Australia from 2003 to 2008, and former Commander of the SAS regiment Michael Jeffery, has seen action in the Malaya conflict and Vietnam War, and regards mentoring as having philosophical, parental and spiritual foundations. The last imperative reflects his own deeply-held Christian beliefs. When I asked him about the reasons for a spiritual connection to his mentoring, Michael replied:

> "I have never met an atheist in a foxhole."

On further enquiry as to what he meant by this, he said:

> "I have encountered a number of men about to die in the field of battle. At this final point in their lives, they generally cry out for two things – their mother, and their God. As a society we would function a lot better if people came to terms with the second of these deeply-held sentiments much earlier in their lives."

Michael believes the fundamental spiritual beliefs that most people have are being suppressed and intimidated by a world of increasing political correctness.

Another perspective on the spiritual and also the parental side of mentoring, comes from former Prime Minister of Australia, Bob Hawke:

> "Together, my mother Edith Emily and my father Clement Arthur (Clem) were two of the most critical mentors in my life. Clem was

> also a member of the clergy, and whilst my own beliefs in Christianity changed later in my adult life, I always remembered and followed my father's statement to me that – 'if you believe in the fatherhood of God, you must necessarily believe in the brotherhood of man'.
>
> That gave me four critical reckoning points on my career compass. First, I believed a working Australian had every right to want to provide adequately for his or her family, and to see growth in their real wages from their own efforts over time. Second, a businessman had every right to expect to make the best profit he could in return for putting his capital at risk. Third, any citizen who fell on hard times should expect some reasonable support from a society that saw itself as both humane and compassionate. Finally, my parents Clem and Edith encouraged me to always be absolutely honest in my dealings with all people I encountered. These four beliefs defined not only the nature of my life, but also what I did when the opportunity came to be Prime Minister of this great country."

Another great mentor interviewed for this book has a different but complementary take on spirituality in mentoring. Colin Carter is a very successful business strategist and company director who serves on the board of the AFL Commission, SEEK and Wesfarmers, and is also President of the Geelong Football Club. According to Colin:

> "Being involved in different places has helped me to be useful as a mentor. For example, I have been able to bring the principles of working in a partnership into my church life, where hierarchy can become too important. And I have been able to take the principles of servant-leadership and pastoral care back into the world of business leaders."

For Australia's Indigenous people, it's also about all three sets of principles, but they are seen as being indivisible – the elder philosopher, quasi-parental and spiritual behaviours provide lessons to the people of our Indigenous nations that are seamlessly integrated. As Jason Mifsud, Head of Diversity for the Australian Football League (AFL), states:

> "That's a key difference with western civilisations – you split them up. For Indigenous Australians, they are all one and the same."

To many others the perceived value of mentoring may have only one or two of these features. As we shall see, all combinations can be very powerful, depending on the person, and their needs and creeds.

In successful mentoring relationships, mentees will often say their principal learnings have come from putting themselves in the mentor's shoes. Listening to how the challenges of the mentee would have been handled at a similar stage in the mentor's own working life is hugely powerful. Li CunXin, author of the best-selling autobiography *Mao's Last Dancer*, eloquently expressed this, but with a subtle distinction which mentees only learn as they move forward in their lives and careers:

> "A good mentor helps you to walk in your own shoes, even if you start out just wanting to walk in theirs."

Many Mentors for the Modern Workforce

The demanding diversity of their future careers indicates tomorrow's leaders will need to acquire a number of mentors during their working lifetime. The most astute mentees will engage with various of these persons longer term, maintaining a continuing network of advice and influence. Notwithstanding that need, the skills to maximise the value of mentoring can be generalised and employed across a broad range of different learning relationships, careers and life experiences. That is what this book is about.

While it is usual for mentors to be a generation in age away from their mentees, peer mentoring is also important. Having close colleagues similar to you in age and interests, but with different skills and career experiences, can be an important source for complementary learning. Peers can also share contemporary values that provide a different bond of strength in a mentoring relationship. In fact, the key for emerging young leaders is to think about having 'One Career, Many Mentors'. Always aspire to find the best person available relative to the immediate challenges you face. A person who is truly a great mentor can take many forms and will be best assessed from the career aspirations and needs that you have at a point in time. By its very nature, the value of some mentors will be time-dated too. How you manage this disconnection respectfully can be a challenge.

The essential value from mentoring comes from the fact that reading and 'doing' on the job won't be enough to equip a modern worker or emerging leader with sufficient knowledge to understand and acquire skills and experiences in:

- Handling complex personalities and human relationships
- Managing stakeholders, power structures and building networks
- Managing strategic, economic and social risk, uncertainty and ambiguity
- Resolving challenging, ethical and moral dilemmas emerging from the rapid fusion of different national cultures or economic imperatives into the same time zone
- Finding new pathways to greater innovation and inventiveness as a leader.

Research for this book has established that these five subjects are the prime matters discussed within modern mentoring relationships. As we know from the annals of Homer's *The Odyssey*, Mentor came to us from Greek mythology and literature. In fact, the Greeks had a lot of useful and enduring contributions to make on the subject of leadership.

As well as Mentor, the Greeks gave us many of the caricatures we meet in our workplaces every day. In particular, they were kind enough to introduce us to the following evergreen characters:

- *Nemesis* – who is always there to trip us up
- *Narcissus* – that reasonably handsome type who is truly, madly, deeply in love with him or herself, but who believes that teamwork without an "I" in it is an oxymoron
- *Echo* – the sycophantic muse of Narcissus, who was ultimately rejected by him to become a lone voice in the wilderness, distracting others every day with false sounds from uncertain directions; that quintessential time-waster and sad lost soul, aimlessly wandering about amongst us
- *Hubris* – the person who is completely and absolutely full of it
- *Achilles* – the self-styled Superman (shame about the fabulously flawed heel)
- *Aphrodite and Adonis* – those dainty beauties, usually unwilling to go outside if it means getting their hair wet. (In fact, it can seem their abiding aim is never to have a hair out of place, and they can become instant drama queens if there is.)
- *Hades* – constantly lurking in the underworld (a bad mother with an evil plan)
- *Chaos* – always keen to produce lots of noise and confusion, but not too much positive action
- *Calypso, Dionysus and Circe* – dangerous romantics and assorted party-goers, whose regular celebrations can seem out of place with robust method and good order in the workplace. Lots of fun to be with after hours, but great distracters on the job
- *Psyche* – that smarty-pants always trying to out-think the rest of us

- *Pandora* – and her mysterious box – why is there always someone milling around the workplace, trying to make everything so frigging complicated?
- *Medusa* – that walking–talking head of snakes, always trying to turn the rest of us into stone with looks that kill.

I have met all of these people in every organisation in which I have ever worked. A new job with a fresh employer never provided me with an escape from any of these characters. They followed me everywhere. They will always be there to greet you on arrival at your new job and then later reappear to terrorise you in your splendid new working pastures. Often, the stereotype you encounter is the dark side of an otherwise fairly normal person who has a particular character trait that happens to irritate you excessively. The challenge is then really to find ways to see past their faults, and also to bring out the best in them, without driving yourself to distraction in the process. You will be the better leader from succeeding at this challenge too.

A mentor can help you deal with all these people. It would be nice if the all-powerful God-figure in our workplace, Zeus, would be there to help too – but he or she is always far too busy with bigger problems than ours. Zeus doesn't like to be seen to play favourites in any event. That leaves Mentor as the one person who can help. The modern equivalents of the teacher of Telemachus can assist you to deal with these dark characters in your everyday (working) life.

In the mentoring programs reviewed throughout this book, mentees have often mentioned being confronted by a 'Nemesis'; not knowing when to be a 'voice'; how to confront negative forms of 'power' (i.e. most of the above characters from Greek mythology); and learning strategies and techniques to employ 'power' positively themselves. Talking with an expert mentor about how that person handled parallel experiences and challenges can help – and often no other form of learning will. The ancient Greeks understood that. The western world is now rediscovering the full measure of the value of mentoring.

Mentoring in the New Generation Workforce

Another reason behind the growing practice of mentoring is the current 'war for talent'. Labour turnover rates in Australian business now average nearly 20%, compared to rates of 2% to 5% in the 1980s. That means workers are only likely to stay with the same employer for about five years. AHRI's research (see Wilson 2010) has tested these trends and believes them to be durable, so in future workers are likely to have between nine or ten different employers over their career. The traditional post-war notion of staying with the one organisation during your working life no longer exists. Mentors can help a person make their longer-term career choices and manage connections in ways that weren't needed in past working lifetimes that spanned one or two employers only.

Furthermore Wilson (2010 and 2014) researched the psychology of younger people and reported that their mental wiring is the same as it's always been for human beings, but with some subtle differentiators:

- Gen Ys like their technological devices
- They have more attitude when dealing with their elders
- They feel significantly let down by failures in ethical business leadership – from the tech wreck in year 2000 to the behaviour of bankers and world business leaders during the 2007 global financial crisis
- They are looking to work for employers who are responsible members of their community

- They genuinely value and seek positive mentoring experiences to help navigate their careers and lives in an increasingly complex and also threatening world.

Another reason for this desire by younger workers to seek out mentors is the fact that very many workplace processes and job patterns have been carefully and closely restructured and re-scripted by armies of consultants engaged by organisations over the last 20+ years. The inheritance of this rigorous work, combined with the new focus of workplace actions and performance based on powerful computing software capability, has meant that innovative divergences away from established ways of doing things are often neither expected nor tolerated. Furthermore, there is much greater turnover at the top of organisations these days. Executives will often feel they are being put through an involuntary career change instigated by those who know a lot more about what they don't like and don't know, than what they do. Such leaders are inherently dangerous to be around. Accordingly, workers and leaders do feel under siege at times today, and seek an independent elder to vent with about "what's going on around here, and what does it all mean for me?"

So mentoring possesses both a defensive and a positive contemporary value to organisations. Defensive in the sense that it can play a role in enhancing engagement and also reducing labour turnover, with its subsequent loss of significant investment made in a person's skills and capabilities. Positive in the sense that it is now a major medium for building human assets and capabilities into the intellectual and leadership capital by which organisations can strive, thrive and indeed survive during the toughest period of global competition that the world has ever seen. Today's top workers are looking for an employer prepared to invest in their skill levels and career learnings. So the demands for mentoring are here, and they are not going anywhere else soon.

The supply of good quality mentors is increasing. Daniel Levinson and Erik Erikson have each written respectively in *The Seasons of a Man's Life* and *The Life Cycle Completed*, about how psychological preferences change with increasing age. Their focus has been not only on the adolescent identity crisis, but also on explaining its context through the 'Seven Ages of Man'. In particular, Levinson states that, at about the age of 42 years, a person's horizon starts to span outwards. The onset of this 'social age' increases the focus on a person's family and community. Erikson further advises that a person's prime psychosocial drivers in this period are 'care' and 'wisdom' (Erikson 1997, P32). Accordingly, the natural desire to mentor others increases significantly. The current bi-modal humps in the age pyramid show that we are growing old rapidly, but also underpin other medical evidence that continued mental and physical engagement are the keys to better health and longevity. In Australia at present, approximately 45% of Australians are over the age of 42 and this percentage will increase to 50% by 2020. 13% are over the age of 65 and this will rise to 20% by 2030. So the supply of older but increasingly healthier cohorts of people who are content within themselves and readily able and willing to mentor and support younger generations is continuing to rise. In business, sports, politics and organisations engaged in public life and the community, the rise of formal mentoring programs is providing a market for this much sought-after human connection.

As Levinson (1978, P221) states:

> "He ('man') has more inner freedom to be himself and is less driven by tribal requirements. This does not mean, however, that it is time at 40 or 50 to withdraw from involvement and responsibility in society. He has major contributions to offer as father, grandfather, son, brother, husband, lover, friend, mentor ... and appreciator of the human heritage. These contributions constitute his legacy."

Why Mentoring? Why Now?

Why mentoring has grown so rapidly in its importance and presence as a formal discipline within modern leadership development:

1. The stress, pace and greater interconnections of world business and social exchanges are producing a lot more relationship, situational and ethical challenges. These are best addressed through an interface with an experienced elder who has 'been there and done that' before.
2. The evolution of post-war western leadership approaches (discussed in Chapter Five) has drawn top executives towards a stronger values-based leadership philosophy to counter the effectiveness of tougher global competition coming from the east with their more co-operative work circles, and the pivotal role played by GuanXi, or an eastern leader's 'powerful connections'.
3. The reaching of limits through organisational use of executive coaches, many of whom are long-term consultants with limited experience in advanced or complex business issues themselves. Emerging top executives have voted with their feet that they want to speak to someone who has actually 'been there and done it' and to discuss and assess their own challenges with someone they respect, within a more informal and flexible work setting.
4. A rediscovery that managing complex human relationships in work and life is still the same as it has always been, and certainly back to the time the Greeks wrote about them. Their solution was eternal – find a good mentor who can talk through the problems with you, reinforce your confidence and who also offers an ability to explore new solutions to your intractable challenges.
5. The breakup and distribution of global work patterns and the higher turnover in jobs, endless restructurings and employer sources, has meant the value of having access to wiser counsel outside your workplace has grown significantly. Older mentors,

and also trusted peers who take a personal interest in you and your career, offer more durable modern forms of pastoral care that we all need.

6. The demands of the younger generation, combined with employer of choice research, show our future top talent expect mentoring to be part of their preferred organisational culture, and something that will help them perform at their best and also develop their careers further.
7. The ageing of the population has seen 45% of Australians rise above the age of 42, to an age at which the desire to mentor becomes strong. So the supply of mentors with positive inclinations to both help and advise has increased at a time when the demand for them has also increased.

The arguments for a spirited renewal of mentoring have been well established in the last few years, and rapidly so. Many corporations are still struggling to put effective mentoring arrangements and programs in place. In part, that reflects the views of many older generation leaders that mentoring need only be a casual game of 'pick-up in your own choice of career expert', which is what they themselves did at equivalent stages of their own careers, 10 or more years ago. In the past, mentoring was mainly done on an informal basis. But as the book demonstrates, formal business and community mentoring programs are springing up all over the place. Unfortunately some of the internal business mentoring activities seem to be little more than 'coffee mentoring', designed primarily to maintain a leadership narcissus syndrome, or to fortify a sense of political correctness at the top of an organisation. Other programs are hardwired to develop learning, support an individual during tough times or a crisis, to strengthen skills of self-reliance and to sponsor candidates to take their next step up in whatever their relevant field of endeavour.

The best mentoring programs are constantly re-evaluating themselves to make sure they continue to improve (as we discover in Chapter Twelve).

About this Book

Make Mentoring Work is designed to assist a more proactive response to both the value of mentoring and the best structures in which to conduct it. The rationale and demand for this discipline to take prime position within organisational and workplace learning have been established convincingly and are expected by a new generation of emerging leaders. But it's a learning technique that can also be mishandled and subverted either through its management or a failure to establish targeted outcomes which are both sensible and achievable.

This book is written for two distinct groups of people with a strong interest in mentoring.

- First there are those who are about to become involved in a formal mentoring program as a participant or organiser, and there are plenty of tips and suggestions as to what they might do in their prospective roles as mentor, mentee, or program manager.
- Second, it is also written for those who are looking to 'self-start' with their own mentoring relationship, but outside a formal mentoring program structure.

Those in this second group will either be trying to find a mentor for themselves, or will be thinking about what they should do if they are asked to become one, following an approach from a new protégé. The 90 Australian leaders interviewed for this book all had mentors whom they had sought out by themselves during their lives, and mostly from a cold start. It can be done, and most mentees will be pleasantly surprised by the generosity of spirit shown from potential mentors, all of whom can be very busy people in their own right, but who will be prepared to find the time to help (for the reasons Levinson has just described).

The book is divided into four parts. Part I introduces mentoring and examines three sectors – business, the police and the public services – where mentoring schemes are in place and are growing and improving.

Part II reviews post-war leadership trends and where mentoring fits in this context. It sets out some of the key skills and needs of successful mentoring including:

- How the mentor and mentee should best prepare themselves
- How to adopt attitudes and styles that will maximise the potential of their relationship
- How best to manage the process of the mutual commitment needed to ensure positive progress is made.

There is an inevitable list of 'dos', 'don'ts' and pitfalls for both parties. This is also a robust menu built up from experiences and observations of hundreds of mentoring connections.

Part III profiles just how powerful mentoring can be at countering diversity challenges – cross-culturally and cross-gender. Several high profile senior mentoring schemes and experiences are documented.

Part IV outlines the impact eight mentors had in my own life, and their advice that still resonates clearly in my mind and forms the compass I use to move ahead in each day of my work and life.

Peter Wilson
Melbourne, April 2015

PART I
MODERN-DAY
MENTORING

1

MENTORING – AN ART, FIRST AND FOREMOST

Mentoring is a well-honed art and craft, and not a science. It is an intergenerational learning experience between two people in an environment that is private and trusting, and which engenders confidence for the big issues to be opened up, addressed and discussed. Mentoring is not, however, a forensic examination of a person's current performance gaps, with an accompanying requirement for hyper-intensive business fitness programs, designed to bring their subjects into superior shape in double-quick time.

Many organisations have encountered stop–start experiences with mentoring. There are some important preconditions and personal attributes required to achieve the right kick-off in a mentoring relationship. Mentors need to have a strong ethical and moral compass; they need to demonstrate a willingness to get to know the person first; clear signals need to be sent to the mentee that they are worthwhile and valued as individuals. Mentors need to telegraph that their purpose is to give unconditional positive support and encouragement to help push back boundaries inhibiting their mentee's development. Without this open mindset by the mentor, a learning relationship with a new mentee won't go very far. If these attributes are missing, the experience will be flawed and terminal.

Mentoring can also be described as a collaborative learning relationship between two or more persons who share a mutual responsibility to help the mentee define and achieve clear and mutually-defined work, learning and career goals. Further, it is a self-directed learning relationship that can be structured on a formal or informal basis. Mentoring requires a commitment of the parties to meet face-to-face every four to six weeks on average – not to believe that occasional telephone calls, emails and blogs are an acceptable substitute. They aren't, and the relationship will fail without the discipline and commitment by both sides to meet through regular face-to-face time. As one of the world's most famous CEOs, the late Steve Jobs of Apple Inc., said in 2011 to his biographer Walter Isaacson (2012, P100):

> "There's a temptation in our networked age to think that ideas can be developed by email and iChat. That's crazy. Creativity comes from spontaneous meetings, from random discussions. You run into someone, you ask them what they are doing, you say 'Wow' and soon you're cooking up all sorts of ideas."

In very recent times, 'mixed media' mentoring is having an increasing amount of success. By this is meant a situation where the prime form of contact is a face-to-face meeting, but with follow-up and reflection coming through an email where a question or a thought is put on notice by one party to the other, for the next encounter. The essential point is that the email is a subordinate, but complementary, form of communication to the face-to-face exchanges. The former should never take over from the latter, but it can be employed to enhance the value of the next meeting. Finally the best relationships are characterised by demonstrated enthusiasm and a proactive spirit to do what is necessary to produce sustainable value from the experience. Sometimes the practice of mentoring is driven by an encounter with a crisis, but such last minute requests to a relatively unknown mentor for assistance can be of limited value and duration. Mentoring requires a strategic approach by the mentee long before a crisis hits. When this is in place, mentoring solutions to a crisis can be found, but that's also the tough end of the spectrum in this art form.

Business Leadership Mentoring

Mentoring for business leadership involves a discussion about the mentee's career experiences that provide significant challenges to the latter's abilities to navigate and survive at work, also with the inevitable tensions across having a fruitful personal and home life. Coaching is more directive and driven from the eyes of the coach. Mentoring must be driven by the protégé or mentee, who needs to be self-aware, ambitious and keen to learn.

Professor Robert (Bob) Wood from the Melbourne Business School has rightly said that leadership is about "maintaining hope". If a leader presents his or her unresolved personal problems within the workspace, the confidence of others will be materially affected and that person's leadership effectiveness will fall as a result. Having a mentor to vent these unresolved problems and issues with will not only help address them, but also improve the mentee leader's confidence and that of the others being led by him or her. Bob Wood says a classically successful mentoring technique is to use the distinction from the following three paradigms to change the focus of the conversation with a mentee. The paradigms involve opening your mind to the extremes between:

- 'Here' and 'there'
- 'Me' and 'you'
- 'Now' and 'then'.

Most mentees in difficulty will often be trapped in the 'here, me and now' domains, and the mentor needs to get them out of thinking this way. The trick is to bump or nudge them into changing gears and thinking instead about 'there, you and then'. It's a classic strategic visioning technique that also has strong personal applicability in mentoring. Many current problems can be diminished in relative weight when the compass is reset and the sights are lifted. A simple dialogue built around 'you, there, and then' can help enormously.

Bob generalises from his own experience that many leaders are mismatched to their roles and feel an "incomplete self". This crisis of identity is often a problem for women in business life, as Chapter Eleven describes. Working with a mentor to re-organise the sources of conflict in your life will help rediscover your true self. With consistent and compatible goals in your life, your leadership posture and style with others will be much more convincing and effective.

Globalisation and the information revolution have converged in the last decade to change power structures in business. Vineet Nayar and Charles Handy have written that the traditional power pyramid has been turned on its head. Particularly in service industries, effective business power is now with those serving the customer and not with those sitting in the executive suite. Thus "reverse-mentoring" – a term originated by the CEO of GE Jack Welch in 1999 – is growing in value as a by-product of the mentoring process. Mentors are finding their conversations with mentees are giving them new insights on critical business issues. Mentoring can also take place amongst peers or groups, although the main form of mentoring in business is 'one on one' and 'elder to protégé'. Steve Vamos, President of the SKE and a Telstra Corporation Limited board member who serves as an informal mentor to many young executives, says:

> "They [mentees] often come to me with career crossroad dilemmas, issues or choices. I don't ever tell them what to do, but rather serve as a confidential sounding-board to help them work through the issues and their relative merits. At the end of the day, my aim is to help them with a sensible passage through to their own decision-making."

Steve's philosophy on mentoring was developed early in his career with IBM where, for 12 months of his 14 years with the company, he was attached as an executive assistant to two Asia-Pacific top functional executives within the company.

> "My job was simple – I attended meetings with them, got to see and appreciate the senior executives' focus, and spent time at the end of each day sitting with my mentor reviewing what had happened, how they responded and the decisions they took and why. IBM had no greater expectation of me than to observe and learn in this way for those 12 months. However, after I began to attain more senior responsibilities in IBM, and later at Apple and Microsoft, my mentors more often became people outside of the company that employed me."

The drive for more mentoring activity is reflected in the emerging profile of a modern business leader. Mentoring isn't needed as much to drive a command and control approach to leadership, or an organisation characterised by either fiercely competitive personal rivalries, or factionalism. However, understanding personal and group psychologies, juggling complex ethical, moral and cross-cultural dilemmas, having a well-developed sense of smell for risk and ambiguity, all require a sharply developed intellect and intuition acquired from an exposure to a wide set of experiences that a mentoring relationship can bring forward effectively and efficiently. Furthermore, many young leaders – particularly women – are still predisposed to think that a thorough and soundly technical completion of assigned tasks is the key to career success, and that wider relationship development and management, both inside an organisation and outside with a broader set of stakeholders, is unnecessary. Mentoring has shown itself to be a useful method to dispell these notions from younger female leaders, as nothing could be further from the truth. Late in your career is a very painful and frustrating time to find all this out.

Zachary (2005), Johnson and Ridley (2004), Clutterbuck and Megginson (1999) and Klasen and Clutterbuck (2002) have defined basic elements and phases for mentoring when it's well underway. More organisations are starting to develop large and in some instances cross-organisational mentoring schemes, where initial matching and providing for a provisional period in which to build up the relationship have warranted an extra investment of care and diligence. At the very least, a golden rule for mentoring is that it must be "outside the chain of command (sic)". Many bosses think of themselves, and describe themselves, as mentors to their employees, but this notion is limited in its potential to the mentee. Cross-organisational mentoring is proving to have more durable stretch and benefits than in-house mentoring schemes for three reasons:

1. In-house mentoring arrangements can be complicated and inhibited by the political structures of that organisation, whereby the mentee in particular feels constrained in his or her ability to be completely honest for fear of jeopardising their career potential. A common experience is the mentee feeling unable to discuss a difficult professional relationship with someone who is seen as a friend or internal ally of the mentor – these situations are known as 'tortuous triangles' or 'terrible trios'.
2. A fear amongst mentees that candour necessary to produce full value in a mentoring relationship requires them to reveal

deep doubts, personal weaknesses and apparent failings that could be seen to be more career-limiting than enhancing.

3. Insufficient stretch and diversity with the in-house mentoring conversation because too many assumptions are taken about a person's potential, or because familiarity serves only to blindside the relationship on pathways worth exploring.

Factors for Success

There are two critical success factors in mentoring programs. The first is adequate training for mentors and mentees. In an interview for *HRmonthly* (AHRI, August 2012), the eminent UK author on mentoring, David Clutterbuck, advises that in his experience only three out of ten mentoring relationships will succeed if there is no training for either mentor or mentee; that number rises to six out of ten successes if the mentor receives training; and eight or nine out of ten where both do. The second success factor is an early provision for a mutual exploring and confirmation between mentor and mentee of mutually-held and consistent values. Both the UK and Australian experience confirms the critical nature of this second key success factor.

Organisations contemplating the establishment of a mentoring initiative related to a life at work for their co-workers should also check their intent, purpose and proposed actions against the International Standard for Mentoring Programmes in Employment (ISMPE) which has six core principles, as follows:

1. **Clarity of purpose**
    - The intended outcomes and benefits of the programme are clearly defined and understood by all the stakeholder audiences
    - The outcomes are translated into viable and well-understood objectives for each mentoring relationship.

2. Stakeholder training and briefing

- Participants and stakeholders understand the concept of mentoring and their respective roles
- Participants are aware of the skills and behaviours they need to apply in their roles as mentors and mentees; and have an opportunity to identify skills gaps
- Learning support is available throughout the first 12 months of their involvement in the programme.

3. Processes for selection and matching

- Mentors are selected to meet the specific needs of mentees
- Both mentors and mentees have an influence on whether they participate and who they agree to pair with
- The experience gap permits significant learning by the mentee
- There is a process for recognising and unwinding matches that do not work and for reassigning the participants if they wish.

4. Effective processes for measurement and review

The programme is measured sufficiently frequently and appropriately to:

- Identify problems with individual relationships
- Make timely adjustments to the programme
- Provide a meaningful cost-benefit analysis and impact analysis.

5. Maintains high standard of ethics and pastoral care

- All parties have access to and understand the code of conduct and ethics
- Performance against the code of conduct is monitored, and there are procedures for dealing with breaches of it
- Participants understand clearly the hierarchy of interests

(mentee, mentoring pair, organisation) and have discussed the implications for managing relationships and the programme.

6. **Supports participants throughout the process/systems of programme administration**
   - Participants have adequate support throughout the formal programme and, where appropriate, beyond
   - The programme is managed professionally.

(International Standard for Mentoring Programmes (2011))

Mentoring succeeds best when it produces 'outside the square' thinking. The lessons of experience in Australia demonstrate that it helps when the two participants in a mentoring relationship also live outside the nine dots of the mentee's workplace.

Types of Mentoring

From the post-war period until recently, the evidence shows that the vast majority of mentoring relationships are developed on an informal basis between people with mutual interests and/or compatible values. Over the last two and a half decades, and particularly the past eight or so years, public and private organisations, not-for-profit companies and professional institutes have adopted facilitated mentoring programs and related initiatives.

The predominant form of such facilitated interventions is called 'traditional mentoring,' a 'mentoring pairs program' or 'one-to-one' mentoring. This structure involves a pairing of an elder/mentor and protégé/mentee. More often today these programs are formally sponsored and organised, whereas in the last half of the twentieth century, they used to be informally arranged. The Australian Institute of Company Directors (Company Directors), Business Council of Australia (BCA), Australian Human Resources

Institute (AHRI) and Financial Executives International (FEI) of Australia schemes described in the next chapter are traditional formal schemes.

Other forms are 'peer mentoring' or 'co-mentoring' where individuals in complementary professions, e.g. law and business, meet to review complementary knowledge and experiences to help each other (Coutu in *Harvard Business Review* 2011). A case study of peer mentoring based on the author's own experience is discussed in Chapter Thirteen. An extended form of this is known as 'circles mentoring' or 'group mentoring', where groups of peers meet together in mutual support (another example is Mary Woodridge's peer CEO group given in Chapter Eight).

More advanced mentees also employ 'needs-based' mentoring, whereby they acquire an extensive network of contacts, each with specialised skills and experiences that are selected for engagement in response to the particular nature of the demands being placed on the mentee.

Mentoring can be cross-cultural in its nature or through the intended targeting of participants. Such initiatives may aim to promote advancement of different cultural groups in business and professional life, or simply assist the transition of one culture into an environment where another dominates. The Clontarf and Australian Football League (AFL) programs for the development of Indigenous young footballers are clear examples. With One Voice, Melbourne Sings is another example that appears more universal in its nature at first blush, but actually targets women who have recently immigrated to Australia, and seeks to pair them with community leaders who can help them gain a 'voice' in their new world (see Chapter Ten).

Other diversity-based mentoring programs are also on the rise (examples are the BCA–AHRI and the Company Directors' programs for women emerging as senior executives and potential board directors respectively).

Best practice employers find ways to capture the benefits of their various mentoring programs so that the overall learning of the organisation can advance as well. Victoria Police (VicPol) does this particularly well by using alumni mentees who have graduated from previous programs as syndicate chairs within the current year's program. These syndicate heads report to the Leaders Mentoring Program (LMP) Steering Committee which oversees changes and enhancements to future activities of the VicPol itself. The main concern is not to do this in a way that breaks the confidentiality of individual mentoring relationships. The 'Syndicate Chair' method has proven to be an effective filter for this to happen, without a compromise being inadvertently generated to the integrity of discussions amongst individual mentoring pairs. Another innovative aspect of the LMP was the use of two mentors for each mentee – one from business and one from the general community via the Rotary International organisation. As the program evolved, however, this aspect of it also changed (see Chapter Three).

The next two chapters of the book attest to the popularity and value of modern mentoring; each covers a sector where mentoring is thriving.

2

MENTORING IN BUSINESS

Rather than individual employers all creating their own mentoring schemes, professional bodies are taking up the challenge and providing mentoring assistance to their members. Two examples are mentoring programs for emerging Chief Financial Officers (CFOs) offered by Financial Executives International (FEI) of Australia and for emerging Chief Human Resources Officers (CHROs) offered by the Australian Human Resources Institute (AHRI). These current best-practice mentoring programs are reviewed below.

Senior Financial Executives (CFO Mentoring by FEI Australia)

The CFO mentoring program, run by FEI, started in 2003 with six well-known CFOs mentoring aspiring young financial executives from outside their own company. The program has grown significantly since then, reflecting its success as measured by the feedback from mentees, mentors and their companies. In 2014-15 there are 56 mentoring pairs on the program across Sydney, Brisbane and Melbourne.

Overall satisfaction with the program has been excellent. In recent years, about 90% of participants have ranked the scheme as very good or excellent.

Nearly all of the mentees are nominated by the CFOs of Australia's major corporations. Some 80% are from listed entities, with the others being from the Australian subsidiaries of overseas listed companies, private companies or government-owned companies.

Most mentees in each annual intake of the FEI program are up-and-coming financial executives and many of them are potential CFOs of the future. Since the program began, the age range of mentees has been from 28 to 51 years, the average age being 38. The positions of the mentees vary: they usually report directly to a CFO or one or two 'levels' below; sometimes, they are new CFOs. The mentors are nearly all experienced group CFOs of large companies. Most are still in that position, although currently about 15% to 20% are ex-group CFOs who are usually a CEO, a COO, a non-executive director or in another senior position. The mentors are all volunteers.

One of the FEI mentors for the past 12 years has been Peter Day, formerly CFO of Amcor, and now a director of SAI Global, Ansell and Multiple Sclerosis Limited. Peter says the FEI program is not well known publicly, but it is widely known and respected within the finance profession. Peter said:

> "There is a lot of support for it at senior levels amongst CFOs like John Stanhope, the [now] retired CFO at Telstra."

The program works on an annual cycle. FEI launches the program with a lunch in each city, preceded by a briefing for the new mentees by the Secretary of FEI, who runs the program. Before then, FEI has asked all the nominators to submit résumés of their proposed mentees to help in the process of allocating mentors. All relevant details of the current position and responsibilities as well as all previous jobs held, professional qualifications, education, age and outside interests are required. The nominators are also asked if they have any particular objectives for their mentee, so that these can be taken into account during the allocation process and provided to the selected mentor.

FEI makes an initial allocation and tries to make the best allocation it can, based on the data available and avoiding any potential conflicts of interest. Each mentor is then provided the résumé of the selected protégé and any related objectives given by the nominator. Each mentor is asked to agree the allocation of the mentee to him or her, and when all have agreed (and any changes that are necessary or desirable have been made) the allocation is finalised.

FEI is not prescriptive on how the mentoring program should operate, apart from a few key conditions for participation which include:

- **Timely contact of the mentor by the mentee:** This must occur as soon as the formal email confirmation of allocation of a mentor has been received, in order to make arrangements for the first meeting.
- **Feedback** is required at three points in the FEI program:
  - Within two months of commencement each mentee is required to provide feedback in general terms to his/her nominator as to how the mentoring program is proceeding and whether there are any issues or problems.
  - Brief interim feedback on an open, honest, full and prompt basis is required mid-term to the FEI Secretary. Feedback is treated as confidential.
  - Near the program's end, FEI requires all mentees to complete a questionnaire to provide feedback on their

experiences. This feedback is seen as essential to help improve the program for future years and to keep it relevant. Individual feedback is confidential and quotes are not attributed or identified.

- **Networking:** Mentees are strongly encouraged to attend the regular FEI lunches during the year wherever possible. This is not only to expose them to interesting talks, but also to provide them with networking opportunities.
- **Continuous improvement:** All mentors and mentees are requested to help identify what works in the program and what requires improvement.
- **Job mobility:** If during the year the mentor or the mentee accepts another position, either within their company or elsewhere, they are required to notify the FEI program director and their own mentor/mentee/nominator (as appropriate) with details.
- **Confidentiality:** It is a condition of participating in the program that confidentiality be maintained. On rare occasions, mentors may require their mentees to sign a confidentiality agreement regarding the mentoring process and the information exchanged during it.
- **Employment of mentees:** It is recognised that a problem would occur if the mentor's company were to offer employment to the mentee during, or within a reasonable period after, the mentoring year.

Mentees are encouraged to contact other executives in their company who have been on the mentoring program to discuss it with them before their own participation begins; and the mentors are encouraged to contact the CFO nominating the mentee to see if there are any particular objectives held in relation to that mentee. Once the mentoring has started, contact between the mentor and the nominator that relates to the mentee is assessed to be difficult by FEI. Peter Day says:

> "It's often usual for the mentor to have a discussion at the outset with the mentee's nominator, but that's the last one on the subject, because otherwise confidentiality within the mentoring relationship may be placed at risk."

The mentees are encouraged to be the driving force in setting up meetings, as they are the ones who stand to gain the most. The average number of meetings is about six. Some of those with fewer meetings appeared to get less out of the program, although sometimes fewer meetings were usually due to special circumstances, such as job relocation or longer individual meetings.

All mentors and mentees are strongly encouraged by FEI to schedule regular meetings at the outset for the full year of the program. As some scheduled meetings may be cancelled because of work priorities, scheduling is suggested to exceed the total target number of meetings. Feedback has suggested that this works better than organising meetings on an ad hoc basis. Peter Day says the program organisers are rightly concerned that you need to schedule regular meetings early in the process:

> "It's a lot about discipline and meeting frequency, and you find that the relationships really build by the end of the program year when strong bonds have been established."

At the first meeting, nearly all of the mentees discuss and agree with their mentors the outline of what each expects from the mentoring process and how it will be achieved, inclusive of a list of all matters which the mentees wish to cover over the year. This is not set in stone, but participants are advised to agree some broad objectives with the mentor and to provide a framework from which subsequent meetings can develop. Based upon participant feedback to the FEI, the most successful mentoring relationships appear to be where the mentee thinks through what he or she wishes to gain from the program.

Mentors and mentees are encouraged to meet at a venue where both feel comfortable. Mentees report satisfaction with all venues, and two-thirds meet in the mentors' offices some or all of the time. Two-thirds of the mentees report some meetings over coffee or a meal, and coffee shops appear to be getting more popular as a venue. Some meetings take place in the mentees' offices and a few mentors (for special reasons) hold some meetings satisfactorily by phone and video-conferencing. The typical meeting lasts about an hour.

Over half of the mentees make some written notes after each meeting and nearly all of those who do so find it very useful. In a number of cases, mentors and mentees agree the topics for the next meeting at the close of each meeting.

In addition to the mentor–mentee meetings, some mentors arrange for their mentees to meet others connected with the mentor's company. The mentees who meet others consistently find this part of the program very useful, so discussion of this prospect is now being encouraged by the FEI with all program participants. People whom mentees meet include the CFO's direct reports, the chairman of the board, the chairman of the board audit committee and other non-executive directors.

A wide variety of topics are covered by the various mentors and mentees. The four broad themes seem to be:

1. Understanding the CFO's role and how he or she fulfils it
2. Technical and business issues facing the CFO
3. How the CFO relates to others and dealing with people
4. Personal development and career planning.

The positive nature of the program is attested by the following comments in the FEI's own internal review from past mentees, on what they have gained from their participation:

> "I gained more confidence in my ability, a clearer direction of where I am heading and the benefit of having an inspirational mentor who was willing to share knowledge and wisdom with me."

> "The benefit was being able to discuss issues with someone who had been there before and receive sound advice on what I should at least be considering when making decisions."

> "I gained from discussion on areas that I had little experience with – which helped to demystify them. I also benefited from the insight into the character of a successful CFO and from some clear guidance on what I needed to work on in terms of my career exposure."

> "My mentor provided me with ideas that I had not previously considered. We were able to have open conversations including issues that I would not be comfortable discussing with colleagues."

> "My mentor was a female CFO to a large organisation who understands the issues faced by other women in trying to get to the top. She was a great sounding-board for issues and how to approach them."

Mentors also gained from the program and some comments from the mentors are:

> "Stepping outside my day job and focusing on someone else helps put some of the day job issues in perspective for the mentor as well."

> "Mentoring people helps you focus on what is and is not important."

> "A better understanding of the challenges and risks facing generation Y."

> "The ability to offer advice and experience on where I had made mistakes in my career path, etc., and developing a good rapport

> with the mentee who put a lot of thought and effort into the meetings, knowing what he wanted to get out of them."

> "I got a greater appreciation of how other organisations manage their business and was able to test my own company's approach against another."

According to Peter Day, two significant problems to managing a mentoring program like the FEI are the (thankfully very few) situations when a bad match seems to occur and also saying goodbye – especially when the mentee wants to continue.

> "But that's two small problems only, relative to the very significant benefits that have emerged from the scheme in the last ten years", says Peter.

Human Resources Practitioners

The AHRI mentoring program is another example of a well-developed and well-executed professional mentoring scheme for hundreds of HR participating members. It follows a similar structure to that described for senior financial executives organised under the aegis of the FEI.

AHRI started this scheme in 2008 with about 50 pairs nationwide. It now exceeds 500 participants or 250 pairs annually! AHRI provides matching facilities comprising:

- Preparation of bio data and career interests, and professional needs and specialisation
- A telephone interview to assist matching
- Discussion and confirmation of rules of engagement
- Timetable and program duration/termination date.

The AHRI mentoring approach involves a supervising program committee in each state to assist and troubleshoot as required and an orientation program for both parties. It also involves a set of program guidelines for participants, including some 'getting started' suggestions. There are Q&A notes for getting value out of the relationship which include tips for building a strong and productive relationship early, setting goals, expectations and – as appropriate – a mentoring agreement, measuring regular progress, managing conflicts. There are checklists for learning and development objectives, resource materials including books and e-learning modules for mentors and mentees in order to sharpen the necessary skills. Furthermore, to encourage dynamic learning, networking functions are organised which have proven to be particularly valuable, and can be for all program participants, mentors only, or mentees only. Throughout the five years of its operation, surveys have shown the significant majority meet at least every two months, and 85+% satisfaction is the norm for participants.

In AHRI's experience, up to between 10% and 15% of mentoring pairs will fail for reasons related to a mismatch of expectations; different mindsets on meeting frequency and style; or simple interpersonal chemistry mismatches. Further, the seeds for the majority of such failures are evident to either or both parties within the first two or so face-to-face meetings.

Accordingly, any mentoring relationship should allow itself a proving ground or an initial testing period of up to three meetings for both parties to formally validate the relationship. If the desire is not there for it to continue after such initial exchanges, a rematch is sought from the person directing the program. Mentees in particular are encouraged to speak up if a mentoring relationship is not working, and not to be either forced to suffer in silence about the malfunction, or be intimidated about confronting this because the mentor seems too great a power figure.

As a general guide from the AHRI mentoring program experiences, astute probing and alertness to malfunctions in the early relationship development stage is required by the mentoring program director. As it is usual for there to be more nominations for mentee positions than mentors, AHRI believes it is worthwhile holding up to 20% of matched mentees in reserve after the initial pairings have been made as a back-up capability for an inevitable fallout, and for a rematching of pairs to occur without seeking to disturb the 85% that are off and running, and working well. All parties need to recognise and accept this initial risk of failure as normal and that it is not a matter to be ashamed of or embarrassed about when encountered. Given the usual excess supply of mentees, those who drop out due to an initial mismatch encounter may need to be assured of a rematch in the next regular program being scheduled.

3

MENTORING IN THE POLICE AND PUBLIC SERVICE

Service in the nation's police forces plays a critical role for public security and safety. How police officers are developed beyond the traditional three-year Academy programs for new recruits has remained somewhat of a mystery to outsiders. Research for this book has revealed that mentoring has been forming part of the lifecycle development of an officer all the way from raw recruits through to Commissioner ranks, for several years now. This is certainly the case in our two most populous states, Victoria and New South Wales. Further, both police services in these states have undertaken some innovative approaches and techniques with mentoring – not only to advance the modern concept of community policing, but also to ensure a better integration between police work and the various cultures in mainstream Australian society today.

Victoria Police Mentoring Scheme

After a successful three-year pilot, Victoria Police (VicPol) in association with Rotary International and the Victorian business community has committed to delivering the Victoria Police Leaders Mentoring Program (LMP) for its members. The LMP is for those considered to be leaders within their field who have the potential to take up senior executive roles in the future. The program was set up with the strong support of then Chief Commissioner Christine Nixon, who had been pursuing a philosophy of community policing during her tenure. In outlining her original expectations for the LMP, Christine said:

> "I wished we had done this earlier. It's about the kind of management you need to have for the future, and the sooner you work on that the better. The LMP scheme introduces police to another world. It really did serve to reinforce those relationships with the community. The police mentees realised that these people, their business and community mentors, were there for you and that it was genuine. Mentoring is also about changing the culture. For example, police today get exposed to a number of high-risk, cross-cultural situations. On visits to detention centres, police will arrive via a trip to McDonald's, and have bought them Maccas. They then sit down and talk to them in a way that leads to a two-way street of thinking and understanding. These are the sort of tips you get from mentors."

The successful pilot program was conducted over a nine-month period in 2007. It involved 15 police leaders (at the Inspector rank or above) who demonstrated leadership potential, and 15 mentors from the Victorian business community along with 15 Rotary mentors. So it was a unique formula – a pairing of one mentee with two mentors. Later, the Steering Committee broadened the target audience to Superintendents and executive level police officers. As a consequence, more recent changes have seen a move back to one mentor—one mentee, either from business or the community, depending on the mentee's rank (we discuss this later in Chapter Twelve).

Mentoring is assessed by VicPol Command as an important

leadership strategy for assisting police leaders to transition into more senior roles within the organisation. This Leaders Mentoring Program is conducted over a 12-month period and its specific aims are to provide police leaders with a development opportunity to:

- Gain a better understanding of different organisational cultures as well as the challenges, roles and skills of senior Victorian business leaders
- Form stronger links with the Victorian community and Rotary.

The responsibility to drive the LMP was initially assigned to an Assistant Commissioner, People Development, at the Victoria Police Academy, Kevin Scott (AC Scott), who supervised the program until his retirement in 2014, after which responsibility passed to AC Kevin Casey. AC Scott had a Steering Committee to monitor and measure progress with the program, and all mentees were sub-grouped into syndicates of six or seven current mentees, with each syndicate led by a former mentee from a previous year's program. These syndicate leaders were charged to stay on the pulse of their syndicate group, to assess progress and to report regularly to the Steering Committee that matters are on track or if not, why not.

On completion of the program, participants were expected to have had opportunities in:

- Broadening their understanding of, and confidence in, strategic leadership and new organisational approaches to leadership
- Building an effective professional business network and gaining insights into, and connections with, the senior leaders from the business sector and the community through Rotary
- Engaging Rotarians and business leaders who have a better appreciation of Victoria Police and its role within society

- Creating additional development opportunities for high potential police leaders by participating in an innovative and cost-effective program
- Raising awareness of further skill gaps that require development.

AC Scott completed a Churchill Fellowship which he used to assess how staff development schemes worked in other countries, and the potential for a mentoring scheme like this to help police gain a broader perspective. He says:

> "One of the biggest risks to the development of a police officer is an over-exposure to closed-shop thinking. The advantage of this program is that it opens our senior and high potential police to approaches used by senior business and community leaders which they would not otherwise be exposed to."

Linking to the Community

The reason for working with a Rotary mentor was to gain a greater understanding of and nurture links to the community. The purpose of having a business mentor was to be exposed to business perspectives, challenges and problems.

In the early years, both the Rotary and the business mentors were critical to the overall success of the program according to Kevin Scott. In particular, the community perspective to policing that came from the Rotary participation was invaluable, said Kevin:

> "It was the Rotary members from the Melbourne Central Sunrise Club that came to me with an offer to assist with a way to engage with Victoria Police.
>
> "They have continually sought to have the best involved, and also continued to ensure that those involved are accountable. For many [mentees], an understanding of the breadth and depth of the work of Rotary has been really enlightening. Individual Rotary Clubs have

> then gone on to support local police initiatives related to community wellbeing."

Mentors in the program were encouraged to be good listeners, able to express empathy, and have a keen sense to make a contribution. They had to be flexible in their approach, display good communication and people-development skills and have a good network.

Mentees were advised by the VicPol organisers that they needed to practise openness and honesty; develop trust; be prepared to be quite honest about their mistakes, past and present; learn from mistakes; be receptive to feedback; commit time to prepare for each session; and be responsible for their own growth and development. There was a competitive selection process and applicants needed to demonstrate their leadership capabilities, by displaying aspiration, ability and engagement through examples that show initiative, ability, commitment to achieve and give back to the workplace. They needed to exhibit strong interpersonal skills and an understanding of the commitment required for this development opportunity.

AC Scott explains:

> "We encourage the mentees to drive the program. They need to have high levels of emotional intelligence (EQ), and are strongly encouraged to set demanding objectives for their one year on the program. There is great enthusiasm to be a member of the LMP at both the mentor and mentee levels, and we have been very impressed with the progress and value from this initiative in what has been its relatively short history."

The time commitment expectation for mentees in meeting with each mentor during the program is about 40 hours (or five days) over twelve months. It is encouraged that the specific dates and times be decided between the mentor and mentee. However, it is expected that each session will run for a minimum of one hour, depending on the issues and activities involved.

The Victoria Police Leaders Mentoring Program is based on the practice of *Profile-Based Pairing*. The questions on the mentor and mentee expression of interest forms are designed to provide a detailed profile that identifies areas of expertise in the mentor and areas of required learning in mentees.

Using this information, as well as matching those with similar expectations, motivations and a commonality in leadership aspirations, the selection panel pairs up mentors and mentees as appropriate. A number of LMP mentors have joked that this is the first time they had been the subject of a 'police profiling', and yet they also speak highly of the beneficial outcomes this has had on their lives and also careers as humble civilians (sic).

Social events are used to launch the program and this is where the ice is broken and an introduction is given to the relationship that is to be developed. Briefings for mentees and mentors are also programmed.

Learning is a Two-way Street

The mentoring program is structured as a means for both mentors and mentees to achieve something that is personally and professionally important. Learning is clearly meant to be a two-way street. Mentors share their expertise and contribute to the personal and professional development of Victoria Police leaders. In turn, they learn about the capabilities and operating environment of the Victoria Police in general.

The LMP members are advised to expect that each mentoring match will be different. However, there are some common stages that most matches will experience. These are cautious knowledge- and confidence-building; selective risk-taking followed by professional and personal sharing, and ultimately a positive personal relationship develops.

For both mentors and mentees the program organisers recognise the first meeting may be a bit awkward, and some opening questions and lines of mutual discovery are suggested to participants. Specifically, six approaches are recommended to break the ice:

- **Introductions.** Share information about your background, experience and motivation to help establish common ground and build rapport.
- **Ground rules.** Discuss early on, the boundaries of what is acceptable or not acceptable to each of you, including confidentiality issues.
- **Objectives and expectations.** Outline objectives for the meeting and your expectations for the mentoring relationship.
- **Practicalities.** Agree on times, duration, locations and frequency of meetings.
- **Action.** Make a date for the next meeting and decide what you both need to do before it.
- **Mentoring agreement and action plan.** Collate this information into a mentoring agreement and action plan.

Program support and enquiries from participants are provided for through guidelines and nominated contacts, many of whom are past graduates from earlier programs. There are networking functions throughout and the Steering Committee produces a regular online magazine called 'Grapevine'. This keeps participants abreast of key milestones, information on matters of interest from the program, some good news reports and also advice of key community speakers who are brought in to address the LMP members on critical issues affecting the community and policing. These speakers are also used to stretch the boundaries of thinking, and often initiate subsequent topics for discussion amongst each mentoring group.

Participants are encouraged to compile a reflective journal – or a learning journal – an important part of the mentoring process as it allows identification of both planned and unplanned learning.

It is essential to the success of the mentoring relationship that mentors and mentees agree on achievable objectives for the time-limited relationship, so that misunderstandings are minimised.

In this VicPol program, the process of clarifying mutual expectations through an 'agreement' or 'contract' is an important aspect of the communication that takes place between mentors and mentees. It is also important that the mentor 'reality-checks' and agrees that the outcomes that the mentee would like from the relationship are appropriate and achievable.

The experience of this program suggests that mentees should be able to appraise their achievements at the end of the mentoring program, so the strategies/actions can be defined within the bounds of both sets of expertise and resources.

The success of the LMP has encouraged the VicPol Command to take the potential value added from mentoring further into the VicPol learning and development system.

AC Scott said the Police Academy at Mount Waverley for training recruits now sees internal mentors attached to each new police recruit on a group or individual basis as required:

> "As soon as police cadets begin, we instil into them that they cannot have a bystander mentality as future police members. When an issue or event arises on the job, they need to be active in addressing that. Moreover, mentoring gives them contexts and situations for how and why difficult events can arise – through the eyes of more experienced police members. This guidance from those senior colleagues has helped the quality of the young cadets' trained responses enormously. By the time police members have advanced their careers to be demonstrating the potential to accede to higher roles, the LMP then offers a further broadening and career growth opportunity. Mentors provide the key to both stages, and we think there is much greater potential to use mentoring in other valuable ways, and in the future as well."

The Victoria Police LMP is a national first of its breed, and relative to almost any other business mentoring program, it is very close to best current operating practice. I take a look at how the program has evolved in Chapter Twelve).

Other interstate police organisations have heard of the good news reports emanating from LMP participants and are conducting their own feasibility studies to establish similar programs in their state. The sponsorship of the Victoria Police mentoring programs sits at the highest level within its executive command structure.

But it's also true that there are different strokes for different folks. The NSW Police have demonstrated that in the next section, and have done so very effectively as well.

Mentoring in the New South Wales Police

Speaking on what a mentor had taught her about policing Catherine Burn, Deputy Commissioner of the NSW Police and also Telstra Business Woman of the Year 2011, said:

> "Sometimes you must get battle-scarred to gain a valuable experience."

The philosophy for mentoring police in Australia's largest state, NSW, has many similarities to the Victorian model, but they have also been undertaking their own innovations, some of which are being imitated elsewhere as a result of the observed successes.

Mentoring has been part of Deputy Commissioner Specialist Operations Catherine Burn's career but the value for her has been acquired on a more informal basis than what can be expected in future. Notwithstanding Catherine's own informal mentoring background, she is now a very positive champion of the NSW Police experimentation which has seen some new and more formal approaches to mentoring being adopted over the recent years. She anticipates the major gains from mentoring will come from enhanced confidence to do a tough job well and also to build positive relationships. Catherine regards these as critical learning acquisitions for women in policing, as she would like to see the percentage of sworn female officers in NSW continue to increase.

The NSW Goulburn Police Academy has an informal mentoring scheme and it introduces various strategies as part of the training program for young police recruits, just as the Victoria Police does at Mount Waverley. The mentors for these recruits are internal, i.e. they are other more experienced policemen and women. The Goulburn Academy is also linked to a university-based tertiary qualification. The NSW journey is designed to build up the professionalism of policing, and mentoring is a key part of that.

Commencing a new working life within the learning environment of the Goulburn Police Academy provides its new recruits with a number of opportunities to appreciate the broader social and community context influencing their future careers. This is particularly the case with Aboriginal and Torres Strait Islander (ATSI) students, for whom mentoring is hardwired as a major learning medium applied to their development within the Academy. As Catherine Burn remarks:

> "As an example, the Police Academy provides informal mentoring for ATSI students with on-site staff to mentor, guide and support ATSI students during the police recruit training program. This support consists of an Aboriginal police officer and an Aboriginal Charles Sturt University representative. In addition, ATSI policing students are mentored through the program with particular facilitators and are provided with resources to ensure they have a smooth transition with being away from their families and support mechanisms, as most are away from home for the first time. We endeavour to provide positive role models at the Academy so students realise their future career choice has a purpose. We have introduced Local Area Commanders and senior staff who play key roles in the attestation parades and this provides students with unfettered

> access to senior police during their training. These types of strategies and initiatives really hit home with students and they aspire to emulate these key police officers.
>
> "We also have the Field Teaching Officers' (FTO) role to support probationary constables after their attestation from the Academy. The FTO component is a large part of the recruit training program. FTOs are both mentors and coaches to the new recruits, [working] intensively for the first three months, and then [in an] oversight [role] for the last nine months. Sometimes this mentoring relationship lasts an entire career."

The NSW Police also has a Command Leadership Training Program with a formal mentoring component in which senior operational Commanders mentor new Inspectors and Superintendents in Operational Command. There is also a formal mentoring program involved in the Strategic Leadership Program and the Women's Leadership Program, through the use of internal mentors.

Within these approaches to police career development in NSW, mentors are sourced from both internal and external sources. The increasing use of external mentors is seen as a developing component of future mentoring activities in NSW. Catherine Burn says that:

> "One of the key issues is to have a group of external mentors who have gained some real appreciation of what policing is and for people like me to understand the demands that can be placed on a formal mentor. That's why I am involved in mentoring five younger policewomen in the NSW force, as well as being a mentor in the university LUCY mentoring scheme. Furthermore, we see the potential for a future supply of external mentors flowing from our Community Awareness of Policing Program (CAPP)."

The LUCY mentoring scheme is for university female undergraduates in the final year of their course. LUCY's objective is to help the mentees shape their career choices as they are about to graduate from the tertiary education environment. Catherine's mentee, Rita, was a student in accounting who spent 35 hours over a six-month period working in the NSW Police finance area. She also attended a three-day CAPP session. These two on-site experiences gave Rita an excellent understanding of what police work in general and in the financial field was like. The formal work assignments were interspersed with regular discussions with Catherine as her mentor as to what it all meant.

The Community Awareness of Policing Program is a major NSW Police innovation that is being assessed for application in other states following a presentation on CAPP at the 2012 Australia and New Zealand Commissioners Conference.

CAPP has broader objectives than just building an external mentoring supply source. The NSW Police has followed the model of the FBI Citizen's Academy in the USA. Simply stated, CAPP puts leading citizens and community leaders "into the shoes of the police" for three days – usually from a Friday morning to a Sunday evening. Past CAPP graduates include Steve Waugh, former Australian test cricket team captain, Catholic Archbishop George Pell and Anglican Archbishop Peter Jensen, Margie Osmond and many others. The course covers real-time experiences at the Parramatta Police Centre – a working police station – at a firing range and in some hypothetical simulations of dealing with armed offenders, where decisions may need to be made concerning the defensive use of firearms, capsicum sprays, water cannons and taser guns, within a split second. The CAPP participants learn that police often are forced to make choices about using these alternatives with quite limited information, and precious little time to consider it. To reinforce the point, CAPP members are often asked to take roles as commanders in these simulations to 'see what it's like'. Some aren't comfortable with taking a leadership role in such life and death situations they might have to face – even hypothetically. "This is a great melting pot to see what policing is really like," says Catherine. It has a number of unanticipated advantages whereby community leaders get to appreciate how tough it can be on front line police officers. One example quoted by Catherine was where support and understanding was provided to the police community by a CAPP graduate after the accidental death of a NSW police officer.

> "I see a related benefit of CAPP enabling and informing high profile people in the community to speak out with knowledge and authority about issues such as police shootings, tasers, police pursuits, etc., as and when they may occur in future," Catherine says.

The CAPP will undoubtedly produce many high quality informed citizens and external mentors to work with serving police officers in future. The LMP in Victoria will also fuel some flattering imitation in other jurisdictions as news of its success travels far and wide.

Our society will be much the better for both of these innovations in policing and their use of mentors to drive them.

Public Service Mentoring

Mentoring programs in the public sector show some common features to schemes employed within private organisations and the professions. Across public service life, there seems to be a series of contrasts that can be drawn between the structure of mentoring within policing and the military, and those used within more general public service life.

Over the last decade in particular, there have been significant reforms to the identification and development of leaders within the mainstream public service in Australia. Probably the stand-out region where modern leadership trends are visible is Victoria, and to a slightly lesser extent in Western Australia. The Commonwealth is now also pursuing these approaches, following the report of the Review of Australian Government Administration entitled 'Ahead of the Game'. These trends are likely to be taken up by Australia's other six State and Territory governments over time.

Mentoring for Executive Public Sector Leadership (ANZSOG)

Following his retirement from chairing the high profile Australian Competition and Consumer Commission (ACCC) in 2003, Allan Fels took up a role as Dean of the then fledgling Australia and New Zealand School of Government (ANZSOG), a position that he held until 2013. Now it is a large and significant player in the development of future public sector leadership in the Federal and State Public Services of Australia and New Zealand. The peak development experience at ANZSOG is the two-year Executive Masters Degree of Public Administration (EMPA), which has about 130 students from around Australia and New Zealand.

A core component of the EMPA degree is a best-practice mentoring program for students. Mentors are usually officers at Deputy Secretary level in the Department sponsoring an EMPA student at ANZSOG, but not someone who is a boss. The role of mentor is a broad-ranging one, and it is to help the ANZSOG student mentees:

- Understand the nature of higher level leadership roles undertaken by the mentor in their department
- Advise on work-life balance issues for mentees who complete the EMPA part-time, and have to maintain continued service within their employing Departments, and to their families
- Have a sounding-board on complex strategic policy choices, issues and relationships that they confront both at ANZSOG and on the job in their department.

Allan Fels appreciates the value that mentors provided to his own career. In fact today, Allan saw himself as more of a mentor boss with the senior executives and teaching staff when he was Dean at

ANZSOG. He also worked on candidates for his own succession, and had some introductory and advisory discussions with the new ACCC Chairman, Rod Sims.

Allan sees a significant part of his role as being able to listen actively to his mentees and to try to engage with their problems, and identify experiences from his own career that might help.

> "My value as a mentor is to help them identify the issue and prospective solutions themselves. They say that helps their thought-processes. Sometimes I'm not too sure that I do that well enough, but if they find that to be helpful, I'm happy. One of the points I emphasise with my mentees is that your own career will be well served by finding some good mentors early on. It worked well for me."

The ANZSOG EMPA mentoring program sits across a well-developed culture of mentoring throughout the major public service departments in the Commonwealth and States. In particular, mentoring is very well developed in the Commonwealth, and the States of Victoria, and Western Australia. ANZSOG has drawn on this culture of mentoring and been able to utilise existing mentors from departments where EMPA students are drawn from, and so achieve a level of more co-ordinated effectiveness in structuring ANZSOG's own mentoring efforts, by drawing upon existing structures and reshaping them with objectives more aligned to the EMPA program itself.

Mentoring in Universities – Monash University

Mentoring is catching on within Australia's publicly-funded university system. A leading example of a tertiary institution with a very comprehensive set of mentoring programs is Monash University (Monash). This university leads and/or is involved with five major mentoring programs.

Deirdre O'Neill is an Associate Professor of Public Sector Management at Monash University, and formerly Academic Director at the Australia and New Zealand School of Government (ANZSOG). Deirdre is a strong proponent of mentoring for both an academic career, and also for one in public sector leadership.

> "Mentoring is very active at this university. It is seen as an important part of supporting the development of an academic career. It's not just about publications. There is a whole series of complex relationships that must be mastered within an academic environment if you are going to be successful, and Monash has a particular focus on encouraging women to develop their academic careers, and grow to take on senior leadership roles within the university. Mentoring is a key strategy to make that happen."

Access Monash Ambassadors

The Access Monash program uses Monash students to support the university's work with school students through the Schools Access Monash (SAM) program. SAM works with schools with a significant number of students from disadvantaged backgrounds or low rates of progression to university study.

Monash searches for university students who have 'been in their shoes' from similar disadvantaged backgrounds and been able to progress to university to act as mentors to young people.

The following attributes are sought in mentors on the program:

- An enthusiasm for higher education
- An ability to explain the benefits of higher education to young people
- Strong interpersonal and communication skills
- An ability to facilitate group work and encourage participation
- They must be responsible, reliable and professional
- A willingness to talk about their own educational experiences.

Mentors are matched with students in years 11 and 12 based on comparative fields of study. Their aim is to provide specific support and course and career advice to students. Mentors are expected to visit mentees in their schools throughout the year and provide online e-mentoring.

Each mentor commits to a program of approximately 30 hours of work during the academic year per mentee on a flexible (as agreed with the mentee) basis. Hours of work are also flexible and negotiated between mentors and mentees/schools. Mentors are paid at a casual hourly rate.

The mentor program is offered to selected schools in outer metropolitan areas, within reasonable proximity to the main Monash campus at Clayton, Victoria.

Peer Mentor Program

The Peer Mentor program focuses on health and wellbeing of students from overseas who may find tertiary life in Australia either lonely or disorienting. Its aim is to help new international students settle into their studies in a country that is new to them. Current students act as mentors and guide new students through the first six weeks of their course. Social events and seminars are part of the program. Students can apply to be mentors and are asked to undertake 1.5 days of training before they are accredited and also commit to being available to their mentees on a weekly basis for the first six weeks of an academic year when the contacts are to be arranged. Whilst the program supports mentees and their understanding of Australian culture, the mentors also receive skills in team work and communication. Upon completion of their training, mentors receive a certificate in leadership and cultural awareness.

Alumni Mentoring Program

Monash provides mentoring support at a different stage of the professional lifecycle – from the university stage of a person's life to the commencement of a working career. Each year the university works with its faculties to partner alumni mentors with student mentees. Through the alumni mentoring program, mentors develop a one-on-one partnership with a student and the aim is to strengthen links between graduates, industry and current students. The program started informally as an initiative run by Monash alumni for more than 10 years, but now there is active ownership and sponsorship of these efforts by the university itself, through its Alumni Relations office. The alumni mentors draw on their experiences to guide students through discussions about career goals, the availability of networks and support, and workplace dynamics. The alumni office matches and supports mentors and mentees throughout the academic year.

Monash's Partnership with the Australian Indigenous Mentoring Experience

The Australian Indigenous Mentoring Experience (AIME) has grown from a small program working with just 25 Indigenous high school students in 2005 to a large operation with 10 university partners across the east coast of Australia, working with approximately 1,000 Indigenous students. Monash is a major university partner with AIME, which uses unique structured education-based mentoring to connect university students with Indigenous high school students. AIME's goal is to see Indigenous young people finishing school and going to university at the same rate as all Australians.

AIME has programs for students from years 9 to 12 of high school and also Learning Centres and an Outreach program. As a mentoring program focused on Indigenous growth, it is reviewed in Chapter Ten later in the book in its own right.

Any Monash student can apply to become an AIME mentor and

so make themselves available to help close the gap in Indigenous inequality. Mentors are encouraged to raise awareness of the opportunities and possibilities that tertiary education can offer by providing a direct and personal link to the university experience for mentees. Student mentors are also given the opportunity to engage with the local Indigenous community and support an Indigenous student as they navigate their way through high school.

Monash Mentoring Scheme for Women

The Monash University Mentoring Scheme for Women aims to increase women's academic and professional access to the learning and developmental opportunities provided by a mentoring relationship.

This matches each successful mentee applicant to the program with a more senior male or female mentor from another area of the university, usually for a period of six months.

Mentees are at the level of Assistant Lecturer and above, and mentors are Senior Lecturer and above. Both members of the mentoring partnership are required to attend a preparation session where the structure and process of the scheme is explained. Pairs then meet at negotiated times throughout the program.

Mentoring Programs for Ethical Leadership

Australia has a world-class executive education program for ethical leadership – the Vincent Fairfax Fellowship (VFF) program, sponsored by the Vincent Fairfax Ethics in Leadership Foundation and delivered by the Centre for Ethical Leadership (CEL) at the Melbourne Business School. The CEL Director is Professor Robert Wood, one of Australia's world-class thinkers and leading teachers in the field of ethics within business, government and community organisations today.

The Fairfax Fellows attending each annual program are

immersed in a comprehensive field of studies, workshops and experiences that include exposure to leading community business and government speakers from Australia and overseas. The mentoring program is a core part of the course activities, both in clarifying challenges and issues, and in supporting leadership development for each of the individual Fairfax Fellows.

The mentoring component continues on beyond graduation from the VFF program through an 'embedding' project, so participants can consolidate the one year's VFF learnings into the leadership practices they adopt during their later life at work. The embedding project logic is based on learning research that much of the knowledge acquired from 'off line' business courses is forgotten within two to three months of returning to the normal job (sic). The embedding program is based around implementing an ethical leadership project in the Fairfax Fellow's workplace, and the assigned mentor works with the Fairfax Fellow to discuss difficulties and challenges encountered along the journey. The evidence is that the mentor's inclusion in this post-graduation activity is critical not only for securing positive project outcomes, but also for more permanently embedding the knowledge acquired from the VFF program studies. The positive psychology implications are there – develop new skills, new instincts and then practise, practise, practise, like Roger Federer did – but with your mentor never far away.

The Twelve Musts for a Mentoring Maker

The mentoring 'maker' or independent third-party that directs, manages and matches participants in these programs needs to have a number of core attributes if that role is to be successfully executed:

1. Clear program objectives and a code of conduct that includes acceptance of the confidentiality protocol; transparency in the program timing and outline of application and selection processes; availability of adequate induction, briefings, training programs and support from the beginning; continuing feedback processes and networking opportunities.
2. A robust program structure to ensure relationships are selected, formed and advanced in a positive professional way, and where the core responsibilities of each party are understood and then acted upon sustainably.
3. A profile of the mentee's career progress, development needs, and objectives – notwithstanding the value of reverse-mentoring, the prime customer in the relationship is the mentee.
4. Functional and industry compatibility – the mentor and mentee should arguably have similar or comparable origins that enable an understandable and empathetic wavelength to be established between them.
5. A common and consistent set of values. A mentoring relationship simply won't be able to go very far without this 'compatibility of values' being established very early in any mentoring relationship, and to the satisfaction of both parties.
6. A capacity for the mentor to stretch the mentee – this might come from having been in the mentee's shoes through holding a role of comparable or greater complexity some years before, or through posing a connection that brings the mentee up against customer or related stakeholder thinking, not available in-house.

7. Sufficient time for respect to be established on both sides, trust to be built that the confidentiality of these discussions will be maintained and that they can be conducted in an apolitical way.
8. Mutual acceptance of the commitment and a disciplined business approach – to meet face-to-face regularly, to set objectives and also to pursue critical and relevant matters together in depth. Beyond the initial bonding phase, casual coffee catch-ups to shoot the breeze simply don't work.
9. Enthusiasm for the 'new'. Participants need to embrace the prospects from this new learning relationship and also its 'outside the square' potential to acquire new knowledge, strategies and approaches for both.
10. Consider and test the underlying need for training and support of participants in any program, at both a group and individual level. If either mentors or mentees are untrained, the risk of failure will be high. Receiving presentations from past mentors and mentees is a very powerful medium, particularly if time for informal networking and connections is made thereafter.
11. An appropriate level of continuing support for the participants, in the form of a program director, and resource materials that both give focus and direction to the relationship, and also enable resolution of conflicts or roadblocks to progress, as and when they arise.
12. Every mentoring program should be the subject of a formal evaluation – to assess compatibility of pair-wise selections, learning progress, support needs and responses, networking opportunities, sponsorship actions, and evidence of personal and career advancement and success.

4

MENTORING PROGRAMS: RESEARCH SURVEY RESULTS

In 2012, the Australian Human Resources Institute (AHRI) surveyed the most senior human resources practitioners in nearly 200 of Australia's largest public and private organisations to find out about the nature, extent and utilisation of coaching and mentoring programs and activities across Australia today. There were 111 responses covering well over half the organisations surveyed. This means the results had material statistical significance in terms of activity within the nation's largest companies and institutions. Results revealed that 75 of the respondents had experience with their own corporate coaching scheme and 71 had a mentoring program in place. While this is the first survey of its type, there is no doubt that the results indicate the growing popularity of formal organised mentoring programs within organisations, as these were virtually unheard of five or more years earlier.

The survey results on coaching confirmed the traditional use for this activity is still relevant (i.e. as a remedy for current performance-related issues) and include:

- The objectives of coaching were recorded as: development of certain skills and capabilities (78% of respondents); addressing a performance issue (68%)

- The coachee's needs assessment was drawn from an existing performance assessment in 69% of cases
- 71% of participants saw the results of coaching to be beneficial, or better
- The effectiveness and outcomes of the coaching process were assessed by the HR department in 39% of cases and by the coachee in 27% of cases
- The main key success factors for a coaching program were listed as: support from management for the coaching program (67%); matching of coach to coachee (47%); relationship between coach and coachee (44%); follow-up after completion of the coaching program (44%); confidentiality and ethical conduct of the program (41%); formal measurement and reporting process (41%)
- Nearly 30% of respondents advised they didn't have a coaching program because they were too small for one, or because they believed their needs were covered by their induction and general management processes adequately.

As a corollary, the 69% of survey participants (71 respondents) who organised a mentoring program described its essence as improving the career potential of the participant mentees.

62% of the respondents said their programs engaged internal mentors, whilst 49% engaged external mentors. The overlap indicates 13% used both internal and external mentors.

The prime reasons given for use of internal mentors were to transfer knowledge and skill; build a common culture; help identify high potential candidates; and encourage general and career networking.

The prime reasons given for engaging external mentors were to give a genuine, confidential and independent focus on the mentee's future career; to improve the mentee's work-related confidence; to ensure feedback was comprehensive and transparent. Another reason provided was to assist retention of key talent. A significant minority of these respondents stated that external mentors were more successful than internal mentors because of the independence, confidentiality and expertise that they offered the mentees. 40% of respondent organisations participated in an externally-organised mentoring program – 7% with the BCA; 7% with the Company Directors; 20% with a relevant professional association; and 6% through a program run by an independent external person. The majority of respondents replied that their participation in an externally-run program had been "successful" or "very successful". Whilst only 34% of respondents matched mentor and mentee through an independent party, the rigour of the match was based on four criteria in a majority of cases by the 71 respondents:

1. Reference to the mentee's CV (83%)
2. Formal assessment of mentee potential (75%)
3. Aptitudes and interests of both mentor and mentee (92%)
4. A capacity for the mentee to be stretched by the mentor (79%).

In terms of the structure and success of these mentoring programs:

- 65% had a formal code of conduct for the program
- The majority of the codes of conduct clarified three criteria:
  - confidentiality (63%)
  - the business objectives of the mentoring relationship (59%)
  - recommended frequency and duration of meetings (59%).
- Supported the mentoring program (73%) through having both mentor and mentee briefings to kick off; 53% reported

having formal mentor and mentee handbooks, and also regular informal networking events

- The major benefits of the mentoring program to the mentees were reported as gaining:
  - better insights and new ways to manage difficult issues and interpersonal relationships (61%)
  - greater confidence (61%)
  - clearer perceptions of more senior responsibilities (49%).
- 66% reported major reverse-mentoring benefits to the mentors
- 84% reported that the vast majority of mentoring relationships succeeded
- 75% of programs were evaluated either yearly, or more frequently
- 69% said the program was run by the HR department, and four-fifths of that number had a separate mentor program director
- 11% of mentoring arrangements ran for six months, 45% ran for a year and 12% for longer
- about three-quarters of respondents without a current mentoring scheme reported it was likely or possible they would introduce one soon.

There is little doubt this survey indicates the use of mentoring programs by large organisations is now approximately equal in size to the use of executive coaching, which has been part of organisational learning and development programs for nearly 30 years. Furthermore, the evidence is that mentoring has had a beneficial impact on realising a mentee's career potential, and that the superior value of using an external mentor is gaining both recognition and prominence.

The next part of the book puts mentoring in the context of the broader discussions on leadership and psychology. We review post-war leadership trends to discover why and how mentoring has come back into vogue. Chapter Six considers mentoring in the context of neuroscience and positive psychology. We then examine the roles of mentor and mentee and the mentoring relationship.

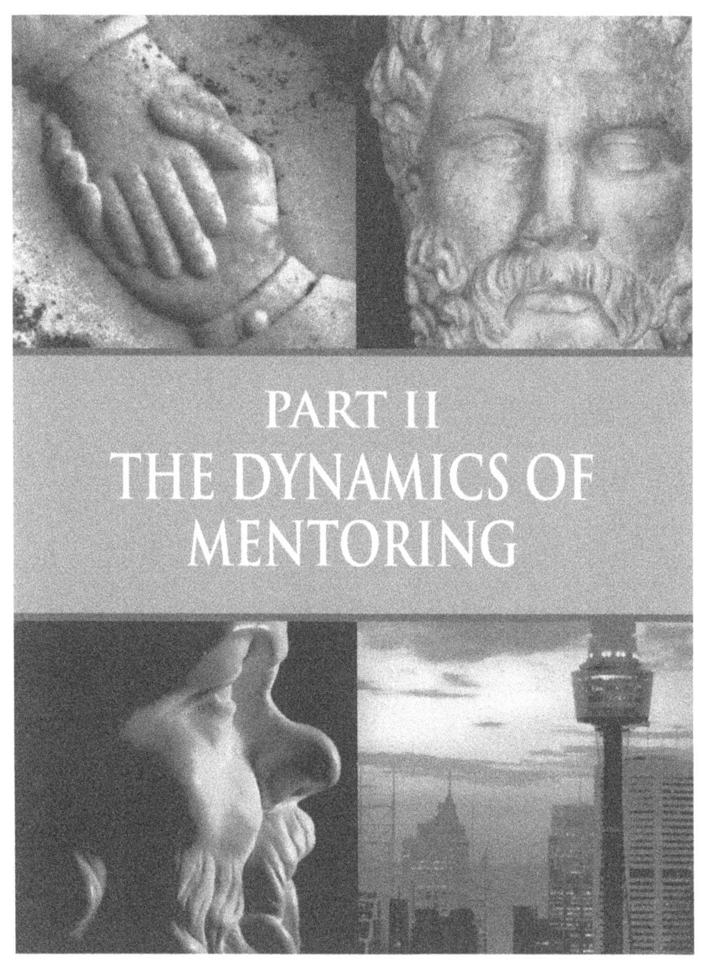
PART II
THE DYNAMICS OF
MENTORING

5

MENTORING AND MODERN LEADERSHIP MODELS

Before advancing too far with a review of mentoring techniques and skills, it's worthwhile to review why mentoring has grown as an integral part of the journey of leadership philosophies and approaches since the end of the Second World War. As well as the recent changes to traditional workplace learning methods that encourage a greater reliance on mentoring, the complementary notion of what makes a leader has also changed. The profile of a successful modern leader has evolved dramatically over the last 60 years. Each approach fitted well with its own era but had to evolve with the pressure of changed environments, competition and societal needs. That history forms the necessary prototype against which contemporary mentoring needs to be conducted if it is to have material relevance and maximum value.

There is extensive literature on leadership which is all about the description of theories and ways for a person to organise other people to achieve a common goal. Plato's *Republic* and Plutarch's *Lives* were the first places to attempt a definition of what a leader is. Subsequent authors have focused on a leader's natural traits, their display of positive behaviours, and with engaging the tools of psychology to effectively mobilise, motivate and muster the support of others in achieving the common task.

Command and Control Leadership

In the post-war period, the Harvard Business School restructured its Master of Business Administration (MBA) degree for the needs of a new era of world peace and to assist reconstruction in Europe and Asia. Notwithstanding that, Harvard's leadership modules were based on the 'command and control' strategies and approaches of the US military. Role models were drawn from its celebrated war heroes like General George Patton. These modules occupied only a small part of the MBA course content during the 1950s. The predominant focus was on finance, accounting, as well as business, technical and operating skills. For the most part, it was thought if these disciplines were mastered and executed well through clear commands, leadership followed axiomatically, and so would those being led.

So, leadership was all about setting and following directions and orders from the top, as in wartime. In this world, mentoring was not so critical. As a current and future leader you simply had to learn all the rules and follow your orders. The immediate post-war business environment suited this style of leadership learning. Reconstruction of Europe and Japan were critical social and economic objectives and regulation of economies to substantially close them off to freer world trade was seen as the preferred operating context. Russia and China were ensconced by choice behind the Iron and Bamboo curtains respectively and India was a poor over-regulated agricultural economy. World business and trade focused initially on Europe, the USA, and then the emerging tigers from Asia.

By the early 1960s, management by objectives (MBOs) became essential to a life in post-war leadership. Like the military, the tasks of doing business required close definition by the senior team and procedures were written and 'cascaded down from above' to make it easier for any and all employees in an organisation to do their job. The father of pre-war management, Frederick Winslow Taylor (1911) moved over to share pride of place with military leadership approaches in post-war business school thinking up until the mid-1980s. This culture was reinforced by the enactment of new corporations legislation in developed countries, which set out the responsibilities and duties of 'directors' (the top brass) and 'officers' of the company. Blue-collar workers had a parallel with enlisted ranks, in both mindset and management practice.

As western trade patterns began to grow post war, new leadership role models emerged in Europe and these were captured in teachings and publications of other leading world MBA programs, like those of the London Business School and INSEAD in France. However, the 'command and control' philosophies remained in vogue and so the underlying content didn't change all that much. However, the great feats of European generals, like Charles de Gaulle, were added to the free world's MBA curricula to try and diversify away from the rapid 'Americanisation' of the global business literature. The title of the leadership bible used in the élite Ecoles Nationales in France said it all, *Le Grand Patron* (The Big Boss). The look down the long nose of Charles de Gaulle became a global signature statement of excellence in French leadership. Well, it did to the French anyway!

Eastern Leadership Influences

With an initial focus by both business and government on post-war reconstruction, supported by heavily protected international trade barriers, these approaches to leadership and business conduct proved reasonably durable. However, as new international powers like Japan grew significantly during the 1960s, and pressure for trade and economic liberalisation gained momentum, new ways of competing, leading and winning emerged. Opening up world trade became the principal way to allow the reconstructed economies of Europe and Asia to keep growing. Business philosophers of the day believed the resulting integration of world trade and production would facilitate world peace as well. Japan was the first to really benefit from this philosophy, but in doing so it broke ranks with traditional western leadership approaches. Fortunately writers like W. Edwards Deming captured well these new business and leadership notions from the east within the mainstream English language literature. Deming wrote of the conduct and value of Japanese work circles and their successful team approaches to performance, execution and delivery. The first sets of peer mentoring experiences were being harnessed for major economic value in Japan. The dramatic benefits to productivity and competition by superior cost management and innovation – or at least rapid imitation of practices elsewhere – produced extraordinary economic growth numbers, as the Japanese economic miracle gained pace in the 1970s and 1980s. The Japanese were keen to make a point to the world, and especially to France, after de Gaulle called the then-Japanese Prime Minister a 'transistor salesman'. (For gen Y readers a 'transistor' was a small portable battery-powered radio, and the top branded product was then produced by Japanese manufacturer Sony.)

This Japanese miracle was closely followed by the success of large private and family companies in Asia, most usually led by the 'Overseas Chinese'. These people were ethnic Chinese émigrés who had fled China after the establishment of the communist political system in 1949. The Chinese business revolution hubbed itself in two major Asian financial centres – Singapore and Hong Kong – and each put a different emphasis on collegiate and family-based leadership approaches. Many of the bigger emerging Asian companies during the 1970s and 1980s were privately owned, and so it was harder for the west to gain a fix on what was actually happening within them. Nor was it easy to see how successful they really were, as there were no listed financial and other accounts that measured their performance. The influence of Confucius, and his focus on the family, local community and the importance of strong relationships amongst your GuanXi (or powerful connections) began to feed into western business thinking and teaching. Another step towards mentoring was beginning in the east. Nurturing by fathers in family businesses was also proving very powerful. Business mentoring was recognising its parental and quasi-parental roots in Chinese and south-east Asian enterprises.

The impact of guerilla warfare techniques during the Vietnam War, which later advanced into global terrorism, had already cast major doubts on the traditional 'command and control' military leadership approaches. In business, western firms noted the use by Chinese businesses of Sun Tzu's classic text entitled *The Art of War*, translated by Giles in 1910, which led to a further rethink and updating of both military and business strategic and leadership models in the west. Asia had arrived with a quite different formula for commercial success. Much of its relative progress was taken at the expense of western firms. These firms eventually took the hint and went back to their drawing boards to rethink what should constitute modern international business leadership. Going back to the origins of one's own history, and rediscovering the sources of a well-functioning and productive society, assumed a critical new importance to future economic growth and wellbeing. In *The Art of War*, the Chinese had gone back to their Confucian roots and used that text to outline the great progress that could be won against the enemy on both the battlefield or in places of commerce, by winning first the battle of the minds.

Ancient Leadership Inspiration

While Confucius and Sun Tzu had their impact on western business thinking, academic and business leaders in Europe and the USA began to search for both parallels and leadership paradigms from their own history. The journey went back to the relevance of philosophers like Socrates, Plato, Aristotle and modern philosophers and psychologists who wrote about the importance of values and motivation of people, rather than an over-reliance on 'just giving them clear directions'. These wise elders were the world's first mentors. Even overlooked episodes like the Hawthorne experiment at the Westinghouse factory during the 1920s were rediscovered. The Hawthorne study of a group of women in the wiring section of the business, found that if leaders established a positive working environment with good lighting, practical seating and the odd rest break, both productivity and morale rose as a result. Much of this progress came from asking the workers themselves what they thought and wanted, and then giving it a go. Hawthorne showed the benefits of reverse-mentoring, at a time when command and control approaches were beginning to fail, (for example the strikes in the Ford factory, which were much about Henry Ford's traditional authoritarian management style).

Modern Business Leadership

In the mid-1990s, Daniel Goleman wrote two seminal books – *Emotional Intelligence* in 1996 and *Working with Emotional Intelligence* in 1998 – which applied major psychological precepts to the field of business leadership. The core thesis was that innate intelligence, or IQ, was not enough to make a good leader. Inspiring leaders needed emotional intelligence, or EQ, that had four main components:

- **Self-awareness** – the ability to read your own emotions, recognise their impact on others, and engage intuition to guide your decisions.

- **Self-management** – controlling your emotions and instant reactions whilst adapting to changing circumstances.
- **Social awareness/empathy** – the ability to sense, understand and react to others' emotions, having regard to the importance of relevant social networks you are operating within.
- **Managing relationships** – the ability to inspire, influence and develop others whilst often engaging in conflict resolution.

Subsequently Goleman extended the thinking to social intelligence – investigating the importance of social networks in more depth – to how we do things on the job. With some criticisms that his work was overly Darwinian, authors like Dana Zohar added works on spiritual intelligence (SQ), which opened connections to mainstream religions and spiritual thinking, and also total intelligence (TQ) which completed the approach by rolling all these concepts in together. These developments are now being used extensively as standard techniques to gain relevant data that can advance the mentoring conversation.

The essential shift taking place to leadership thinking over the last 20 years has been for objectives, and management by objectives (MBOs), to move over and make room for an assessment of 'reasonable values and modern behaviours'. As Goleman's writings were discovered for their relevance, business organisations introduced 360 degree feedback processes that measured their leaders for not only what they achieved, but the behaviours they displayed as they went about it. These moves emphasised a redefinition of leadership to be more about 'outside–in' than 'inside–out' approaches, i.e. how others saw you, rather than how you saw yourself, which was the predominant pillar of command and control. This gave rise to a new principle of seeking and respecting inputs from outsiders on one's own leadership – another key enabler of the subsequent rise of mentoring as a critical mode of learning about leadership.

The literature on what makes good leaders then consolidated the burgeoning alphabet soup of acronyms into simpler terms like:

- *Authentic Leadership*, best characterised by Professor Bill George from Harvard in his book of the same name and also by Jim Collins' 'Level 5 Leadership', as described in his modern business classic *Good to Great.*
- *Servant Leadership* by Robert Greenleaf (2003) which he said took inspiration from Herman Hesse's *Journey to the East.* Many have extended the rebirth of this style of leadership thinking into a reconsideration of the value of traditional religious texts, e.g. that the substantive notions of traditional servant leadership probably have more in common with the life of Christ, as set out in the New Testament of the Bible, than Hesse's private eastward trek. Whilst Greenleaf was happy enough about his source of inspiration, John Maxwell and others took the concept further back in time and linkage to its more spiritual foundations.
- *Ethical Leadership* – in response to the reliance of eastern firms on Sun Tzu and Confucius, western leaders reached back to the philosophical underpinnings of the new values-based leadership literature of the 1990s, to Aristotle, Plato, Kant, Bentham and others.
- *Positive Psychology in Leadership and Neuro-Science* developed by Martin Seligman (2011) and David Rock and described in Chapter Six.

All these contributions to the thinking around modern leadership are quite complementary. They open up the thinking of leadership to be both an art and a science that encompasses the attributes of mentoring. The tests of success in practising these new schools of thought can be found in organisation-wide 360 degree feedback surveys, as well as those measuring culture and engagement right across the workforce. All of these schools have given strong evidence to the notions that employees work best when they have clear roles, understand what the organisation is trying to do and where their contribution fits, and finally, are inspired by those leading them. There are well-established metrics now available to assess whether, how and where this is happening. These techniques are widely practised by employers of choice. The power and conditions for positive leadership, discussed further below, have now also become much more subject to the workings of an industrial democracy. Through the force of online engagement surveys, workers at the coal face can now vote with their fingertips and their feet as to whether they are being exposed to good leadership and are part of a great place to work, or not.

A powerful example of this was a recent study by Dave Ulrich in conjunction with the global investment bank, UBS. Dave and Wendy Ulrich found that the World's Most Admired Companies – a global survey of leading multinational enterprises with strong authentic leadership practices – outperformed others in shareholder value growth by 7% per annum during the decade to 2008 (see Ulrich and Ulrich, 2010, P6). Great authentic leadership also means higher performance than traditional command and control approaches. A review of these companies' leaders shows that mentors are most commonly present behind the curtain of that leadership stage. The 70/20/10 ratio (mentioned in the Introduction) was soon promulgated, only to now move to 50/30/20 which heightened the importance of mentoring.

Furthermore, in conjunction with Charles Hampden-Turner at Oxford University, Fons Trompenaars (1997, 2000 and 2004) also assisted the future of leadership in a globalised world by drawing on the great philosophers from east and west to develop a simple but powerful set of seven pair-wise differentiators that would underpin analyses for better cross-cultural understanding, and also for a reconciliation of different perspectives present across workforces with increasingly diverse cultural origins.

Ethical Leadership Roots

A further critical update to the recent literature on leadership has been a rediscovery of the importance of ethical leadership in its broadest sense. The re-emphasis of modern leadership towards its ethical roots has supported a re-emergence of the importance of mentoring in the development of future leaders. Reading and on-the-job experience simply aren't sufficient means to embed these learnings. Rather they require face-to-face discussions between someone who knows from being there, and someone who is keen to make the journey ahead.

There are three main schools of thought in the history of ethics. First, Aristotlean ethics was encapsulated by that ancient philosopher after whom it is named. Aristotle believed a set of guiding moral principles could be identified that would enable human beings to reason their way through the key ethical and moral dilemmas of life. About 300 years ago, philosophical leaders sought simpler reduced-form theories to deal with life's major ethical problems. So at this time a second approach known as 'Deontological' or 'Kantian' ethics was developed by Immanuel Kant. This focused on the importance of duty and strong absolute values like honesty. Third, a little after Kant's writings were published, Utilitarian ethics was first articulated by Jeremy Bentham. This focused on achieving the greatest good for the greatest number. Outcome rather than duty was the way utilitarians believed we should sort out our ethical challenges. This third school of ethics drove business thinking from the time of Milton Friedman's writings at the University of Chicago in the 1980s when he said:

> "businesses had no other responsibility to society than to make the biggest profit that they possibly can."

The lessons of the tech wreck of 2000, and the failings of companies like Enron showed up the fallacies of such an overly simplistic approach. This became even more pronounced with the meltdown of major financial institutions in 2007 and the beginnings of the global financial crisis that still leaves many European economies in a faltering recovery zone. Both these periods of the new millennium saw major ethical failures in leadership amongst "the smartest guys in the room", then managing some of the world's biggest marque corporate institutions and brands, some of which like Lehman Brothers are no longer with us today. Leadership thinking has been updated with the inclusion of the need for leaders to be transparent in, and accountable for, their ethical beliefs and also their actions.

Many organisations search for the latest thinking on business ethics. But therein lies a fallacy of thinking. There is no such thing as business ethics. There is only ethics itself, and that relates to one's own sense of personal responsibility and duty. As Maxwell (2005) has summarised – probably the best expression for the essence of ethics is the 'golden rule' – do unto others as you would have them do unto yourself. Whilst this rule is often associated exclusively with Christian thinking and western societies, Maxwell (2005, P17) demonstrates the golden rule is also found to be a core component of teachings in Islam, Judaism, Buddhism, Hinduism, Confucianism, Baha'i, Jainism and Yoruba (Nigeria). So it's a robust principle for the new world of global business, as well as the mainstream cultures now underpinning the conduct of that. Whilst the golden rule is a widely accepted principle, its practice by workplace leaders is not – often because it entails higher costs than people are prepared to tolerate. Research for this book has established that discussion of ethical and moral dilemmas is a large part of modern mentoring conversations, where the mentees know they need help.

As the French philosopher and poet, Molière, said:

> "Men are alike in their promises. It is only in their deeds that they differ".

Notwithstanding that challenge of practice, ethical leadership fits enormously well with the principles of high employee engagement in a modern workplace. Surveys by the Human Synergistics group show that high engagement is strongly correlated with high performance and profitability. These results are the same as those emanating from the annual surveys of the World's Most Admired Companies conducted by the US *Fortune* magazine. High engagement occurs where the leaders are transparent, honest and ethical.

Elliott Jaques (1997) described what people are seeking at work in his seminal text *The Requisite Organization*. In this work, he established that all employees searched for clarity in their role; an understanding of what was expected of them; a picture of where they fitted within the organisation; and a light on the hill, i.e. where they were headed as a group. They also sought the following personal treatment on the job: to be valued, appreciated, trusted, understood, respected and not to be taken advantage of. The golden rule is therefore a very robust short form of ethics that applies well in business. It also circumscribes the type of leadership behaviour that is both acceptable today and the most effective.

Modern workers are looking for strong ethical characteristics in those who lead them. It's also a major precondition to be an effective contemporary mentor. Making ethical decisions consistently is found to be most difficult when the following features are present: many people are involved in decision-making; the prospect of an individual's pleasure or gain at the expense of the group is high; there is a threat to pride or power held; the costs or consequences of any decision are large; and where the pressure of meeting priorities starts to swamp an organisation's core values. Unfortunately, these characteristics are found today in spades within all organisations and are critical to how we function as an economy and society. So there is no escape from the confrontations posed by major ethical dilemmas each day we are at work.

As this book shows, the best mentoring approaches and case studies draw their contemporary thinking from these post-command and control leadership approaches. Part of the occasional resistance to mentoring amongst older generations, who are still in significant leadership roles, reflects the lack of relevance that organised mentoring programs have had to their own training as leaders from their pre-1990s business school origins. Add to this the failure of many older leaders to understand the relevance of mentoring to our emerging generation of business leaders and the new iWorld of competition in which they must operate.

It's clear that time will partly solve that problem. But the prospects for a more timely recognition and acceptance of the value of mentoring, followed by faster adjustments to capture its potential at work, remain.

Expectations of a Modern Leader in a Mentoring Context

A profile of ten modern executive leadership expectations has developed over the last 65 years, as follows.

1. Demonstrate a positive purpose and a desire to lead others positively in achievement of a given set of goals, primarily through inspiring and engaging your colleagues psychologically.
2. Possess strong self-awareness and consciousness of your style and its impact on others (EQ).
3. Have a moral compass or 'true north', and 'walk the talk' on some basic moral philosophies that others will assess your leadership by. Be prepared to practise mental toughness on yourself to get there. At the same time always aspire to show respect and humility, not only about your own vision, but also with the challenges being faced by other people in your company.
4. Manage complex ethical dilemmas, where sets of values, moral principles (Aristotlean ethics), rules and duties (deontological ethics) and broader outcomes (utilitarian ethics) all need to be considered together and acted on in a systemic, integrated and compassionate way. When it all seems difficult, ask yourself 'does this accord with the golden rule?'
5. The Golden Rule now applies in a more complex world of triple bottom line management of a broad range of stakeholders related to the life of business, including shareholders, employees, customers, suppliers, government and regulatory authorities and the communities all need to be explicitly accounted for by current and next generation leaders.
6. Value and seek out strong relationships in business and life that can sustain not only your personal career progress, but also your physical and mental health in the career journey ahead.

7. Seek out 'win–win' rather than 'directive command and control' solutions by embracing different cultural approaches in an increasingly interconnected global business environment. Particularly consider the confluence of western and eastern cultural traditions in business.
8. Understand and lead others through resolution of significant challenges incorporating risk and ambiguity in a global world where conflicts of interest amongst different value systems are more likely to be encountered than ever before.
9. Human beings have great potential to both respond to and recover from significant stress, but that requires prior identification and practice of alternative and more resilient leadership strategies and approaches. Such applications have shown improvements to use of a person's powers of intuition, and greater rates of innovation have occurred as a result.

6

MENTORING, NEUROSCIENCE AND POSITIVE PSYCHOLOGY

The last and most recent material contribution to the world business literature has come from the new field of neuroscience and positive psychology, through the writings of David Rock and Martin Seligman. Underpinning the importance of neuroscience, the *Harvard Business Review* (January 2005) wrote about a new phenomenon called ADT – Attention Deficit Trait – whereby today's executives have largely overloaded circuits in their mind. ADT is becoming a worldwide phenomenon and emerging leaders now appreciate they have to learn how to combat ADT themselves and also its related effects in others around them. Rock and Seligman address this issue in their writings. Part of the inspiration for their work also came from the contributions of Daniel Goleman, who described the pressures of modern life causing an 'amygdala attack' in the mind and inducing a traditional fight, flight or freeze (FFF) response. The amygdala is that part of the brain which alerts us first to the presence of people or events likely to threaten or cause us harm. The FFF response is the most typical to result. Its anecdotal origins stem from when Neanderthal man first confronted the sabre tooth tiger. McLennan (2007) extended that thinking with the FEAR – false evidence appearing real.

Neuroscientists like David Rock have written that the hardwired circuits in our brain that have produced fight, flight and freeze responses since the Stone Age can be changed because of the brain's neuroplasticity.

The recent research of neuroscientists using Medical Resonance Image (MRI) technology, has demonstrated the emotional impact on working people of not only different styles of leadership, but also how such approaches engage, inspire or turn off co-workers. The neuroscientists have also been able to measure some classical response patterns to sources of inspiration from the words and actions of others, and also to sources of stress producing fear, and typical responses to the latter.

MRI technology can measure the responses in each critical segment of the brain:

1. **Pre-frontal cortex.** The section behind the forehead where inspiration and innovation emanate within us
2. **Limbic system.** The section below the pre-frontal cortex, in the middle of the brain, which holds the primary drivers of our emotional responses
3. **Sometimes referred to as our 'autopilot'.** The section at the back of the head includes various structures relating to our memory and experiences that have stored our past responses under sudden fearful or threatening occurrences, or the responses we have observed in other authority figures – a parent, teacher or boss. Critical episodes in our past life are stored in this 'autopilot' segment, as either the foundations of our unconscious thoughts and things that drive our unconscious bias, in response to certain life events we have experienced. For example, if a very young child sees a parent scolding or mistreating an animal, they may be

either expected to behave that way themselves in later life, or at the very least to tolerate such behaviour in others without a desire to intervene, because of the implied acceptability in seeing a past authority figure behave in this way.

These sections of the brain provide important underpinnings to how we respond across the performance stress curve shown in the diagram below.

Performance Stress Curve

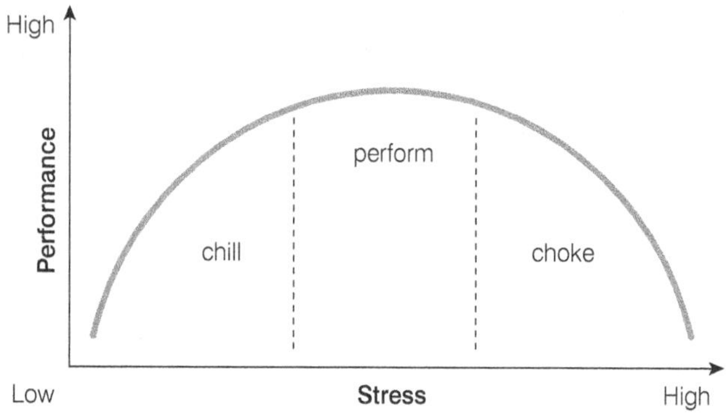

Most of us will be able to relate to the relationship drawn here between performance and stress. When we are at work and the jobs ahead of us are sparse or don't contain much challenge by their very nature, the tendency is to 'do it easy', and perhaps 'wing it' a little, because what is expected doesn't take much out of us, and there aren't additional pressures around to lift our overall performance. This is referred to as the 'chill' zone. The place we generally prefer to be is the 'perform' zone where we are challenged by all that we have going on and know that we are working to full capacity. However, our adrenalin is well aligned to what we need to do, and we feel 'it's all OK' – even if we go home fairly tired out, because we have used our energy, emotion, capability and resources to do what we have to, and usually will have enjoyed doing!

The place we hate to be is the 'choke' zone – when there is far too much on, and we feel the stress acutely. In this zone, we don't complete all we need to do thoroughly and to the best of our ability (and we know it). Here, the stress levels go up and force some critical mistakes, or we drop the ball and fail to complete key projects, or just complete them badly and probably with resentment. The likelihood of workers in this zone experiencing illness and then taking sick leave is very high. Too much 'choke' and we are overloaded, feeling horrible, and about to spin out of control.

Three sections of our brain are active in this performance stress curve. As we move up from chill zone to the perform zone, our prefrontal cortex (the inspiring creative source) and limbic system (our emotional triggers) are interacting highly. We are positively engaged in what we are doing, and are able to be innovative in our performance, that makes our emotions feel very positive. All good, so far. "Can the requests to do more and faster simply stop coming through the door?" we think to ourselves. But perhaps no luck there. As the load keeps rising, the emotional brain feels more under pressure and the thinking brain becomes exhausted and is progressively unable to source any further innovations.

We then start to drop into a choke-zone hold on our brains, we are drawn more and more into autopilot responses which may or may not be appropriate. In fact, continued overload makes it almost certain some of them won't be, compared to situations that we would have handled well and easily in the perform zone.

These features are often encountered in the mentoring experience. A mentee will raise issues with a mentor that are stressing the former at home or work. The mentor may not identify with them in the first instance because they don't usually cause a stressful response in themselves. Nevertheless, the mentoring challenge then becomes to recognise the mentee has a different problem source to the mentor, and to drill into what happened and why, in the mentee's mind. The following analysis can give some clues as to what a mentor should look for.

Sources of Stimuli to our Brain and Emotions

Incoming information impacts on the performance stress curve in either a positive (happy face) or negative (sad face) way. A succession of positive stimuli may actually lift the curve along the thick dotted line – through the effect of experience enabling us to manage more when the overall cumulative impact is positive (see diagram (a)).

(a) Positive Stimuli to Performance

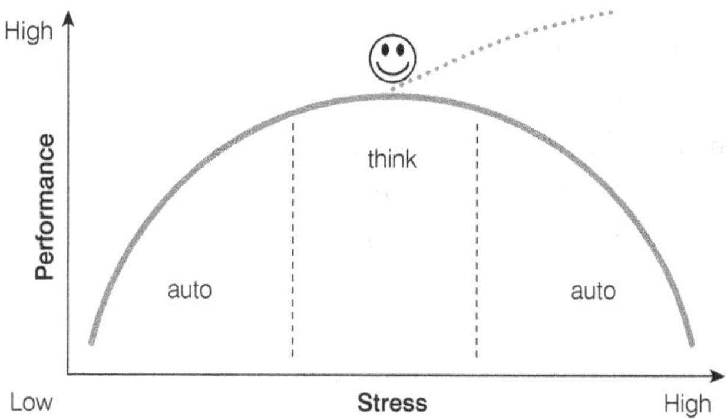

(b) Negative Stimuli to Performance

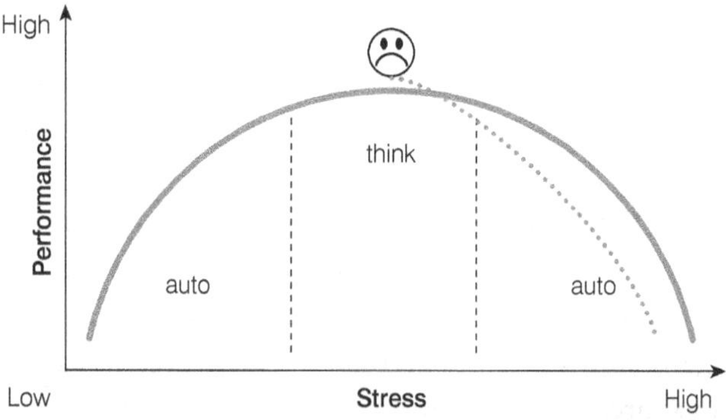

As you can see from the lower diagram (b), the reverse can also occur. Successive challenges that are threatening and of a negative nature can force us down the curve, or even cause a more rapid deterioration than normal, which in its extreme might usher in some mental health issues from total overload.

The links to mentoring can be further clarified. For many of us, the signs of a threat are identical. If for example, we were walking through a remote part of the Northern Territory and encountered a five-metre crocodile on the edge of a river bed, most of us would see this as a threat. Those who don't, probably aren't still with us today. Alternatively, if most of us stopped for a coffee break after a particularly demanding period of work, and a colleague offered us a piece of Swiss chocolate, we would generally see this as a reward. Those not on a diet at the time, that is. However, if we encountered a small chihuaha in a local park, many would see that little dog as a positive symbol, and one we might like to stop and pat. Except those who might have previously encountered the same breed of dog during their childhood, and been attacked by one for infringing its territory.

So the art of being a mentor sometimes requires a careful probing of the mentee's fears in order to understand what they are based upon. The challenge then becomes to develop a set of strategies to rewire the mentee's brain that this is not usually a threat source, or it's one that confidence can be built through role-playing with the mentor that significantly marginalises if not eliminates its negative magnitude in the mentee's mind.

How the Brain Copes with Rewards

Another piece of neuroscience that can help mentors is how the brain copes with expected and unexpected rewards. As mentor, you are also the mentee's cheerleader, especially on efforts they take to overcome their fears.

The diagram below shows how the brain responds when it expects and receives a reward.

Dopamine Response

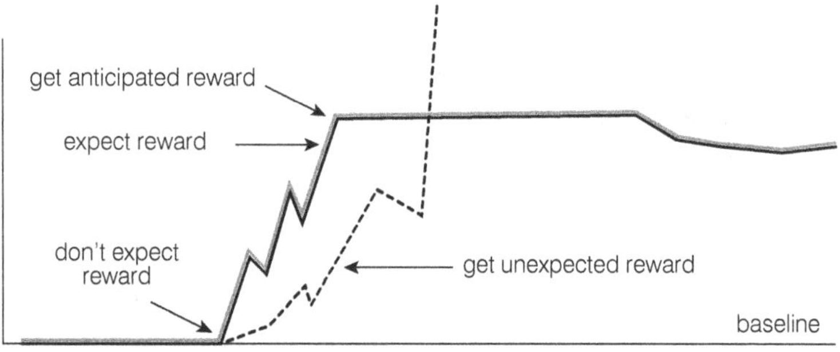

The grey line shows a positive expected lift in adrenalin and positive sentiment called the 'dopamine response'. The black line shows how we actually feel when that expected reward is delivered. It's exactly the same as the expectation with the delivery of an expected reward. No more, no less.

What is far more interesting is the dopamine response when we receive a reward unexpectedly. You can see the impact is almost 'off the charts' (dotted line). And so it is with the mentee. If they come back to you at a later meeting and relate how they have tried and succeeded with conquering a fear or addressing an unusual challenge, your spontaneous positive and congratulatory response will be received with great excitement. And it will reinforce the value of the changes in behaviour and application you have been seeking as their mentor.

It's worth trying. And it's the same in the general workplace. Bosses who say an unexpected thank you to co-workers for their efforts often don't realise what a positive impact that can have to engagement and also loyalty.

This means we are possessed with abilities to develop new response circuits throughout our life – subject to our own continued attention, and then development and repetition of remedial approaches in our response to perceived threats. The remedy implied here is not unlike how Roger Federer had to develop his backhand shot from what won him Junior Wimbledon in 1998 in order to progress successfully through a life in professional tennis and secure his first of 16 Grand Slams from 2003 to 2010. The same applied for golfing great Gary Player, who said "the more I practise, the luckier I get." Federer, for example, had to change by rewiring his brain to develop different techniques and produce superior responses to faster curving balls, returning rapidly over the net, and to experiencing different and more difficult physical playing environments. These metaphors are similar to the pressures faced by all global executive professionals. They also apply to other professional walks of life, where courage and new skills need to be developed to cope with higher order pressure situations. As Robert Frost wrote in his 1915 poem 'The Road Not Taken':

> "Two roads diverged in a wood, and I –
> I took the one less travelled by,
> And that has made all the difference."

The SCARF Model

Rock's work has made an important contribution to addressing ways to accommodate this necessary rewiring of the brain through his SCARF model that sets out the five areas where 'amygdala attacks' can originate in a potentially threatening way, or so it may appear:

- **Status** – a major driver of how many people support their own self-image. Threats to this, like the prospect of a job loss, can cause very negative instantaneous responses.
- **Certainty** – a fall-off in this characteristic can cause panic, e.g. expectations of a recession induced by the European

sovereign debt crisis from mid-2011 and its impacts to world financial markets.

- **Autonomy** – we all like to work with the freedom implied by this and without the suffocating supervision of a micro-manager overseer. Finding countervailing strategies, rather than producing spontaneous adverse reactions, is another key learning from neuroscience.
- **Relatedness** – being removed from the game is a major fear at work. We all want to belong to the pack in what we do. Leaders need to observe and manage this tendency to exclude others.
- **Fairness** – people expect to be treated fairly and will produce counterproductive responses when they aren't.

Accordingly, modern leadership models take a number of cues from neuroscience, particularly these paradigms of FEAR–FFF reactions to SCARF situations. The science of positive leadership is built around the development of simulations and case studies to help workers and emerging leaders rewire the brain to defer spontaneous FFF responses and create new ways to seek out and apply better choices, through what McLennan (2007) calls a set of well-developed "re-appraisal" skills. The final part of this new approach from positive psychology is termed "mindfulness" where participants are taught to develop a non-judgmental awareness and acceptance of the present. Seligman has studied the US Armed Services in the last few years and has written about post-traumatic growth (PTG), where US servicemen have experienced enormous physical, psychological and emotional stresses in the field of battle, but have found ways and strategies to survive and grow as a result. This is the other end of the spectrum to post-traumatic stress (PTS), but Seligman argues with training and the development of certain mental skills of invention and resilience, PTG is a plausible outcome, and one worth aspiring towards in business, politics, sport, community, or life itself.

A major impact on another issue of concern in leadership today is the encouragement of more innovation. Rewiring the brain can facilitate a greater propensity and openness to innovation, through a sharpening of a person's intuition. As Albert Einstein once remarked:

> "Intuition is more important than IQ – I never discovered anything with my rational mind."

These strands of rational thinking that sit behind ethical leadership, the western and eastern schools of ethics, and also neuroscience and neuro-leadership can be drawn together into a simple diagram for both mentors and mentees to use, particularly for mentors.

In its basic form, ethical leadership reduces to the Golden Rule – and this applies across all major civilizations and cultures. For us all that can be simplified in the Ethical Diamond shown in the diagram below.

The Ethical Diamond

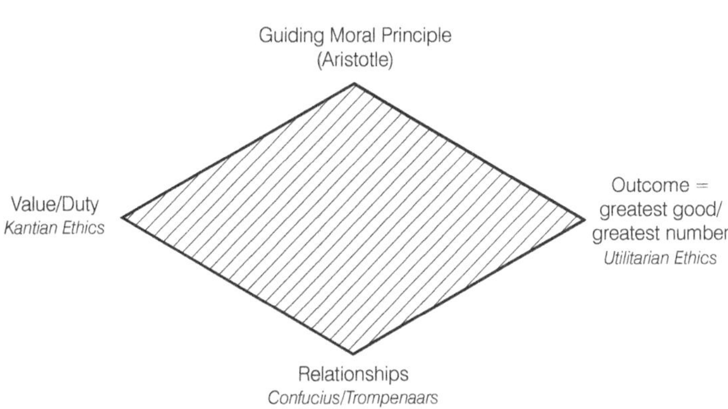

To be effective at the Golden Rule of ethical practice, leaders need to optimise their behaviour and actions across the whole plane of the diamond in the diagram. In other words, our leadership style and actions need to walk the talk on sound values, practical outcomes of maximum benefit, overarching guiding principles, and enhancing and respecting relationships across a wide range of cultures in the workplace.

That all sounds quite compelling, and few would argue with it. The main problems occur, however, when we are confronted by a material adverse event that triggers our fears into gear. Then the drivers of SCARF within us combine to form a fear frontier that cuts across this ethical diamond and forces us back to one or two points on the spectrum, e.g. to rely on values and some outcomes in a way that compromises a range of critical relationships. That situation is further compounded when the source of our fears arrests our creative thinking and we allow unconscious bias to kick in at any or all points on the ethical diamond, so that for example, we may rely on a sense of values at the expense of outcomes and relationships, but also select and rely on inappropriate values that have formed in our minds at an earlier age.

Confronting Fear Frontiers

Two examples will clarify the types of dilemmas that arise from fear, and our fear frontiers that push us back and force us to operate only at one or perhaps two points on the ethical diamond.

The first instance occurred when I was an executive at the ANZ Bank during the 1990s. In those days, there was no such thing as "carer's leave", and a subordinate staff member in my group had a mother who was terminally ill. She needed time off to care for her during the working week. The staff member had used all her recreational leave for this and other purposes during the previous few years. I believed the absence of my colleague was best characterised as sick leave, and so I granted her that form of time off to attend to her mother in hospital. These sick leave absences occurred at a time when my employer was cracking down on spurious leave-taking and sick leave was the prime target. One of my colleagues learned of what I was doing, and first warned me to cease but then later reported me to our superiors for "breaking the Bank's sick leave rules", which technically I had done. In other words, that colleague took a limited view on the event as constituting breach of a Kantian rule, and his fear frontier came into play. My perspective was that the sick leave rule could be stretched to give a valued and high-performing staff member time off now to look after her mother, on the basis that this granting of leave would enhance the working relationships and empathy within my group, and that the staff member taking the leave would make up lost time in terms of her considerable output at a later stage. But I did break the sick leave rule, even though I didn't believe I was breaking the Golden Rule of ethical leadership. Needless to say, I was cautioned by my superiors, and my competitive peer who reported me felt he had taken a relative step up in the succession-planning stakes for senior executives. I was chastened and would have approved sick leave again, were that to have been necessary, but it never came to that – the staff member's mother died the following week. She and her work colleagues were very grateful for my actions, and support – even though there had been enormous pressure to comply with the rule on sick leave taking, (for some in the place, anyway).

The second example is a more high profile and public one. In May 2013, during a match at the MCG, a 13-year-old Collingwood fan racially vilified Sydney Swans player Adam Goodes by referring to him as an "ape", following which Collingwood president Eddie McGuire apologised to Goodes "on behalf of the Collingwood Football Club and on behalf of football". McGuire said that Collingwood had a "zero tolerance" policy towards racism, but also said that the girl did not appreciate that she had made a racist slur.

The following week, McGuire himself made an on-air racist

reference to Adam Goodes and the new stage play about to commence in Melbourne "King Kong", by also using the word "ape". McGuire apologised on air after making the reference, but prefaced his apology by stating "I wasn't racially vilifying anyone". He was widely criticised for that lame excuse. In a later interview that day, he admitted he was guilty of racial vilification. He also offered his resignation as Collingwood President, but the Collingwood board expressed their support for him.

Initially, after the first event of racial vilification took place, McGuire had acted responsibly, promptly and comprehensively. His words and actions sustained the League's zero tolerance on racial discrimination (values and outcomes); he had directly spoken to the two parties involved in the slur to reconcile them (relationships), and to apologise for such behaviour on behalf of his club (outcomes); and he had made public comments directed at the broad community (all three points).

Unfortunately, it didn't end there. Barely a week later, on the prime-time, early morning radio station Triple M, Maguire made his own racial vilifying remarks.

But why such an apparent backflip?

Presumably given the pressure to perform in the very competitive morning radio environment, McGuire slipped back to say something instinctively which he thought would be taken as a contemporary and insightful joke. Almost immediately after saying that live on air, he recognised a serious mistake that had unwound all the positive ethical leadership he had shown in the days immediately after the May incident. His fear frontier was invoked to shut down the balanced perspectives and focused him primarily on outcomes, i.e. continued top radio program and celebrity ratings. These words sacrificed his earlier credibility in support of League and Club values for zero tolerance on racial vilification; and it ended his personal relationship and friendship with Adam

Goodes. Goodes stated a year later that he had accepted McGuire's own apology but that he could never again call him a friend. Nearly a year later, on 5 May, 2014 Goodes was quoted in the Melbourne *Herald Sun* and Sydney's *Daily Telegraph* as follows:

> "I harbor no anger towards the young female fan," Goodes said.
>
> "I would like to have called Eddie a friend before that incident," he said further.
>
> "To have a friend and someone there that night shaking my hand and consoling me in the rooms, I was disappointed and unfortunately that's how friendships end. Friends don't make jokes like that."

The reason for this analysis and the two case studies is that often a mentor will be confronted by a mentee's fears. They will hear stories of the mentee's more challenging experiences where their own fear frontier has cut a more balanced display of ethical standards down to one or two characteristics, fuelled possibly also by some unconscious bias. Exploring and sensitive probing of these events by the mentor to help the mentee re-wire their future responses to similar situations and pressures is part of the mentor's role. As it is for the mentee to identify and acknowledge where fear and unconscious bias have inhibited them.

So the mentor's role is learned counsellor, friend, part psychologist, and also part ethicist. And very trusted friend too. Always!

Mentoring Tips from Positive Psychology

1. The mentoring conversation often comes down to issues of fear in the mind of the mentee, and stress caused by that.
2. Fight, flight and freeze responses can be combatted by the natural neuroplasticity in the wiring of our brains, and with development of a positive and conscious set of skills and responses that anticipate the fives sources of amygdala attack.
3. Mentors will need to probe what causes the mentee's fear and stress, and work on strategies with the mentee to help lift their ability to perform to the level which they aspire to, or ultimately to accept they are shooting 'too high' in terms of the person they really are, and that this is OK!
4. Mentees need to confront their own fear frontiers. Mentors should role-play how mentees behave, and what values they show when they are fearful. The 'Ethical Diamond' should be used with the mentee to encourage self-reflection as to how they are responding to fear and stress, and then ways that can be overcome.
5. Mentors should be honest and direct with statements on similar situations where they have been fearful, and how they worked to overcome that.
6. As a mentor, you are well advised to boost the dopamine response in your mentee by congratulating them, and where appropriate rewarding them when they least expect it.
7. Targets for unsolicited rewards by the mentor to the mentee should be selected in ways that serve to reduce their fear(s), and will therefore be likely to help the mentee's confidence in combating these.
8. Mentees need to be confronted with sources of their own unconscious bias, and the impacts they can have on other people. Self-awareness is a precondition to self-management. Even just cutting out adverse behaviours driven by unconscious bias will be positive for the mentee.

7

THE MENTOR'S STYLE, SKILLS AND ATTITUDE

There are a number of traits for excellence in mentors. The usual starting points are for a mentor to have significant experience relevant to the mentee, as well as wisdom, credibility and patience. An ability to communicate directly and clearly is also recognised in the literature on mentoring, having regard to the interrelationships of mentor experiences with mentee challenges. Of critical significance is a positive mindset by the mentor that the purpose of mentoring is about the development of increased business, organisational and leadership strength in the mentee.

Regular (and Crisis) Mentoring Meetings

A preparedness by mentors to make themselves available for the mentee in a reliable and consistent way is very important. This can come through having the discipline to set and adhere to a regular meeting schedule. It is also necessary to establish high standards for the mentoring exchanges and this comes from the mentor's demonstrated willingness to set objectives for the relationship and also to identify key challenges about where the mentee needs to go 'into the deep'.

As well as regular, scheduled meetings, mentors should be available informally when crises arise for the mentee and the need for assistance is more immediate. At these meetings, listening in a reflective way is often a good approach as it demonstrates to the mentee a belief that the issue is significant but also it may warrant patient consideration by the mentor of alternative pathways forward.

Peter Day, who has mentored for more than a decade under the FEI program for emerging Chief Financial Officers (discussed in Chapter Two), found mentoring at a time of crisis to be the biggest challenge for his role as a mentor.

> "Some mentees don't come to you until they have a huge problem, and usually they are right – it is one that's huge. So as a mentor you need to give yourself enough time to absorb the challenge faced and to ask them the questions you would be asking yourself in their situation. But that context of a crisis can make it very tough to be a mentor, particularly if it occurs early in the life of this mentoring relationship."

In dealing with any crisis, there is the issue of not only dealing with its substance, as Peter Day has remarked, but also the timing of the mentor's intervention. Deputy Commissioner Catherine Burn of the NSW Police said on one occasion late in 2011 she was having a very tough time with an issue that had gained media attention. Out of the blue, a former mentor telephoned her to express support and encourage her to "keep working through it and not to get disillusioned". Catherine said:

> "It wasn't that he had the solution, it was more that he was there for me and I hadn't needed to ask for that support."

The best mentors establish clear protocols for the relationship: that confidentiality will be maintained; differences in values will be respected; and that there is a declared readiness on both sides to identify and resolve any prospective or real conflicts of interest. Sometimes the mentor may want to seek outside counsel about the mentee's progress or needs. If so, any such approach, and the reasons for it, must be made very carefully. Consent must be gained from the mentee for the matter to be discussed, and with whom, and a commitment made to give subsequent full feedback with the mentee later. If there is ever any doubt in the mentee's mind about the value of this, such an external approach should not be pursued at all.

Mentoring Language and Demeanour

Mentors need to demonstrate their own honesty in their conversations with mentees and use simple language in communications – not ambiguous or in-house jargon.

A willingness by mentors to disarm themselves of any 'power' body language is also critical. Mentors with poor self-awareness can fail to realise they are power figures in the eyes of the mentee, and they should work hard to take any explicit hallmarks of their formal authority out of the conversation. For example, having meetings in the mentor's office with that person sitting behind a big mahogany desk, arms folded with an overly-steely or poker-faced demeanour is likely to be a giant turn off for the mentee, or a source of intimidation not to talk about anything meaningful.

Mentors need to work hard but subtly to be, and appear to be, open, enthusiastic, relaxed, welcoming and positive about the mentee, and to develop the necessary chemistry and sense of humility to enable the relationship to work best for the prime customer of it – the mentee.

Patient explorations by the mentor are critical as to who the mentee is really – both as a person and as a professional. This will be vital in establishing a comprehensive baseline on the protégé that will underpin the potential to draw full value from the forthcoming explorations around the mentee's challenges. Mentors also need to be active listeners, committed and caring counsellors, career advisers and a critical friend. They need to give conversations with mentees a sense of meaning and purpose. As Elizabeth Broderick, Australia's Federal Sex Discrimination Commissioner, says:

> "A mentor and mentee need to have a shared sense of humanity, in order for the relationship to be effective".

As a consequence, mentors need to have a strong interest and a genuine commitment in developing others. Without this, they will get quickly found out. These elders must place themselves in a position to help their protégés explore questions and issues that they otherwise would not be willing or able to do.

A related, but very effective approach used by mentors, particularly early in the relationship-building phase with a new mentee, is humour. Former Deputy Prime Minister and former Ambassador to the Holy See, Tim Fischer is a classic example of this. He sees humour in all parts of life, and uses that to great effect in putting those whom he is mentoring at ease. As an example, when I asked Tim how his Akubra was received at the Vatican, and what were the major lessons for a former politician in the world of diplomacy, Tim replied as follows:

> "There are just four words that define the world of diplomacy:
>
> - Protocol
> - Vitriol
> - Alcohol
> - Panadol.
>
> But to be serious, there is also much endlessness. There are:
>
> - Endless meetings
> - Endless networking
> - Endless representation
> - Endless nation-building."

Setting time to assess the mentee's previous experiences with mentoring will provide significant value to the mentor, as will an outline of their expectations for this relationship and particular issues or concerns they might have 'up front'. Sometimes the mentee is facing specific challenges on the job and a large amount of time may need to be devoted to addressing these before any big-picture career issues can be tackled. Don't assume to know where the mentee is at. Ask probing questions that reveal it. The 80/20 of being a good mentor relates to the percentages of air-time devoted to active listening/speaking, and not the other way around. Reversing the 80/20 here will almost certainly guarantee mentor and relationship failure, respectively.

Listening and Questioning – but not Fixing

It is important the mentor resists any temptation to reach over and fix the mentee's problems with direct intervention and 'checklist style' advice. This is often the hardest characteristic for mentors to manage. As established business and organisational leaders, they will have spent a majority of their time assessing situations, defining performance gaps and deciding on necessary corrective actions and timetables.

The essence of good mentoring is active listening, followed by an account of parallel experiences in the mentor's life and what he or she did to address them. Peter Antonie, Olympic Gold Medalist in rowing at Barcelona in 1992, spoke of how one of his mentors, the late Stan Nicholes used this technique

> "I sometimes found myself talking to Stan in his kitchen, where he would discuss other élite athletes he had helped but who had not achieved their full potential. Stan would discuss where they had strayed away from what they needed to do in order to succeed. He wasn't talking critically about me in any way, but I got the message about lost opportunities – which is what Stan hoped would not happen with me."

The mentoring will be a success when the mentee derives their own 'ah ha' moment and takes away, from listening to the experiences of others, new ideas as to how they might confront a certain issue or predicament in their own way.

John Colvin, CEO and Managing Director of the Australian Institute of Company Directors (Company Directors) and father of that Institute's very successful Chairmen's Mentoring Program agrees mentoring is:

> "at least 80% listening, and not about trying to prove yourself to the mentee. They are already sitting there in front of you, and they are after some help because of who you are! As a mentor, you need to work hard so you do actually come across as helpful".

The mentor may also need to serve as a guardian in the relationship, and work to protect the mentee's interests as and when they may be subject to bullying, harassment or intimidation by a stronger party. This can be a two-edged sword and a moral hazard for the mentor, whose best role is really to be conducted behind the curtain of the mentee's career and life stage. But sometimes the mentor must emerge to protect the protégé, particularly when there is no alternative.

Mentees are often embarrassed about outlining matters they can't fix, or where they feel cornered. They really don't want to be told reproachfully, or to feel belittled in the process. To deal with these situations, Peter Day says:

> "Then sometimes you need to slow them up, distinguish the relative nature of issues and get them to work through matters in a slightly different way."

Again, related stories of inspiration that they can use to pursue in their own way and time, can often help.

Mentors need to be honest when they don't know the best way to help, and should consider offering to ponder the matter separately, or to consult other sources of advice that may be more helpful or qualified on the challenge itself. A quick bad decision by a mentor could damage the confidence and trust between the two persons materially. The relationship is meant to be about business but it's usually one that's also voluntary in its nature. The mentee wants to walk away from any meeting feeling positive and inspired, and not having demonstrated reluctant compliance until the session is finally over and they have been able to escape.

Vogt, Brown and Isaacs (2003) elaborate on the Art of Powerful Questions in their publication of the same name. Powerful questions from a mentor will elicit curiosity in the listener, stimulate their reflection and can open pathways to come up with creative or innovative means to address key problems. Moreover, they can enable detection of breakthrough insights by the mentee on their own – which is a key success factor in mentoring. Questions can be in areas related to the reshaping of priorities for the mentee; assessing or reviewing third-party impacts; questioning all relevant underlying intentions and connections between issues and relevant participants; and finding breakthroughs for the seemingly intractable challenges in the mentee's current life.

Peter Reith agrees on the importance of framing powerful questions with his mentees seeking careers in politics. Peter is a former Commonwealth Minister for Workplace Relations, and later Defence, and is currently a political mentor and an active political commentator in the media. He comments that:

> "Despite the temptation for me to fix the mentee's problems directly, I resist and instead impress upon them the importance of following the arguments on any issue through to their inevitable conclusions. It's also critical to put yourself in the place of your political opponent and break down their own position to its core principles. That homework will support the powerful questions you will be able to ask them... As a mentor, you have to be a role model in active listening and probing questions, which themselves are the key foundations for a successful political career."

A Positive and Sensitive Approach

A sensitivity by the mentor as to differences between the parties related to race, gender, origins or beliefs is also fundamental. The mentor must have an internal code of conduct to do 'no harm' to the mentee, and must be conscious that any behaviour in the relationship might become a source for disrespecting the other, if care is not used in their conversations. This is particularly the case with Indigenous mentoring programs in Australia. Jason Mifsud, leader of the AFL's Indigenous development programs believes Indigenous athletes want to be treated equally, but also want to have their mentors appreciate and respect their traditional culture.

> "It doesn't take a lot," says Jason, "but simple mistakes can get in the way. That's why some education about Indigenous culture and values can be very important to effective mentoring."

The Monash and AIME initiatives take this prior learning need on board in how they approach their mentor training.

Good mentors constantly remind their mentees that their 'glass is half full'. The conversation is usually structured to reinforce positive behaviours and approaches the mentee is already taking, and then to suggest alternatives that the mentor would have used to take those challenges further. One test mentors can undertake is to constantly probe what issues are holding the mentee back from dealing with their challenges during their discussions and alternatively what options or approaches might take them forward.

The best mentors are supportive of the mentee and always encouraging about their ability to grow further. They are also innovative or creative in their thoughts and strategies. At the end of the day, the mentee will or won't practise these ideas when the mentor isn't there, so there is no way of controlling outcomes. Further, a directive coaching approach by the leader can create a moral hazard or dependence between mentor and mentee which can become counterproductive to the relationship's intended purpose and value.

Research undertaken for this book shows that the greatest share of value in business mentoring usually comes over a finite period of up to, say, a year or at most 18 months, in any relationship. It is common for that to be followed by a willing longer term association, but one that is much less frequent and less formal. So it is important for the mentor to get the positive psychology and chemistry working early for the mentee so he or she will want to apply the indicative learnings before the natural use-by date is reached in the relationship's production of value.

Conquering Fear of Failure Means Success in Mentoring

A good mentor also needs to be honest about their own failures, where these have occurred, and what their own learning experiences have been from them. No human is perfect. Revealing one's own blemishes, in a positive and transparent way to the mentee, is likely to produce a more enduring and constructive bond between both parties. Leadership requires a person to know what failure is like and to assess and understand the risks and consequences. To experience and survive failure requires humility, persistence and mental toughness to get through to the other side. Accordingly, there needs to be willing and transparent self-disclosures about the mentor's own failures, misgivings and foibles encountered during their career. This form of action will also build confidence in the mentee to make the necessary declarations about sensitive and private concerns held about their own lives and careers. Declarations and discussions about failure are a major key success factor in mentoring relationships. Perhaps counter-intuitively, failure will drive success in mentoring.

John Bertrand, Australia II's skipper, won the America's Cup in 1983 which was recognised by the Confederation of Australian Sport as "the finest team performance in 200 years of Australian sport". John says invariably life's lessons emanate from failures – the three America's Cup challenges preceding 1983 included, followed by his 1995 One Australia Syndicate challenge where his yacht broke up and sank in 47 seconds.

> "The 1995 One Australia Syndicate, which I led, is the only entrant in America's Cup history recorded as having lost a race due to shipwreck!" John mused. "Failure is what we all face at various times in our lives. Life's deep lessons are remembered via failures, so one should not shy away from discussing them, analysing them and learning from them."

Professor Fiona Wood, 2005 Australian of the Year, and Director of the Burns Service of Western Australia sees confrontation of failure as critical in dealing with her mentees.

> "To be honest, and baring your soul about failure is a critical part of any mentoring experience. In our situation, the most profound negative we face is with the death of a patient. It is my belief that we must learn the utmost from those extreme situations, so that no critical information is lost."

Fiona Wood has learned more about the skills in managing failure from one of her mentees outside of medicine:

> "I had the privilege of being mentor to Darren Glass, the Captain of the West Coast Eagles AFL team… a football club [that] has experienced a lot of negative off-field incidents and had a very poor reputation for both its values and behaviour. I have learned a lot from mentoring and watching that young man. He had to confront and harness what positives he could find amongst a barrage of negative energy, and then get the team to summon the internal strength and discipline to get past all of that."

Humility, persistence and mental toughness are three characteristics of a Level 5 Leader described in Jim Collins' book, *Good to Great*. John Curtin, one of Australia's two great war-time Prime Ministers from 1940 to 1944, was jailed for protesting against conscription in 1916. Coping with that ignominy in the First World War didn't detract from the leadership he showed nearly 30 years later. It's clearly arguable that the first humbling experience with Curtin helped make a more positive mantle for his future leadership. The same applies to Nelson Mandela's period of service as President of South Africa, after being incarcerated for 27 years on Robben Island.

Many readers will probably regard some of the leaders interviewed for this book as both flawed and unpopular, and may question why their record of public life has been covered at all. Individual perceptions on leadership and its significant value (or lack of) are bound to vary across a wide spectrum in a diverse modern democratic society. However, the broader evidence available confirms that all leaders included in this research have made significant positive contributions during their time at the top. All have experienced some failures along the way, some of which have been quite spectacular in both nature and consequence. Nevertheless, none of that was proven to be criminally unlawful, even if their failures served to dent personal popularity or reputation for a time. What's more impressive for them as mentors has been their willingness to share and openly explore their own failures with their mentees. Every mentee's turn will come to face very tough and at times insidious events in their own lives. Their ability to navigate those times will be enhanced by such open, honest and forthright exchanges with their mentor. Some future leaders may hope they have eternal good fortune in their own careers, but that's unlikely in this new global iWorld that catches and disseminates any misstepping or worse, both widely and rapidly.

Nick Greiner, former NSW Premier and now successful company director admits he would have been better off with a group of strong mentors around him earlier in his political career. Nick now mentors a number of business people and former politicians and tells all his mentees:

> "...to go back to basics on themselves and decide what your strengths and weaknesses are, and allow that to help point your way forward. That way the risk of failure is significantly lessened," he says.

Adding Career Value

A good mentor needs also to sponsor relationship networking with others. One of the major gains from these arrangements is the mentor's demonstration of the career value available from networking, and from building a wider set of relationships that can assist a mentee's growth. Introductions are often facilitated by the mentor and many will pre-rehearse strategies with the mentee to 'break the ice' when such external parties are encountered. The results of such events can also be a worthwhile review point for subsequent mentoring discussions. This is an objective that is explicitly assigned to mentors in the FEI program for future CFOs referred to earlier, for example.

Peter Collins is a leading national professional coach and mentor to a number of CEOs, politicians with senior portfolio responsibilities and élite sporting leaders. He believes the role of a good mentor is to give their mentees:

> "A sense of meaning and purpose, and to find ways for them to address the threshold moments in their life, which they must cross in order to be a leader."

Collins said in particular that military leaders understand this distinction. He said that:

> "World War Two Allied Forces Commander in Europe, US General Dwight Eisenhower, stated that '15% of the people landing on D Day will be killed.' That's an enormous responsibility of power and leadership when you know many of those under your command will surely die. He possessed this knowledge before the D Day landing started, but also knew there was no escape from this consequence."

Mentoring grows in other particularly important ways within military careers. Former Head of the Australian Army Lt Gen Peter Leahy AC stated:

> "Reflecting on my description of mentoring by subordinates (Sergeant to Lieutenant), I would definitely call it reverse-mentoring. In this situation the junior rank is actually the more experienced and he is expected to support, train and assist the new officer in learning his trade.
>
> "Another form of mentoring in the army is the formal system of having a second-in-command for nearly every appointment. In theory the 2IC is there to assist the Commander but in reality he or she is there in case the Commander becomes a casualty. The 2IC then steps in and takes over command. To make sure that he or she is prepared, the Commander usually involves them in all matters and ensures that they are familiar with what is going on. A 2IC is expected to deputise for the Commander and can speak on his behalf. This method institutionalises mentoring."

This military analogy has a much broader application. Mentors should approach a mentoring association with a positive expectation of reverse-mentoring. The best mentoring relationships all have two-way streets of learning. Most mentors want to come away with some new insights themselves, and they usually do.

Peter Collins believes mentors must try and show the importance of understanding the implications of leadership. Sometimes the ritualism in a leader's actions can send a strong message to all parties, including the leader him or herself.

> "For example, in a more positive respect, the first act of a new CEO at BHP Billiton is to sign the company's values statement. It's a simple but positive sign that says 'these are now my own' and I must accept and respect them, whilst I am in this role."

Peter Collins also believes that business mentoring is still in a somewhat underdeveloped state. He has observed the existence of trivial 'coffee mentoring' which "doesn't delve into the necessary challenges or issues in sufficient depth", Collins says. As a faculty member and the mentor's leader in the Vincent Fairfax Fellowship program at the Melbourne Business School, Peter Collins exposes the participants to derailment exercises early in the course.

> "It's a combination of narcissism, hubris, Achilles-heel-style behaviour and no fear of failure all coming together as one very powerful force. All participants recognise the reality and applicability of this to their own lives. Having mentors around you is a positive way of identifying and then actively managing yourself through this major trap in a life of leadership. Knowing the risks of derailment and failure in senior leadership positions, and exposing this to your mentee in a positive and considered way, is a major component of the mentor's role," says Collins.

Ontological Learning

Collins speaks of another critical characteristic of a good mentor. It is to expose their mentee to some ontological learnings. Ontology is a branch of philosophy where one is exposed to learning across matters of being that are fundamental to life. This comes from exposure of mentees to events that open their mind to other realities or possibilities in life not encountered before. They are issues that hopefully any leader will never have to deal with but a reflection on what someone once had to confront can be very powerful.

For example, the former CEO of Cricket Australia, Malcolm Speed, describes how he worked with then-test captain Steve

Waugh to take his team to Gallipoli on the way to an Ashes test series in England. The purpose was to expose the élite of Australia's cricketers to what that tragic battle had meant to their own countrymen nearly 90 years before. Such a first-hand experience puts a person's current struggle against the odds on a sporting field into a quite different perspective, and it also makes them think about what comradeship and teamwork really meant in a different and most extreme theatre of life. Hawthorn Football Club coach Alistair Clarkson took his AFL team to hike the Kokoda track in the year before they went on to win the 2008 AFL premiership. The same objective, but a much stronger learning message was delivered as these footballers had to climb the mountains and experience first-hand the actual physical hardship of Australia's World War Two soldiers in Papua New Guinea.

A similar ontological learning opportunity has come from visits by some of our élite athletes and leaders to Robben Island – the site of Nelson Mandela's imprisonment for 27 years, before apartheid ended in South Africa. Another very effective ontological venue on racial prejudice is Gandhi's house in India, or Anne Frank's house in Amsterdam. All three sites leave indelible marks in the mind and heart as to the pernicious magnitude and level of cruelty that racism and cultural colonisation had reached in relatively recent human history. Again the impact of these experiences can change the mind as to the hurt that racial vilification can cause in life itself, but also in the sports arena.

A simpler and quite valuable ontological experience is called shadowing or 'to follow the leader' for a day or a week or more. By following the mentor or another leader of their choice, the mentee sees first-hand what the responsibilities of senior leadership roles are actually like. Former Victorian Police Commissioner Christine Nixon employed this technique in reverse by engaging one of her mentors and Professor of Diversity and Organisational

Change at the Melbourne Business School, Amanda Sinclair, to shadow her at work for a number of days and advise her on how well she was managing herself and others – or not! It proved a very valuable learning technique.

In developing their mentees, the mentor needs to be conscious that leadership skills are ingrained, but also trained for. The value of ontological encounters is that many important learnings can be 'caught' this way, when they can't be 'taught'. Exposure to the right experiences, encounters and thinking are critical for a mentee to understand what leadership really means.

Delivering on commitments is also a key driver of mentoring credibility. Often a conversation will spur the mentor to dig out a reference or book that might help the mentee at the next meeting, or sooner. Ensuring that such commitments are delivered is an important foundation to trust, respect and integrity in the relationship.

As Ken Blanchard wrote in the *One Minute Manager*:

> "There is a difference between interest and commitment. When you are interested in doing something, you do it only when it is convenient. When you are committed, you accept no excuses."

Building Confidence

The mentoring meeting is the safe haven to develop an approach to some workplace trials in areas of difficult tests and challenges. Reviewing progress subsequently becomes mandatory, as does a conscious desire and display by the mentor of positive recognition and acknowledgement of successes when they have occurred. Mentoring is much about building confidence which can wither if it is not nurtured progressively, as and when it is needed. As a mentor you need to show uncommonly positive attitudes. There is a parallel to dealing with a child. A child who is shown unconditional love and loyalty will accept criticism. One who is not loved will always rebel against it. As mentor, you are the safe haven and you have to live that with your mentee always. Peter Day, a non-executive Director at SAI Global and Ansell says:

> "Mentees want to feel they are on safe territory, before they fully open up".

Clutterbuck and Megginson (1999, PP 18-22) provide a useful framework for a mentor to assess a mentee and guide that person through the components of the emotional intelligence framework pioneered by Daniel Goleman (discussed in Chapter Five). Specifically the mentor will explore the mentee's knowledge of their own emotions, in terms of questions from the former about how they might have felt during difficult moments, and strategies they would usually employ to manage those emotions. As a corollary, the mentor will explore how they might assess and manage emotions in others; where they might have difficulties in doing that; and their broader skills in relationship management. The parallels of such an approach are also there with positive psychology. The mentor's assignment is to explore defensiveness to criticism – whether the mentee plays the blame game or is overly excuse-driven – and factors that might drive their unease or anger in certain situations. Once the bases of the mentee's difficulties in self-awareness, self-management or managing others are spotted, the mentor can suggest alternative remedial strategies that the mentee might employ to 'accentuate the positive and eliminate the negative' in how they conduct themselves under stress or challenge.

Role-playing with the mentor is a useful component of the mentoring encounters, as it provides a safe situation for the mentee to explore alternative ways of handling matters. The mentee's responses can then be reviewed on the spot and re-played in a new exercise until their confidence starts to lift. Alternatively, the mentee's psychological code might suggest the need to go further and set out possible challenge encounters at work. These can then be rehearsed and alternative approaches that the mentee might later apply at work may be explored in order to gain more confidence in being, for example, a 'voice' in the relevant team, or able to negotiate more difficult situations.

Very often a mentor will be the key to a mentee gaining insights on the relevance of recent developments in the field of positive psychology and the need for instructive learnings in how to rewire the latter's brain in order to avoid the amygdala attacks discussed earlier in the book. A very good example of a mentee who learned this skill from his mentor is former Prime Minister John Howard.

> "Today's crisis is often tomorrow's old news. My mentor, John Carrick, impressed on me that you had to keep cool in a crisis and be persistent until you had batted the issue through to a resolution, or completely away."

Whilst the mentee really needs to drive the agenda, the mentor must be an astute listener and also examiner of what is heard in order to elicit related issues of importance. As Steve Vamos, President of the SKE and a Telstra non-executive Director, stated:

> "A mentor can give you what you can't give yourself – an independent look at you. Mentors must have two prime characteristics above all else – sincere personal rapport, and a genuine interest in you and your career. On the other side, mentees need to make the effort to listen openly in order to get the most out of the relationship."

The mentor will be a significant beneficiary in the relationship. As well as discharging Levinson's thesis that all of us want to put back into the next generation at some stage of later adult life, the knowledge acquired can also be very useful both personally and organisationally to the mentor.

In summary, the mentor should see his or her role as: to assist the development of strategic thinking by the mentee; be a careful and caring active listener; to hold up the mirror on the mentee's own behaviours, or impact on others; to positively reinforce and encourage the mentee; to celebrate the mentee's successes; to point out opportunities for growth and development; to role-play and counsel on difficult situations or interpersonal relationships the mentee is experiencing; to expose the mentee to new learning experiences; and where appropriate to sponsor the mentee.

Similarly the mentor will probably be the first to realise when the value potential of each meeting is starting to drop, when a potential 'running on empty' point is being reached. The mentor therefore must have the courage and the respect to state that it is time for the mentee to move forward from the formal and intensive period of this relationship. For some mentors this means being the first to spot the point of the need to say goodbye, reflecting both the value of this journey and the mutual respect established.

Twelve Traits of a Great Mentor

A good mentor can be summarised as a person who displays the following style and characteristics within a mentoring relationship:

1. Recognises the fundamental business nature of the mentoring relationship and the standards and conduct necessary to deliver primary value for the mentee.
2. Works hard to make themselves be and appear to be honest, friendly, open, trustworthy, confidential, accessible, encouraging, consistent and dependable for their mentee, particularly when the latter's needs are how to respond to a crisis in their career.
3. Exercises patient due diligence on ascertaining the mentee's needs through active listening and exploration in order to encourage mutual establishment of objectives for the relationship and to explore pathways that are likely to be of most value to the mentee.
4. Resists the temptation to fix the mentee's perceived problems through directive interventions, but rather acts to reinforce existing positive behaviours and approaches by the mentee and to provide alternative suggestions about ways they might best want to take the next steps forward … for themselves.
5. Sets written objectives for the relationship with the mentee but encourages the latter to initiate these. Ensures the goals are measurable, appropriate, have stretch but are attainable. Monitors progress at reasonable intervals throughout.
6. Willingly discloses themselves and their own experiences – including failures and consequential learnings – to the mentee, in a way that enhances mutual trust, but also encourages the mentee to believe that their journey has a parallel with that of the mentor.

7. Draws out and explores the mentee's career dream and encourages innovation and creative thought as a way to help realise that aspiration. Celebrates victories and achievements of the mentee against plans of action, as and when they are reached.
8. Brokers useful relationships, expanded networks and shadowing experiences for the mentee, and reinforces the value of them doing this in a sustainable way for their own career development.
9. Facilitates exposure to ontological learnings and experiences to upgrade the mentee's insights, thinking and experiences of life's most extreme challenges, (e.g. Gallipoli, Kokoda, Robben Island).
10. Walks the talk on maintaining integrity with the mentoring relationship: maintains confidentiality; delivers on commitments to the mentee; actively manages any conflicts of interest that could do harm to the mentee; is prepared to engage in 'hard talk' when the mentee is demonstrating avoidance behaviours or being blindsided on some core realities. While always being honest, also commits to doing 'no harm' to the mentee.
11. Recognises and rewards progress in appropriate ways.
12. Knows when the major potential from the relationship has been reached and transforms that as a positive opportunity for the mentee to move forward on his or her own, or with a different form of advice or assistance.

8

THE MENTEE'S BEST MINDSET

The mentee is the primary customer of the mentoring relationship, so that person's needs, expectations and objectives require early identification and attention. Often those needs, however, are only known to the mentee and kept within their own minds. Accordingly, a corollary of this primary customer service imperative is for the mentee him or herself to be fully transparent about these needs and to be proactive in seeking the mentor's help to address them. Assertive customers who are clear about their needs and expectations will always get the best results.

Confronting a mentor for the first time, especially one who is a significant power figure in a mentee's world, can be a bit intimidating and that needs to be recognised for what it is. However, the mentee needs to remind him or herself that the mentor has already made a commitment to be there to help. To do that productively they need your professional database, personal bio script and career expectation menus. Many of the best texts on mentoring, e.g. Klasen and Clutterbuck (2002), advise the mentee to pursue the mentor's assistance to chart a personal development plan after a few weeks. That is a valid conclusion but it also needs to be tackled like a large change-management program, where you expect later encounters and experiences will cause necessary modifications to the plan.

The responsibilities of the mentee flow naturally from the expected benefits such a program is intended to have for them. Mentees are expected to:

- Gain experiences from outside their current business area of responsibility, from someone in a senior role who has 'reached a peak' in that business to which the mentee is aspiring
- Develop new skills and approaches to dealing with the senior echelons of complex organisations
- Accelerate their own personal change and growth expectations
- Identify professional growth and development areas relevant to their career path, and improve employability and potential as a result
- Be inspired to set and realise new goals, strategies and processes, and to achieve these effectively and efficiently
- Capitalise from excellent networking opportunities.

Accordingly, mentees need to be prepared to both initiate and sustain productive relationships with their mentor. In particular, they need to be mindful of the following initiatives successful mentees have taken in the past.

Proactively Seek out Appropriate Mentors

Mentees must take proactive responsibility for their own career development and be purposeful with initiating contact with the mentor. The value of proactively searching for appropriate mentors is perhaps best expressed by Federal Liberal Member for Goldstein, and Minister for Trade and Investment, Andrew Robb, who has a strong belief in the value of mentoring:

> "I had just assumed everybody stumbled across mentors throughout their life, or maybe I have been fortunate because I'm naturally curious and a good listener ... I found that if you could get to people who really were the sharpest in their area, invariably they had distilled the essence of their business or area of expertise down to some very simple principles." (Robb 2011, P68)

Searching out mentors can also be very valuable when you have just taken on a major career change. When he moved from a career in professional basketball administration to one in Australian and then world cricket, Malcolm Speed started his professional life in the latter sport well aware of 'knowing what he didn't know'. He wanted to seek out mentors who would help him fill in the gaps, in order for him to be a better and more effective leader. It was an early priority for him, and one he capitalised upon.

John Bertrand, successful business entrepreneur and skipper of 1983 America's Cup winning yacht, Australia II, agrees:

> "I have always sought mentors out during my career. What an opportunity to learn from motivated successful people! To be able to tap into life's lessons via a mentor is an incredible opportunity."

As business entrepreneur, former Wallaby Captain and twice Rugby World Cup Champion, John Eales said "I have had many mentors", and he is always looking for a new mentor who can challenge and push him to think differently.

Adopt a Strategic Approach

Mentees need to have a strategic approach overall in dealing with their mentor. An excellent example of this is Jason Clare MP. While he had been a protégé of former NSW Premier and Federal Foreign Minister Bob Carr early in his career, Jason Clare saw the material value of mentoring most clearly while he worked for the large ASX-listed infrastructure group, Transurban. That company successfully utilised mentoring arrangements amongst its senior executive team.

Jason has a personal objective to bring into his political career those ideas and approaches he saw working well in business. In particular, he wants to be quite strategic about his political objectives and vision during his longer-term journey in parliamentary life. He has a mentor with whom he meets every three months; someone with whom he can share challenges, thoughts and review alternative ways of tackling critical political issues. He notes other senior political figures he admires, like Paul Keating, always had key figures around them.

> "Paul was mentored early in his career by former NSW Premier Jack Lang, (who had been sacked by then NSW Governor Sir Philip Game during the Great Depression), and later Bill Kelty of the ACTU was an important influence to his political thinking. A good mentor can provide skills for what you are doing, and also critical advice on how to manage the broad range of relationships you must master for a successful career in politics and government."

Former Prime Minister John Howard agrees with this perspective to have higher level objectives in your political life, and using the safe zone of a discussion with your mentor is a very useful way to define what that means for you. One of the most important lessons he received from his mentor John Carrick, was to make and practise a distinction in his career between matters that were proactive and strategic, and those that were tactical and would emerge on a daily basis. During an interview for this book, John Howard said to me:

> "My political mentor John Carrick had been a prisoner of war during the Japanese occupation of Singapore at the now infamous Changi prison camp. John told me he had physical challenges to face every day – whether it was dysentery, infections, diarrhoea or any one of a host of other illnesses; the harsh treatment meted out by their captors; or to support a mate who was suffering. But John

really only had one mental challenge. And it was a simple one – to survive and go home. And so that lesson provided a parallel distinction that I used in my political life. Problems or issues were going to emerge on a daily basis, many of them unanticipated in their nature, but they had to be dealt with – just as John Carrick had to in his daily life as a POW. That was a separate matter to the strategic longer-term objectives I would set for myself during a life in politics. They were always there as well, and I was able to achieve many of them, but only by being patient, purposeful and also waiting for the right time to go after them. That's a very important lesson I received, and it's one I encourage others to search for and discover in their own way. John Carrick had to be patient to achieve his mental challenge, but one day he did and he came home."

Smarter mentees also need to be flexible and responsive to fitting in with the mentor's demanding schedule. They can use a variety of methods to initiate contact with the mentor or that person's office – telephone, email, face-to-face – always mindful of the need to be polite but persistent when confronted with any 'dragon at the gate' behaviour from those who are engaged to protect the mentor's schedule and who may not yet know about the protégé's and/or the mentor's involvement together in this exercise.

Getting to Know each Other

Assume that the mentor will want to know a lot about the mentee personally and their professional and educational background, as well as their career to-date, and personal and family circumstances. Mentees will need to be prepared for this in a detailed way, even if similar details have already been provided to any organisers of this mentoring program.

Mentees and their mentors also need to have a shared sense of humanity and core values. As Federal Sex Discrimination Commissioner Elizabeth Broderick says:

> "Mentoring can't be forced. You need a shared sense of humanity to really make the relationship work. You both need to give a bit of yourself. The greatest impact from mentoring is to share with others who you are, and to care deeply about what happens to your colleague. Building sound relationships will be based on a genuine sharing of experiences."

The draw of core values can also influence selection of an employer, where a young protégé might expect to find better quality mentors during his or her career. An example of this is Mike Fitzpatrick, presently AFL Chairman, but also a former élite footballer with the Carlton AFL club in the 1970s and 1980s.

> "I talked to most VFL (now AFL) teams. Carlton impressed me with their winning culture and financial stability. They stressed what being a part of their club would mean for me. They had a talented side with some iconic players including Perce Jones, one of the best ruckmen in the competition and the legendary John Nicholls coaching. So I could be understudy to Perce and be coached by one of the best ruckmen in the game. Overall that swung my decision in their favour."

At Carlton, Mike encountered another lifetime mentor, his coach David Parkin, who became a great source of counsel to him and is someone with whom he still speaks regularly.

Many leaders interviewed for this book state that mentors in their lives have been critical in instilling core moral ethical and leadership values into their lives at an early stage of their career. Retired High Court Judge The Hon Michael Kirby is no exception to this, but he has taken the learnings he received on values from a key early mentor into a unique direction of practice during his legal and judicial career. Michael has been at the forefront of a relatively recent movement where many judges are being clearer about the values behind the pronouncements and decisions they make. He is one of a number of members on the judiciary who believe it is no longer just about interpreting black letter law.

In any mentoring association, the vision or dream for the mentee's career should be prepared and provided directly to the mentor. Mentees must be honest and clear with the mentor about what expectations are held for learning and achievement to ensure both have an understanding of the mentee's goals. Finally, setting out specific objectives from the mentoring assignment, related to the mentee's career vision, is an important intermediate milestone to be achieved within the first three or four meetings held.

Tania de Jong, Founder of Creative Universe, Creativity Australia and Creative Innovation Global and a leading entrepreneur in the arts, believes that mentors were critical to helping her realise her own career dream.

> "As an entrepreneur and a woman, I have had my detractors. My mentors have been people who have understood me, where my dream has come from, and why I hold that. They have always encouraged me not to give up. Their belief in my own vision and the bigger picture of trying to make a difference has kept me going.
>
> They have also been great teachers and appraised me about how Australian business-thinking works, and have been excellent connectors to open the doors for me that have been relevant to what I am trying to do."

A mentee needs to spend time getting to know the mentor; they will appreciate that as an important feature of the relationship-building that needs to happen. Aim to enjoy the experience and use humour positively to show an ability to be aware of your own weaknesses, but not so flippantly that it betrays an underlying belief that there is no real desire to be able to change or develop.

Never have an expectation of perfection in a mentor. Try and gain a balanced perspective about this leader and who that person really is, as opposed to what they have done. As John Bertrand noted in the previous chapter, mentors should have an expectation to be honest about their failures, so mentees should go into the relationship expecting to find out about this – in particular, how their mentors learned from their failures and how they applied that hard-fought-for knowledge for the future.

Ensure confidentiality is maintained about the nature and content of your exchanges with the mentor, as a mentee may be exposed to matters that are commercially or personally sensitive. As an example, a mentee in the Victorian Police LMP was included in a meeting of his mentor's investment banking employer, and made privy to confidential discussions about a prospective corporate takeover. Later that mentee introduced his mentor to a preparations briefing and rehearsal for a drug raid by the Special Operations Group. Both participants took away some unique perspectives about the work pressures the other party was subject to.

Good mentees also display a willingness to listen and an openness to learn new ways of doing things. Whilst mentors can take their protégés to new environments to broaden their thinking, the mentees have to be alert to take in the potential. As Michael Kirby noted, he received early support from one of his mentors, Lionel Murphy QC who was Commonwealth Attorney-General from 1972 to 1975 and Judge on the High Court of Australia from 1975 until his death in 1986. Michael said:

> "He was a very different personality from me. He was a great party-goer and I was a party-pooper. But for some reason he used me in cases that he had in front of the High Court and that was a great experience."

Mentees Must Kick-start the Mentoring Relationship

Mentoring is a reflective exercise that is best kick-started by the mentee. In the preparation of briefing material for the mentor, consider what events or milestones have had a significant contribution to how your career has developed, and also to the successes experienced and learnings from them. Further, identify a summary of critical challenges you face and areas where you are seeking particular perspectives from your mentor.

As Tania de Jong notes:

> "Whilst my mentors have admired my passion, my persistence and my talent, they have helped me to modify my personality and approach in order to be more effective at getting things done. They have also coached me on better ways to manage my staff and the more challenging interpersonal relationships I face. However, it was up to me to sponsor these issues with them. They can't mind-read about that, although some of them are extremely intuitive!"

An 'outside–in' and 'inside–out' mindset is an important part of the kick-start. If you have your Myers-Briggs Type Indicator result, or have any 360 degree feedback material on how you see yourself and how others see you, be prepared to share these or the key insights available from them, including the external insights of you that you find concerning barriers confronting your career. The mentoring conversation will need to focus on how to break these down very early in the piece. List the ones affecting your career growth or development now and strategies you are contemplating, or have actioned, to address them. Be honest in disclosing the ones that you have tried and that have failed with any ideas you have on why you think they might not have worked. As the relationship develops, expect to hear acknowledgement of failures and shortcomings in your mentor's own life in response to current challenges you are sharing, where failure is a real possibility in your own mind.

Ensure you reveal yourself 'as you are', rather than 'how you might like to be seen'. The second approach will deny achievement of the full potential value from the mentoring relationship. It may even bias it unproductively. A mentee must overcome his or her 'fear factor' with the mentor. That also means the protégé should expect to be challenged and pushed to do things they may have found prior discomfort with. A good mentor won't try and direct a person in what to do, but it can be expected they will constructively criticise the mentee's approaches, giving reasons and suggesting alternatives that are likely to be more successful, based on their experiences.

Former Chief Commissioner of Police in Victoria, Christine Nixon, believes that strategies and skills learned from mentors are important for any person to learn how to conquer their fears.

> "Fear is a massive issue in people's careers today. The more I talk to people and understand what they are afraid of, the greater I see the significance. Many are concerned with the question: 'What will people think of me?' A good mentor can do role-playing with their mentee and review alternatives in learning how to 'face my fears'. I saw the importance of mentors after the 2009 Victorian bushfires. People can experience post-traumatic growth, but you need some helping hands around you to be able to do that too, and to get through the initial trauma reactions."

In the early stages of the mentoring relationship, the mentee's task will often be to study the leader and try to absorb as much of the mentor's life experiences as possible. A challenge will be to keep the mentor's interests on the radar screen, so you are more likely to draw examples from their career that match your own set of challenges. After each meeting, a task is then to think through how those approaches could be integrated into the way you do things. Some trial and error may be needed at work with those learnings. Many mentees take extensive notes from their meetings and use those as a basis for study, later reflection and preparation for the next encounter. Be prepared to show constructive criticism of what the mentor has outlined, based on your own subsequent endeavours, and review these experiences in later sessions. This is often a key to the benefits of reverse-mentoring for the mentor which will also enhance their commitment to the relationship that is a genuine two-way street.

Be scrupulous about actions and plans agreed with the mentor, as this relationship is a self-directed learning process. Implement them and other 'homework' faithfully and with care. Record the objective results and personal observations as to what happened during implementation of any trial or project, and comment on the role and impacts on the mentee and others that transpired during those trials. Be honest on this in subsequent discussions with the mentor. Remember what mentors are advised to do – not reach over and solve your problems but rather to discuss parallel experiences they went through, and how they identified, assessed and ranked their choices for action. Craft questions to draw out this type of information from the mentor.

Ask for regular feedback from the mentor and provide feedback when required. As Kelly O'Dwyer, Federal Member for Higgins, states:

> "Really good mentoring relationships must go both ways. You need to have conversations about your career with people outside that square. We all need that respected independent input on where it is all going, but also some frank exchanges on the big challenges. Politics is also about team-building. In your electorate you have volunteers and a paid workforce, and you must build and lead a strong and cohesive team. Being able to talk about this to senior leaders and people outside politics who are my mentors has been extraordinarily helpful."

Planning for Mentoring Meetings

An astute mentee should plan for any meeting ahead of time, create a list of things to discuss that are relevant to the mentee's development. A suggestion is to identify two challenges the mentee has faced in each of five areas:

- Their commercial or business dealings

- Strategy development and/or execution
- Challenging peer and boss relationships and/or networks
- Corporate governance
- Ethical dilemmas.

Under the cases identified within each of these five headings, the mentee should identify whether the key problems or challenges reflect any or all of the following: their own ability to self-manage the situation; the relationships to their career choices and options; how they learn and organise themselves to solve problems. For one thing, a mentor will be mightily impressed if you have shown this degree of application and preparation for your meetings, and will be likely to treat you and your committed intentions much more seriously as a result.

It's best to telegraph these thoughts and preparations ahead to the mentor, and then to amplify the relevant storyline at the next meeting. Push your mentor to give you assignments, or projects to work on between meetings. Mentoring is a pro-active art and it requires this style of assertive behaviour to be fully productive and not degenerate into ambling fireside chats over coffee.

Maintain awareness about other skills, resources, contacts or relationships that you may need to call on to reap the full potential of this mentoring arrangement. While mentors are meant to be sufficiently experienced so that you can learn from them in most respects, they are not always 'the font of all knowledge' for issues and challenges that may be encountered by a mentee.

If possible employ a group of mentors as a personal board of directors, as Priscilla Claman advises in the *Harvard Business Review* (2011). Mike Fitzpatrick, AFL Chairman did just this to kick off his Hasting Funds Management Business initiative, and he regards this characteristic as a hallmark of its success.

Active networking is a key skill for mentees to acquire. Group mentoring programs like the Company Directors Chairmen's Mentoring Program provide this as a feature. In individual mentoring environments, the mentee will need to continuously update the mix of mentors engaged with, so that value can always be delivered where it is most needed. Classifying relationships in your mind, as to where they are most relevant or beneficial, can help. Cross and Thomas advise in the *Harvard Business Review* (2011) that mentors will also need to be de-layered if they aren't adding value to, or are draining energy from, the mentee, which can sometimes happen.

The distinction between being a mentor and a mentee can converge when there is a peer-mentoring arrangement. Good mentees often have to switch for their peers and become astute listeners and mentors themselves. Mary Woodridge, Shadow Minister for Community Services in Victoria, returned from completing a Harvard MBA to become CEO of a not-for-profit company, and established a peer mentoring group of others in similar situations.

> "We were a group of five CEOs. We all knew each other from the US business schools we had attended. We got together for a weekend every now and then and each of us experienced being both mentee and mentor – that's what peer mentors need to do."

It's not that counter-intuitive to ask your mentor where and how you can help them. The chances of a positive acceptance are very high.

Being confronted with a power figure as a mentor will probably encourage the mentee initially to take on some 'reflective glory' style objectives, and to emulate walking in the mentor's shoes. As author of *Mao's Last Dancer*, Li CunXin eloquently expressed (and we quoted in the introduction):

> "A good mentor helps you to walk in your shoes, even if you start out just wanting to walk in theirs."

Mentoring is not about being a groupie in the mentor's fan club; it is about using their experiences to help find the mentee's own mojo.

Further, mentees must recognise that mentors and mentoring relationships will generally have finite productive lives. As stated in the previous chapter, on average, intense mentoring relationships go for no more than 12 to 18 months.

Mentees also need to remind themselves that mentors are very busy people and be aware of the signs of 'mentor fatigue'. Many mentors will try and deliver effective and intensive value early. Often a point is reached where they may start to feel that the need for the frequency and depth of discussions has reached a natural end – for now. In any career, mentees will respect and manage this deftly, but also retain the mentor as a long-term confidante and begin the search for others who can play different but also valuable mentoring roles.

One myth worth exploding is that you will cease being a mentee around the age of 50 or so. An example is Michael Kirby. Michael has never ceased to pursue mentors in his later career. Following his retirement from the judiciary, Michael has taken an active role in international human rights issues. Michael states.

> "I was blessed with many fine mentors and now in the international arena I know many leaders of great ability, warmth and insight, such as Mary Robinson, a past High Commissioner for Human Rights at the United Nations; Louise Arbour, one of her successors; and Navanethem Pillay, *[the then]* current High Commissioner. Jonathan Mann, who headed the first United Nations global program on HIV, is another inspiration. Mentors are a critical part of a life in leadership."

Mary Robinson, who was also former President of Ireland, is now a member of an esteemed high-level group established by Nelson Mandela and chaired by Archbishop Desmond Tutu, called 'The Elders'. The Elders is effectively a mentoring and advisory group on global human rights and social issues, and it's an environment "where we continue to learn from each other", Mary said.

Twelve Steps to Establish a Successful Mentee Mindset

To summarise, the following steps will ensure you adopt a successful and satisfied mentee mindset:

1. Prepare a mentee's career and life bio for the mentor, to bring that person up to speed with who the mentee is, together with any 360 degree feedback data that reveals image and self-image of the mentee.
2. Outline a career vision and support it with summaries of positive experiences that have worked and challenges not yet overcome.
3. Be proactive, and when necessary, be persistent to establish a meeting program in the mentor's schedule for the full duration of your working relationship, and exhibit flexibility in responding to the mentor's constraints and diary pressures.
4. Allow time for chemistry between mentor and mentee to build, and for the possibility that the directions and value of the relationship may be a little unclear during this stage.
5. Probe the mentor's value sets and determine their compatibility with your own. Beat a strategic retreat if any alarm bells go off on who that person really is. Advise the program director and seek help to address this, as appropriate.
6. Set mentoring objectives after sound chemistry is established with the mentor, and document and implement objectives and plans of action, as they are agreed.
7. Be prepared to discuss the most complex and sensitive relationships and challenges you are facing, as well as ethical and moral dilemmas.

8. Prepare assessments of any trials or experiments undertaken for your subsequent discussions with the mentor.
9. Actively pursue other relationship or network-building initiatives that the mentor recommends, or other resources or people suggested for consultation.
10. Pursue feedback from your mentor, and give feedback on your thoughts and experiences with the challenges and assignments provided for you.
11. Respect signs from the mentor that your mentoring association may be reaching its point of full potential. Seek advice on future pathways you should pursue, and the basis of any less formal continuing relationship that may exist with that mentor.
12. Remember – 'one career, many mentors' – always do your best to seek out a great mentor relative to your present career aspirations and needs.

9

THE MENTORING RELATIONSHIP

The matchmaking phase is critical to forming positive facilitated mentoring relationships. Notwithstanding that, other informal mentoring relationships can be constructed on a self-starting basis and do not need to be intermediated by a third-party. In fact, one theme of this book – 'one career, many mentors' – connotes a dynamic mindset of the mentee initiating a range of relationships with potential mentors who will be able to assist aspects of the person's career. This will be particularly the case when a foundation mentoring experience has concluded and the mentee has proceeded to a new level of confidence about both the workings and the benefits of mentoring.

The first meeting between mentor and mentee is perhaps the most critical. Basic trust, openness and confidence will most likely be established at this time, for the remainder of the learning relationship.

A good mentor will have done as much homework as possible on the protégé. He or she will use that information both to ask questions and seek to fill in missing gaps, and also to draw out the mentee's experiences and so demonstrate the leader's knowledge of whom he or she is dealing with.

In particular, the first meeting will:

- Start off 'getting to know each other' and begin to show the 'personal self', by outlining some aspects of the home lives, family background for each party, etc.
- Outline the mutual commitments to, and objectives for, the relationship
- Discuss what mentoring really is and accordingly set a 'trusted adviser' tone and style for discussions – particularly by the mentor capitalising on opportunities to recount personal experiences aligned to early challenges being described by the mentee
- Establish a hallmark of candour, openness and compatible value sets for both parties
- Show they can both be active listeners
- Set a challenging professional standard for the discussions
- Confirm confidentiality as an early protocol
- Set a calendar of regular meetings, if not already established
- Openly question and probe whether the right chemistry is being established.

Once the right chemistry is established for ongoing discussions after the first few meetings, the mentoring pair should also set clear objectives or goals for the relationship. The ultimate onus for initiating and concluding this really lies with the mentee, as the arrangement is primarily to assist that person's career development. If this is at all unclear, it would be worthwhile engaging a discussion on what each party thinks success might look like by the end of this learning association together.

Some authors, e.g. Zachary (2000), have suggested establishing a mentoring partnership agreement. This requires a level of formality that may be neither necessary nor desirable, but it is important that goals be formalised, discussion themes established and that there be mutual validation of the protocols or guidelines for the relationship, for example confidentiality and two-way feedback. Zachary (2005) has identified three simple stages or phases in mentoring that both parties should remind themselves about continuously: preparing, negotiating and enabling. These stages are well named but also continuously iterating throughout the mentoring relationship. Both mentor and mentee need to prepare for each meeting and the discussions need to take on a negotiating attitude for all key issues encountered so the edges of the conversation are opened and pressed on both sides. At the end of the day, mentoring needs outcomes. These could be most usually preferred, or new, approaches to be taken by the mentee in confronting challenging situations or adopting new strategies and skills for managing complex relationships at work.

There should also be a program of work established that is both purposeful and flexible. A formal agreement to discussing a set of topics not only for the duration, but also for major sub-periods, e.g. quarterly, is a common hallmark of success in mentoring. However, the most fruitful relationships will also reserve a time at each meeting for issues to come up informally – perhaps having a provision for hot topics from the mentee is one technique that has worked very successfully.

Bumps in the Mentoring Road

There are many reasons why mentoring momentum may be thwarted. Any failures with openness, honesty, trust and confidentiality will be critical, but there can be other simple obstacles encountered to achieving fuller learnings from any mentoring arrangement.

Chris Argyris (1991) makes one distinction that is important in this respect. Mentors can focus too much on problem-solving or 'making a change to put things right'. This is called single-loop learning, and it's a trap that mentoring exchanges can fall into, courtesy of the behaviour and style of the mentor. The more astute approach is for a mentor to go beyond a detection of errors, and further into the underlying assumptions and values that underpin them. Argyris calls this 'double-loop' learning and it requires a more comprehensive level of inquiry and questioning by the mentor.

A common misconception of both participants in a mentoring program is that it is a confidential but high level protective friendship. It is expected that a friendly relationship will develop, but that is a side-product. In fact, a major risk to be guarded against in any mentoring arrangement is the development of an unhealthy dependency. The relationship is about empowerment and the career growth of the mentee, and possibly some reverse-mentoring. These prospective benefits will only prove valuable and durable if the mentee's boundaries are pushed. Stan Wallis, formerly CEO of Amcor and Chairman of several leading listed companies and the Business Council of Australia, stated:

> "The prime value of one of my most important mentors in my business life was to help me appreciate the importance of mental toughness and to advise me on how best to acquire and practise it. That doesn't mean you must become a difficult person to deal with, or worse. The key implication is that life's challenges in senior and CEO roles often require that you maintain your mental toughness through to the resolution of some very difficult problems. If your mentee doesn't realise that, a timely but polite wake-up call may be needed."

As we discussed in the previous chapter, the mentee needs to be prepared to divulge his or her innermost challenges and fears about the career prospects and issues confronting them. After sharing insights and parallel stories, the mentor must push the mentee on addressing – and where necessary formulating – alternative strategies to confront such issues in between mentoring appointments, and then later to review and assess progress with the mentor. The best outcomes are where the mentee picks up cues from the mentoring leader and develops these further to articulate new approaches he or she could take in addressing these challenges, all the while with assistance and confidence-building from the mentor.

In advanced business and political circles, however, many of these challenges will be quite complex and daunting. The mentee may return to a future meeting with little progress to report and sometimes it will be because little action has been attempted. Mentors need to be skilled cross-examiners and intellectual, factual and mental archaeologists, uncovering what has happened and why. At the same time they must be mindful that they are the protégé's confidant, philosopher and living conscience. The best changes aren't those instructed by the mentor, they are those the mentee has been encouraged to discover and see as their own inspired ideas. There can be no substantive development without some hard lessons. Growth only comes from positive responses to negative conditions. However, sometimes the questioning of the mentor will need to be quite direct – even bordering on brutally frank – in the same way that a parent shows tough love to an adolescent child.

The skill required to do this is considerable, given the constant need for confidence-building of, and support for, the mentee. However, a life at work sometimes provides 'no easy way out' and must be confronted for what it is – without fear or favour by the emerging leader. Without this ability to confront and handle the tougher situations, the emergence of a mentee to top leadership will probably not occur. How mentoring facilitates that will represent a test of the mentor's skill to hold the mirror up when necessary.

Professor Bob Wood of the Melbourne Business School relates the story of a time in his life when a former mentor rang him up to effect more of a bump, than a nudge. Bob had defied the advice of this earlier mentor, when the two of them had searched through Bob's own strengths and skills and concluded his preferred direction was in research, and not administration. Years later when Bob had accepted the role of Deputy Vice Chancellor (DVC) at the University of Western Australia, this mentor rang him up to ask what he was doing, given their earlier discussions about Bob's comparative professional advantages. This call out of the blue from Bob's mentor caused him to reflect on the wisdom of staying in that DVC role. The view of others was that Bob was performing well as DVC, but he knew in his heart that his mentor was right and that he would be happier in a challenging research field. So later Bob sought out an opportunity to return to what he loved, a career in leading academic research on ethical and business leadership. Sometimes only a mentor will know you well enough to speak the career-resounding truth.

In these situations a mentor can soften the blow of a likely future failure by sharing his or her own experiences of failure under similar circumstances. This sometimes requires considerable courage from the leader but will inevitably strengthen the bond of the relationship, when the mentee appreciates they are being encouraged to tackle situations their counterpart also found to be extremely difficult.

Encouraging Innovation

At senior levels of business and government, mentees will use mentors to help them develop principles to be creative and innovative. A classic example of this was the late co-founder of Apple, Steve Jobs. Steve's mentor in the late 1970s was Mike Markkula, the angel investor who became shareholder 'number three' after Jobs and his co-founder Steve Wozniak. Markkula advised Jobs that he should use three principles to be innovative over time: (1) empathy (placing yourself consistently in the customer's shoes); (2) focus (to break issues down to the three or four things that really matter, and eliminate the rest); and (3) impute (form an opinion about something by both its substance and its appearance, on the basis people will want to feel comfortable with an IT device to overcome natural fears about its apparently inaccessible complexity).

Viva La Difference: Mentoring for Men and Women

One of the major challenges faced in any future mentoring assignment will be related to gender. The immediate needs of men and women are different, as much because their career prospects have been historically different post war, although this is changing in the right direction but very slowly.

The low share of senior executive and top board positions held by women in Australia raises a number of complex issues including the role gender plays in developing leadership potential, the different risk factors behind forming and managing relationships at work, and general attitudes towards sexuality in business.

Global management experts like Daniel Goleman and John Kotter have written that a person's career progress is as much about developing relationships as it is about building stocks of workplace merit or demonstrating knowledge and good practice. Notwithstanding this, there are gender-based differences in the perceived value of developing sensibly-cultivated work relationships.

Recent surveys of top businesswomen and men by the US Center for Work–Life Policy (CWLP) reveal that females are relatively slow to respond to these trends. Whilst 83% of men surveyed conclude "who you know" is at least as important for advancement as "how well you do your job", 77% of women see only the latter factor as critical, in the mistaken belief that future promotions will be based solely on technical merit. A woman's inclination to shun the relationship-capital game in business is pervasive, but also is being exercised at a cost to her own career development. The CWLP survey results reveal different perceptions on the value and objectives of business leadership itself. Men see that leadership positions deliver "money and power", and that strong business connections are paramount. The top leadership motivators for women are quite different and include team quality, job security, being "myself" on the job, and having flexible arrangements. These latter drivers also underpin the low value attached to senior relationship networking by women. Today the selection of more senior executives is driven heavily by identified abilities to handle risk, ambiguity and more complex interpersonal perspectives and challenges, than it is by displays of technical skill and timely job accomplishment. Astute development of senior business connections is therefore critical to show you can handle the pressure and "get to the top".

Both Australian research and the US CWLP results show women are reluctant to ask for help to land a top job. Men are 46% more likely to have a powerful male backer than women. The dilemma in many female minds may be linked to ambivalence over advanced personal relationships developing between the sexes at work.

Studies such as the 2007 Knowledge@Wharton report show that a significant number of co-workers will experience a sexual relationship with a co-worker during their career. Very many of these develop into long-term life partnerships. Increasing pressures of work are dissolving the distinction between weekday and weekend and also head office and home office. Furthermore, high male and female job participation rates are here to stay and so the incidence of not only strong personal associations, but also intimate relationships, forming on the job are more likely. The CWLP also reports 64% of senior men are reluctant to have a one-on-one meeting with a junior female under any conditions. Yet when asked to rank preferred mentors, most women prefer a male rather than a female mentor, in part because there aren't that many women at the top to advise on how to get there. So for women to accede to more senior roles, significant changes are needed in the attitudes of both genders.

Mentoring provides a transparent and formally sponsored key to reconcile these problems – especially if explicit and proactive strategies are included to protect the career and reputational risks of the parties involved.

The modern best-practice solution for this dilemma is to adopt a more direct and positive approach, rather than to put the organisational head in the sand. Leading global companies like Citibank, Deloitte, Unilever and Bristol-Myers Squibb are taking this course and avoiding the pitfalls, as are local leaders like Westpac, CBA and the Business Council of Australia's cross-industry mentoring program run jointly in association with AHRI. These initiatives all take a breakthrough approach by establishing robust in-house mentoring schemes with positive support networks to enable women to make better use of mentor sponsorship to advance their careers. Safety nets are also established to minimise the risk to participants of exposure to office rumour-mills, including active sponsorship of the mentoring scheme under a workplace diversity committee chaired by the CEO; provision of a mentoring director to oversee and report on progress with an open brief to be proactive in raising issues; and a confidential adviser to each mentee who is a peer of the mentor.

Now more than ever, our modern working environments are requiring both sexes to walk the line on gender equality every day, and be more conscious of the workplace sensitivities about sexual relationships and reputational risks. It is critical for high potential women to be more proactive and pursue clearer objectives and strategies to capitalise on the value of networking through mentoring, but also to expect and negotiate provision of reasonable safety nets from their employer. It's also desirable for significant changes to occur in the behaviour of some leading corporate men who have shown a vicarious preference to avoid walking this line.

Moments of Truth

Mentoring can have many 'ah ha' moments – where the mentee gets the mentor's cues and breaks these into more meaningful messages, symptoms and approaches to use when dealing with critical situations. This leads to progressive confidence that comes from sorting through the case studies of mentoring with positive results. These are also called 'breakthrough insights', and are necessary conditions for mentoring success, but they are not sufficient to guarantee this success.

The best mentoring outcomes occur when actual 'moments of truth' are reached by the mentee. Many protégés are guilty of star-gazing about what life at the top can be like. There is much mystery and romance attached to senior leadership roles, and for whoever holds them. A parallel sentiment is that there are often deeply held fears amongst mentees about the stress, pressure and complexity of these responsibilities, and whether the mentee can cut the mustard at this. That is why an experienced mentor provides unique and significant value – because they have been there and done it.

What is hoped for by the end of a mentoring assignment is a longer-term exposure during the relationship to all the problems and challenges faced by a mentee, and a feeling that they have road-tested all the high level challenges they are likely to face in any given top role. Those experiences will have been assessed with private family needs and pressures and whether work–life balance, or more likely work–life integration, can be handled well by the mentee. At this point the mentee will be able to feel that he or she has got what it takes to do the job, and can perform in a way that is complementary to the private life they want as well. At this juncture the moment of truth is clear. The mentee should ask him or herself:

"Do I want this, or not?"

Furthermore:

"Am I OK with either answer, because I have now seen this higher level life for what it is, or is likely to be – for me?"

A very clear example of this occurred in 1998 for Andrew Gaze – probably Australia's greatest ever basket-baller and five-time Olympian, as well as the nation's flag carrier at the 2000 Sydney Olympics. Andrew lists his father Lindsay as probably his greatest mentor in life.

Andrew recalled the occasion was when he had been invited to play a season for San Antonio Spurs in the US National Basketball Association late in 1998, and his father's advice was truly that of a mentor. At the time Andrew felt heavily conflicted about that option and his choices. It was mid-season in the local National Basketball League. His team, the Melbourne Tigers, was doing well and on top of the ladder with a chance at a third championship in the past seven years. Andrew led the League in scoring and seemed on the way to yet another national Most Valuable Player award. Lindsay, also still then head coach at the Tigers, had watched the extensive thought-process of his son, but also the wavering mindset, and finally came to him and said:

> "You cannot afford to pass up this once-in-a-lifetime opportunity."

Andrew will now not die wondering about this opportunity, as he accepted the one-year contract offer and was a member of the San Antonio team that won its first NBA Championship in 1999, returning in plenty of time to carry the Australian flag at the 2000 Olympics, and captain his country's basketball team into the final four of this tournament, up against three of the world's basketball superpowers.

If mentee and mentor reach the point of moments of truth and then agree that to be their desired destination – the arrangement will have been successful. Both parties are then able to say goodbye but as the French say, "C'est au revoir, ce n'est pas adieu". Until we meet again. This is not farewell but it is the end of this intensive journey we have made together. For now.

Notwithstanding its informal and friendly nature, positive mentoring outcomes in business, politics and sport require focus and purposeful discipline from inception to conclusion by both participants.

Mentoring has been an extremely successful tool for managing diversity challenges. Whether you are tackling cross-cultural or gender diversity, mentoring can be an effective approach. We see how in Part III as we discover several thriving mentoring schemes bridging divides.

Ten Disciplines for Positive Mentoring Outcomes

Positive mentoring requires:

1. Solid homework and preparation by each participant on the other, and proactive attention to building early chemistry and engagement with each other in the first two to three meetings.
2. The mentee needs to take ultimate responsibility for setting robust objectives and goals that will materially assist his or her career to advance.
3. The mentor needs to take ultimate responsibility for establishing an environment of strong trust, disarming candour and high confidentiality, but also one characterised by his or her active listening to the real needs of the mentee.

4. Both parties need to set an annual program of meetings every six to eight weeks at least, and be diligent in recovering space for any cancellations.
5. The mentoring assignment needs to be characterised by common values, continual loops of preparing, negotiating and enabling confident applications and trials by the mentee of strategies and desired practices formulated in the mentoring sessions.
6. These trials should be evaluated and enhanced or re-tried as appropriate at subsequent sessions. Any perceived failure to trial, or avoidance, needs to be pursued vigorously by the mentor through skilful questioning and mirror use with the mentor. A mentoring relationship without bumps, shakes and a bit of tough love in the advanced stages is unusual, and likely to produce immaterial benefit in the mentee.
7. Different skills and approaches are needed with the mentoring of men and women, that go back to their possibly different objectives for work and also how they see and value top level relationships.
8. Establishing a level of dialogue characterised by patient probing and powerful questioning by the mentor, as well as non-defensive consideration, responses and reflection by the mentee are critical continuous hallmarks for positive and productive mentoring assignments.
9. The ultimate test of a mentoring relationship is whether it reaches 'moments of truth' for the mentee – whereby the reality of life at the top is fully disclosed, and the mentee decides he or she not only wants it but is confident in their ability to handle it.
10. When all material 'moments of truth' have been reached, the mentoring has done its job and both parties should move forward independently but the parting sentiments should be expressed as 'au revoir, ce n'est pas adieu'. Until we meet again! This needs to be explored carefully at the beginning.

PART III
THE POWER OF
MENTORING

10

MENTORING FOR CROSS-CULTURAL DIVERSITY

Diversity can be an overloaded and sometimes confused term. Often associated with gender, in simple terms it is meant to connote the characteristic of a material 'difference'. So it covers gender, cultural origins, race, ethnicity, physical or mental disabilities, Indigenous and a wide range of other differentiators to the mainstream approach, wisdom or thinking. Research at AHRI and other institutes has shown that diversity improves the quality of decision-making by enriching debate, fostering creativity and alternative views, encouraging independence and constructive analysis of very difficult problems.

Mentoring has proven itself to be a great reconciler of diversity. By that is meant that mentoring programs have been used to embrace particular sets of diverse groups, and teach them techniques to maintain their separateness but also to embrace the mainstream thinking in a given social system. The objective is to produce a 'win–win' outcome.

This chapter reviews seven very successful mentoring programs for recent immigrants of different nationalities and Indigenous Australians.

With One Voice, Melbourne Sings …

Mentoring can take innovative forms, although it usually takes a natural innovator to produce a form that is both valuable and sustainable. Tania de Jong provides an excellent example. Tania is a leading entrepreneur and performer in the creative arts field.

Early in her career, Tania performed with the Victoria State Opera and went on to win the 2006 Ernst and Young Social Entrepreneur of the Year award for her work in creating the Song Room. Many other awards and accolades followed, including an Order of Australia in 2008 for services to the arts as a performer and entrepreneur and through the establishment and development of music and arts enrichment programs for schools and communities. In 2010, Tania founded Creativity Australia to inspire people to find their voice and improve wellbeing, engagement and innovation in the workforce, in partnership with disadvantaged communities, through creative thinking and leadership programs.

> "As a child of a Jewish immigrant family that fled Europe, I had to grow up in an environment of prejudice towards my cultural origins, and also bullying at school because I was different. My parents, family and over time my mentors, always encouraged me to be the best I could be, but more importantly, they were always there to help me get through challenges, tough times and the occasional crisis."

That support and inspiration encouraged Tania to find her own 'voice' and use that to further her career and life in Australia. Tania set up the 'With One Voice' program to help diverse communities from disadvantaged backgrounds. The participants were also new to Australia, and With One Voice helped them to find their identity through joining a local choir. Melbourne Sings is one such regional component of this program, and at last count there were twelve others operating throughout Australia plus programs in Holland.

The prime target audience for the program is adult women, who have recently emigrated to Australia. Many of them were refugees and asylum-seekers not too long ago. A significant number are unemployed and are quite intimidated about what is necessary to go about finding a job. The program isn't just about singing. The choirs meet weekly and during the breaks from singing rehearsals, the participants are addressed by community and business leaders who offer tips on adjusting to this new country, finding employment, and some much needed sponsorship for that. Stories are exchanged in true mentoring fashion amongst the participants and leaders. Even a little bit of expert help with an upgrading of the resume for job applications is on the cards during an evening's activities. This is an integrated program of peer, senior and cross-cultural mentoring at its finest. The essence of the program, and the parallel from teaching participants to sing, is to find and employ creativity in your own personal solutions to confront challenges, and to do so confidently with integrity and honesty about who each person is, and what they have to offer.

Feedback from the program cites improved well-being from belonging to With One Voice and increased self-esteem and reduced anxiety and depression. Participants made new friends, found increased understanding and acceptance of diversity and gained new life and work skills.

Tania said the choirs from the With One Voice program are a:

> "tool for social transformation. They enable participants to build networks, skills and find jobs. It's all about achieving practical outcomes on diversity. In these circumstances, it will never just happen. It's something you have to engineer with astute mentoring connections. It links CEOs to asylum-seekers. In most other respects that connection would never be likely to happen. The benefits include huge reverse-mentoring learnings to these CEOs."

The mentees speak highly of what With One Voice does for them. Here are a two of quotes from program participants:

> "The choir is now a big part of my life – they are like family to me, and are always so encouraging and helpful. People in the choir helped me to get a job." **Thilini from Sri Lanka, a member of Dandenong Sings.**

> "For my first six months in Australia, I was quite isolated because I was sad about what happened to me and my family. I had no family or friends here, and it was very hard for me to adjust. I love arts and music but there were many fundamentalists in Afghanistan and we weren't allowed. The beauty of singing is that it lifts you up and keeps you going." **Abrar Kather, Afghani refugee and a member of Melbourne Sings.**

Big Brothers, Big Sisters

Mentoring programs are also used extensively in the community, not just for professional career development. The essence of mentoring is parental and/or pastoral care for someone young in learning, or undeveloped in a new and strangely different environment. These characteristics can and do apply to young people who need an 'elder' to mentor them, whether that be because they are missing one or both parents, for whatever reason, or if they are coming from a broken home.

Big Brothers, Big Sisters is a worldwide mentoring program which has as its vision, "Every young person who needs a mentor, has a mentor". Specifically that means its mission is to "realise the potential of all young people, through the provision of the highest quality mentoring programs".

Big Brothers, Big Sisters mentoring programs in this country support vulnerable young Australians to reach their full potential. Their programs and activities have guiding principles which include:

- Reaching young people most in need in the community
- Policies and procedures which are non-discriminatory and inclusive of social, cultural and religious diversity
- Sharing of best-practice mentoring models and ongoing research globally
- Accountability to all stakeholders including Bigs (mentors) and Littles (mentees), program delivery partners, corporate partners, donors and government
- Effective program-design based on research, evaluation and consultation
- Substantially increasing and diversifying funding sources to ensure sustainability and growth.

A number of people interviewed for this book have had involvement with Big Brother, Big Sister. Andrew Robb, the Federal parliamentarian was a board member for the program in Australia. Cameron Ling, the former Geelong Football Club captain, is a current mentor for children in the program living in the Geelong area of Victoria.

Indigenous Youth – Future Developments

Australia's Indigenous people represent 2.7% of the nation's population; but also constitute 60% of the 'clients' of the juvenile justice system. The mental and physical health profile of our Indigenous people is similar to that of an underdeveloped economy, and not one of the ten most advanced economies and societies in the world today.

Much has been said and written about this national issue, but little of that has transformed into initiatives of any practical value that identify and sustain a solution to the problem.

However, five programs have emerged over the last decade that have provided a very positive demonstration of the practical ability of Indigenous and mainstream western-based cultures in Australia to work together in mutual respect. These five initiatives have delivered sustained improvements to skill, knowledge transfer, and co-operative behaviours between these two broad cultural groups in our nation. They are the Clontarf Football Academy; the AFL Indigenous Development Program; People Trackers, the Australian Indigenous Mentoring Exchange (AIME), and the Jawun program. All five centres of activity include mentoring as a core component.

1. Clontarf Foundation

The Clontarf Foundation (The Foundation) established its first Academy at the Clontarf Aboriginal College in Western Australia in 2000. The Foundation was established by Gerard Neesham, a former coach in the West Australian Football League (WAFL) and Australian Football League (AFL) who had developed very positive associations with young Aboriginal footballers. Gerard was acutely aware of the cycle of disadvantage confronting Aboriginal people and the largely negative image of them held by many in the wider community.

In contrast to this stereotypical view of the time, Gerard recognised that the football environment was one in which Aboriginal people had traditionally excelled, resulting in very positive impacts upon the self-esteem and personal growth of players, their families and the wider Aboriginal community. Gerard witnessed emerging young Aboriginal footballers who had played in the WAFL and AFL grow into fine men through an environment where they had great success and during playing careers which had offered well-founded support structures.

Gerard recognised the need to surround the boys with good role models and mentors. With this in mind, he acquired the services of former Hawthorn premiership player, Ben Allan to assist with the coaching, as well as other committed professionals with physical education, teaching, and personal development and work preparation skills. In its first term, the Academy trained 15 of the College's 50 students. The program built up to 25 participants, and of the eight graduating that year, three were drafted into the AFL, three gained employment, one commenced a TAFE course and one returned to his community in the north-west.

The Clontarf Foundation program now has Academies in 59 schools around Australia, and engages over 3,000 Indigenous youth annually. A condition of participation is active involvement and progress at the student's secondary studies. Providing a supportive, welcoming and safe environment in schools to engage the Aboriginal boys in education is the Foundation's governing purpose in its partnership with participating educational schools.

However, it is not just about scholastic education. The participants are mentored both in and outside of school hours by the Clontarf Foundation staff, and taught valuable skills in future career selection, job preparation and search. Each Academy is staffed with full-time, suitably-trained men who are often former teachers or professional sportsmen. The evidence from each Academy is clear – these mentors capture the participants' attention and gain their respect and trust.

The mentoring objectives are to develop self-esteem and positive attitudes towards health, education and employment. Mentors expose participants to a wide range of life experiences which challenge and develop them. Achievements are rewarded with camps and exposure to new challenges.

After the conclusion of secondary education, the Foundation works to find employment for graduates and supports them in making the transition from school to the workplace. The mentors act like family and stay in the lives of their participants.

The Foundation achieves consistently good results from participating students, including:

- Year-to-year retention is not less than 90%
- School attendance rates are greater than 80%
- Many participants have re-entered education after prolonged absences
- 75% of graduates achieve full-time employment within one year of graduation
- Enhanced self-esteem, self-awareness and positive goal-setting/achievement
- Knowledge and experience gained to make healthy lifestyle decisions
- Reduced cases of criminal re-offending
- Greater understanding of, and access to, the employment opportunities available to them.

That's enormous progress in 15 years by the team at the Clontarf Foundation.

2. The AFL Indigenous Development Program

From the 2.7% of Australia's population that is Indigenous, comes 10% of AFL élite player participation. The top athletes in today's AFL include many Clontarf Academy graduates. Whilst the AFL executive and board have acknowledged the positive nature of the Clontarf program, they have felt the need to accelerate these efforts to develop Indigenous players themselves. Prior to 1995, there was no real targeted strategy for potential AFL players from Australia's Indigenous communities.

The situation changed that year with the Michael Long racial vilification incident. Michael Long is a former Australian rules footballer of Aboriginal descent and now a spokesperson for

Indigenous rights and against racism in sport. In the 1995 Anzac Day match between Essendon and Collingwood at the MCG, Long claimed to have been racially taunted by Collingwood's ruckman, Damian Monkhorst. The AFL arranged a mediation session between Long and Monkhorst and although Long was clearly not satisfied from the short-term results of this mediation, it seemed to set a beneficial longer-term precedent.

After that incident, the AFL established a dedicated education program focused on racial vilification and cultural awareness. There have been some other more general programs within AFL clubs, but these have been focused more towards the 'on field' behaviour by players. Over the past few years, the AFL itself has taken some giant strides in leading Indigenous thinking for the League and its constituent clubs. In 2007, the AFL had five Indigenous employees working in its ranks. Since then, it has employed 80 Indigenous workers across the nation. The leader of the AFL's Indigenous programs and initiatives is Jason Mifsud, an Aboriginal Australian, and former player and assistant coach with the St Kilda Football Club.

Whilst Clontarf is a big program, the AFL equivalent is now a huge one.

There is an immediate temptation to consider the AFL program as all about the development of on-field talent amongst emerging young Indigenous athletes. It's partly about that but a lot more about educational encouragement, the provision of useful and positive role models and mentoring these younger players to find full and fruitful adult lives ahead of them.

As Jason Mifsud says:

> "Our aspirations are to teach them future life skills. Some of this comes from positive learnings from on-field behaviour, but the roles of our volunteers and 400 professional staff are much broader than that. We aim to provide 'attainable role models' .... [who] work in

> supermarkets, or in the trades, and some will be professionally qualified in areas like commerce, banking and the sciences and even medicine. We try and pair our workers and volunteers alongside our young Aboriginal players to advise and mentor them about their lives in general. We address this need before each annual intake with mentoring training, because that's the required skill. We have no problem finding people to teach them how to run, mark and kick a football. Clearly the participating volunteers are a substantial part of how we solve this mentoring need."

When three bases of western mentoring (Socratean philosophical, quasi-parental and spiritual) were explored with Jason he replied:

> "That's the problem. Indigenous people don't differentiate between those three types. In our culture, they are totally integrated as one."

Jason goes further and sees mentoring as the core part of all Indigenous programs and he defines where the glass is still half empty in what the AFL is doing.

> "Since 2007 some of our earlier efforts had missing ingredients, and we decided to include Indigenous leaders in the development and design of our activities and this produced immediate benefits," Jason said. "It's easy to engage the Indigenous in footy, the challenge is how do you best use that love of the game as a vehicle for the other parts of their life. Sport has many teachable moments on the field that apply to other areas in life, and we know that.
>
> However, our targeted objective with the mentoring is to get directly into how our people can build their future livelihoods. We have four pillars to make the results of this initiative transferable to their future lives:
>
> - Decision-making
> - Communications
> - Resilience
> - Identity."

The AFL's overall approach is very balanced. The League understands that with 10% of top talent coming from 2.7% of the population, the talent return is very high. However, with our Indigenous people having a health, economic and wellbeing profile akin to a third-world country, the AFL also accepts there is an obligation to deliver social value from its efforts as well – primarily through education and employment.

As Jason says:

> "The Indigenous population has great opportunity to excel on the football arena. But we want the participants to get the opportunity to excel in adult life. The success factors for our work are threefold: talent identification; supported pathways for its management; and mentoring the participants to excel in their chosen fields after football."

The AFL Indigenous programs have two arms – an educational component and an adult work training program.

The educational program has no direct relationship to the Clontarf initiative, which is a complementary approach, but also separate in its execution.

Jason explains:

> "We use the same philosophy as Clontarf in having school retention and completion as a condition of continued participation in our national football development schemes. The next generation challenge is how to use the strength of footy to lift academic performance, and not just to drive school attendance and minimum compliance to learning."

The adult development programs explicitly aim to prepare participants for post-élite career adult life. This has been done by engaging with corporate partners, such as Rio Tinto.

The adult workforce training and development efforts place Jason Mifsud as mentor and developer to some of the élite former

AFL players which include some of the greatest Indigenous footballers in AFL history: Andrew McLeod, Chris Johnson, Michael O'Loughlin and Xavier Clarke.

Like all good mentors and program managers, Jason acknowledges there have been stops, starts and shortcomings along the way in this short but concentrated journey of the AFL.

> "We are doing well now but we need to acknowledge and learn from the failures we have had along the way. We need to keep breaking the challenge down, and to build it back up with the right competence and mindset. But we are confident. There is a younger generation emerging with bi-cultural protocols, and you can do a lot with that."

3. CareerTrackers

CareerTrackers is a national non-profit organisation working with Indigenous university students and private sector companies to create career pathways through a structured internship program. Its innovative and comprehensive internship program gives Indigenous university students the opportunity to fulfil their career aspirations and to become leaders in their chosen field, with the ultimate aim of having some of its Aboriginal and Torres Strait Islander graduates reach CEO and board posts within Australia's largest corporations.

The CareerTrackers (CT) website sets out the internship model used, and it's one where mentoring plays a critical part.

Students and their families are supported at home, at university and in the workplace, through mentoring provided by two mentor sources: the staff and alumni of CT who have the credibility that comes from comparable Indigenous origins; and the corporate sponsors who are trained in better ways to mentor the interns, but also exposed to skills and knowledge that support the program and that will also assist them in their future lives as well. The mentoring component is a key element in building trust and providing support where required. By being the main point of contact for employers, CT is able to provide specialist expertise in engaging with students and bringing out their full potential.

Many of the programs reviewed in this book on mentoring, or where there is a critical mentoring flavour, are very young. CareerTrackers is no exception, it is only six years old. Whilst it is an independent Australian not-for-profit entity, it is based on the US program called INROADS. The founder/creator of CareerTrackers is Michael Combs.

Michael said:

> "I am from the USA and went through the INROADS program myself. It changed our family, and INROADS set me up to do my internship with Hewlett Packard (HP) in the States. I graduated in 2002, and subsequently joined the HP global leaders program, and had the opportunity to do an international rotation with HP in Australia. On the second day on the job here, I asked why there were no Indigenous employees working here. I was told it was difficult to find and support Indigenous people to work in Australia. So the next day I showed my Managing Director an outline of a framework that could work here (in Australia) because it had already worked there (i.e. INROADS in the USA). My MD supported me in applying this framework in Australia, but it needed a number of changes to encompass both Indigenous cultural differences, as well as the Australian corporate environment (e.g. the cultural awareness training). We have an informal linkage to INROADS but are also quite independent ourselves."

The program's success comes from its highly interactive nature with its mentees doing their internships.

As well as each internship mentee undertaking 12 weeks of employment during the program, they are asked to aspire to achieve more than one rotation with that sponsoring company; their grades are expected to increase; individual goals and objectives are set for each mentee, and progress is assessed. Michael says that CareerTrackers is also assessed for how well it is acknowledged and embraced in the Indigenous community, including by the elders within the involved Indigenous communities. Michael also states that retention rates are high and improving, as are completion rates. Companies and students are now both embracing the model. An example is Leighton Contractors which has gone from one student, a year or so ago, to more than 30 students.

Michael sees that training for the mentors is essential to its success. The Indigenous business mentors are advised that the program is about relationships and community fundamentals, and ways to strengthen and embed this. The business mentors go through cultural awareness training, and are exposed to techniques with which they can enhance the value of the internship to both the mentee and the people involved within the corporate sponsors for the program.

4. Australian Indigenous Mentoring Experience (AIME)

The AIME program started in 2005. Jack Manning Bancroft walked into the Alexandria Park Community School in the Redfern area of Sydney, with 25 of the first AIME mentors. In 2014, that first partner school began its tenth year in the program. Jack says:

> "I have an Aboriginal mother and a white father. When I was 19 years old and starting out at Sydney University, a lot of people were complaining about the problems with Indigenous Australia and with it a real sense of hopelessness – but not too much action. So a few of us got together and decided to do something positive about it."

Jack is now the CEO of AIME and just eight years on AIME is supporting 1,000 school kids with 1,000 university student mentors. The AIME website www.aimementoring.com is a simple, clear and very admirable tribute to the excellent work done to establish and roll out this initiative over the last seven years.

"I have seen some amazing Indigenous and non-Indigenous people keen to do something positive like this. ... Mentoring has provided those kids with a real connection to a positive future life for them, and the mentors' real life experiences have enabled them to visualise what that future can be like," says Jack.

When the surface of AIME is probed, a very comprehensive learning and development program is uncovered, and it's one that is closely driven by well-trained mentors. AIME is a carefully-constructed, facilitated mentoring initiative, that wasn't allowed to plod forward under a combination of hope and good luck. AIME has a structured learning program that covers years 7 to 12 of high school.

Jack Manning Bancroft says:

"A strong educational content drives our program. There is a course for each mentor and mentee, in every year's program. Our mentoring never takes place in a simple 'one on one' relationship. We decided that the learning process needed to be well scripted and guided, and also that it was important to make the space as safe as possible for the mentors".

"We always have a program facilitator present, who is an Indigenous university graduate themselves. These 'coordinators' serve as the high-quality Indigenous role models, who are there to support mentors and mentees. We use a recruitment firm to hire the best calibre people we can find as coordinators, and there is an intensive process of 17 to 18 days' internal training for our core staff. All our mentoring resources and tools are well documented, and much of this is available on line. As well, we do regular training of mentors: that's two hours on line, and two hours face-to-face.

"They also receive an email brief for each session, and we have 15 minutes of training pre, and post every session. All classes are run at our partnership universities. The coordinators provide the initial two hours of training in Indigenous culture – especially for non-

> Indigenous mentors. They are also there and available when an issue crops up, due to a lack of understanding on cultural issues."

So where does Jack see AIME going next?

> "The next stage of development is working out how to get to the 60,000 Indigenous kids in our high schools today. My vision is that AIME shuts down when we have done this successfully".

When asked about the program's key success factors, his approach was remarkably simple, but also disarming in its nature:

> "We have always had the confidence to be honest about what we expect from the participants. Every time we have raised the bar, they have stepped up. You ask people to put themselves on the line and push the boundaries further, so we can all grow and advance. And they do. They always do."

5. Jawun

Noel Pearson is one of the most prominent leaders of Australia's Indigenous community. Noel is also the Patron of Jawun, which is managed by a professional board of directors from business and Indigenous communities. The Jawun initiative emerged from a summit in 2000 of selected leaders from the Indigenous and corporate communities in Australia. Following that 2000 summit, Westpac and the Boston Consulting Group (BCG) met at Weipa and endorsed the 'real economy' philosophy of Noel Pearson, whereby independent communities and actions were fostered to support reconciliation and economic and social progress for Indigenous Australians. Westpac and BCG agreed to support this approach with secondments from their organisations to work with Indigenous leaders to make the concept work within traditional Aboriginal lands in the Cape York area.

Jawun now has more than 20 corporate partners and its activities have expanded from Cape York, to East Kimberley in WA, to Shepparton Victoria and other regions. 1,000 secondees have now worked with Indigenous leaders under this initiative, and an alumni group has been was established to exchange experiences and ideas on how to advance this initiative practically.

The essence of Jawun is a business partnership program but cross-cultural peer and reverse-mentoring takes place within that. Experienced business leaders can spend up to 12 months working with Aboriginal elders on traditional lands with the aim of transferring skills to them that will make the 'real economy' an accessible and achievable concept. Reverse-mentoring also takes place with the corporate secondees, who take away knowledge of traditional Indigenous cultures, together with the current living and working environment of Aboriginal communities, and the challenges faced. This has not only helped the shaping of corporate Indigenous employment policies and programs but has also established an informed part of the business community, which can speak with authority to governments on Aboriginal issues and policies, better than existed before. On the value from reverse-mentoring, one CEO said:

> "Within KPMG, our involvement (with Jawun) is transforming our people, and as a result, impacting our culture in profound and positive ways." **Geoff Wilson (2010), CEO, KPMG in Australia.** (From the Jawun website, "Benefits to Corporate Partners".)

The Balkanu region of Cape York is an example of how Jawun, its corporate partners and Indigenous Regional Organisations (IROs) have worked to develop the local economy over the last 10 years, and the role mentoring has played in this. This work has involved Jawun's secondment program (that lasts five weeks), in which secondees from organisations such as Westpac, the Boston Consulting Group, KPMG and IBM have worked with Balkanu and individual enterprises to conduct feasibility studies and develop business models for potential business ideas and provide direct advice and hands-on assistance to entrepreneurs. Balkanu has also engaged the Westpac Fellows Program, under which Westpac employees are placed with an IRO in the Cape for 12 months.

Under this approach, for example, a Westpac secondee to Balkanu has been providing extensive business advisory support to local farmers in the Cape York region. His support has been crucial in helping the farmers to gain access to capital, improve their financial management and also to facilitate their access to new markets in Cairns.

Mentoring Indigenous management of enterprises, and providing specialist management advice, is a major part of this approach. Balkanu also operates the Cairns to Cape Mentoring Program, an initiative which brokers connections between Balkanu's client businesses in Cape York and successful, long-standing enterprises in Cairns.

> "The impressive thing is that our contribution is so wholehearted – this is not just about contributing money, this is about contributing hearts, minds and hands." **Gail Kelly (2009), CEO, Westpac.** (From Jawun 2010, "Learnings and Insights Ten Years on.")

Mentoring: An Effective Reconciler of Cross-Cultural Diversity

1. Successful mentoring programs in the diversity field have started with the same objective: to develop 'win–win' outcomes across the definitive difference between the mentor and mentee groups, by engaging them first in an activity where there is a common cross-cultural passion. For Clontarf and AFL IP, western coaches/mentors engage with Indigenous youth across a common passion of football.

2. These programs have three core elements:
   - Mutual recognition and respect for the different value sets underlying the western or dominant culture and the Indigenous or minority culture
   - Companion programs based on reconciling sources of diversity, improving education and skills, transferring effective job application and interview skills to the mentee group, reverse-mentoring on a better understanding of problems and challenges faced by Indigenous youth
   - Building of new and extensive networks that can be farmed patiently for actual opportunities and knowledge to better position yourself – e.g. post career opportunities organised by the AFL.
3. These programs pass through typical natural growth phases: pilot trials; establishment of core working principles and practices; and then a rollout of the core program to new regions, new annual intakes and a broader set of participants.
4. Most diversity mentoring programs encounter second generation challenges – e.g. how to expand the education philosophies to accommodate the natural learning philosophies of the culturally diverse mentees, (i.e. kinesthetic learning by Indigenous people).
5. Some mentoring program organisers realise other tools and resources need to be put in place – not only to help build a pipeline of future applicants, but also to enhance mentoring participants to get most value from their program, before it's over.
6. The final challenge is to generalise these learnings more broadly in society, in a way that expands the reconciliation results to be well embedded in, and to be accepted as, 'second nature' within society itself.

11

MENTORING IN A WOMAN'S CAREER

Since the historic low point in female senior executive and board participation rates of 5% and 8% respectively during 2009, there has been regular high profile media attention concerning a woman's career, and the reasons behind these low rates of participation by women in Australia. The difficulty experienced by top women in obtaining mentoring is a key driver of this poor performance. However, surveys show also that women wrongly put a low value on mentoring as a critical factor to their own future career success.

This situation in Australia is in sharp contrast to that in Asia more generally. Asia's rapid economic growth has led to a significant increase in demand for managers and professionals. In China, Hong Kong, Singapore, The Philippines, Taiwan, Thailand and Vietnam, women typically occupy more senior management roles than their counterparts in western countries, although in this latter grouping Australia sits at the bottom as well.

The March 2014 International Business Report "Women In Business" by accounting firm Grant Thornton found that the proportion of female CEOs in the Asia-Pacific region, excluding

Japan, is much higher than the USA, Australia or Europe. The country with the highest percentage of female senior executives is Indonesia at 41%; followed by the Philippines at 40%; and then China and Thailand which both have 38%. The global average for women in senior management is 24% in 2014, up from 20% in 2010. The 2014 Womens Gender equality Agency Report identified that 26.1% of women were in senior management roles, just above the global average of 24% but still at least 5% behind New Zealand, Canada and United Kingdom. Women, however, are more prevalent in corporate management roles than in line, business, or operational roles. Unfortunately, more CEOs and board directors are drawn from those with direct operational experience, rather than corporate functions.

Within Australia, mentoring programs have started to address this situation and play a pivotal role in emerging progress.

The Australian Institute of Company Directors (Company Directors) is well known to be a key driver to the increase of women on boards, rising from 8.3% of ASX200 directors in 2010 to just under 19.3% at the end of 2014. At the ASX20 level, it's closer to 25%.

Surveys by AHRI show that the top challenge for people in business is the war for talent. Staff turnover rates used to average 2% to 3% in the 1980s but are now averaging 15% to 20% per annum. Female workplace participation rates are nearing 60% and the numbers of men and women working are practically equal. The biggest challenge on gender is to hold women into active senior roles beyond the age of 35 to 40, when those with a family find the demands of managing children too much to sustain full-time workforce engagement.

When challenged with such a dilemma, the mind usually turns to what ought to be done about it?

In March 2011, AHRI joined with UN Women Australia to initiate the first National Gender Equity Summit, with Westpac as the principal partner. Two hundred top level CEOs and senior executives met for a day to hear keynote presentations and discussions on this critical issue in business, and then workshop potential outcomes. A communiqué of key agreed actions from this summit was produced and is available on **www.genderequity.ahri.com.au**. The main conclusions in that report included:

- Establishment of 40% targets for board and senior executive positions in Australia's leading organisations
- Positive action on child care and gender pay discrimination
- Corporate commitment to the UN Women's empowerment principles
- Establishment of scorecards on flexibility and equity.

On the last recommendation, two of the clearest components for organisations to take positive internal action on gender equity were to develop programs to target removal of unconscious bias towards women in the workplace, and to establish programs to mentor senior women, both within and outside their corporations.

The two highest profile, and also very successful, cross-organisational mentoring programs for women were established by the Company Directors for aspiring top women board directors, and the Business Council of Australia (BCA), the peak body for Australia's top 120 CEOs, in conjunction with AHRI for emerging senior executive talent on the way to leading Australia's largest companies. As the late James Strong, former Chairman of Woolworths, Kathmandu Holdings and the Australian Council for the Arts said:

> "There has been noticeable progress in gender diversity on boards, and much more is needed. The leadership of Company Directors, the Business Council of Australia and others on this issue is gaining a lot of traction." ***Company Director*, Monthly Magazine of the Australian Institute of Company Directors, (February 2012, P17.)**

Business Council of Australia's CEO Mentoring Scheme for Women Executives

In 2010, the BCA and AHRI announced the establishment of this foundation mentoring program. The President of the Business Council of Australia, Graham Bradley stated:

> "There is a lot of attention at the moment on the unacceptably low levels of women on Australian boards, but women are too scarce at all senior levels of Australian business. We need to open up pathways for our best women to take on senior positions and open up a strong pipeline of success all the way to the boardroom. The Business Council of Australia's current membership of the country's leading CEOs is 97% male. A simple mark of the success of this project will be seeing more women in the room at BCA forums like this one."

Further, Graham Bradley saw this mentoring program as capable of offering longer-term strategic benefits to improving the nature and practices of diversity in the workplace.

> "The potential of the scheme goes beyond supporting individual women," said Graham Bradley.
>
> "It will also facilitate a valuable exchange of views and ideas between mentors and mentees on barriers to workforce participation and promotion.
>
> "This problem is not unique to Australia but our generation of corporate leaders must make changes to bring our companies in line with community reality and expectations."

The active leader of this initiative within the Business Council was its CEO, Katie Lahey, who emphasised the critical nature of the need, and the relationship that a mentoring program could have in securing the necessary solution. At the launch, Katie stated:

> "I think it's really important that women are given the opportunity to succeed ... a project like this will identify women with potential and

it will give them the support of a very senior CEO who's already in the C-Suite (i.e. top executive group reporting to a CEO), give them an insight into the role, the expectations, the credentials needed to occupy the most senior roles and give them the feeling that this is a possibility."

Following nominations of many CEOs as mentors and mentee candidates from BCA member companies, mentoring pairs were matched up on a cross-organisational basis and with maximum potential synergy for participants having regard to the program objectives. Mentees were targeted to have the potential to reach the top executive team of BCA member companies within the next five years, i.e. to become CEO, executive director, COO or CFO at the group executive level. Most participating organisations sponsored a mentor and mentee, which gave the benefit of reciprocity to CEOs committing their time as mentors, as another top CEO would mentor one of their own. Mentoring pairs were matched by an independent organisation, AHRI, to be cross-organisational in nature and with maximum potential symmetry between matched participants.

Meetings commenced with a formal and face-to-face 'kick off', involving induction briefings. Over the 2010-11 year, significant progress was made in the views of the participants and the program director. The overwhelming majority were assessed to have made very good to excellent progress over their average eight to ten meetings. The strength of these arrangements has been shown by the further commitment of these participants to maintain their working relationships into the future, albeit on a less formal and frequent basis.

Outcomes for Mentees from the Program

The specific and positive outcomes for the mentees from the program are worthy of mentioning.

1. **Positive professional relationships were established from the outset.** All participants commented favourably on the positive and professional way that their mentoring arrangements commenced. In particular the openness, enthusiasm, helpful nature and positive spirit of this very senior group of CEO mentors were remarked upon by all mentees. Mentors were very good listeners and almost all of them asked their mentee up front where they would like help and/or what they would most like to discuss.
2. **Confidence-building was a major mentee benefit.** Almost all mentees stated they felt a lift to their confidence and came to accept that their presence in the senior team isn't part of an 'imposter syndrome', but that they are there on the basis of equitable merit. As Rachel Foley-Lewis further commented that:

   > "This has been particularly important, following my return to work from maternity leave, when confidence can be fragile, and anxiety at being 'professionally left behind' can be significant. That's certainly how I felt".

   All mentees who had responsibilities of motherhood expressed similar sentiments about the fears existing when they returned to work from maternity leave.
3. **Understanding the importance of networking.** In many instances, mentors included their mentees in alternative networking groups and facilitated introductions to other potential mentors and advisers. The rationale and value from this was most commonly discussed and emphasised in later mentoring sessions.
4. **Understanding that mentoring is a key component of senior executive leadership.** The lesson of 'learning to be a mentor myself' encouraged some to take on their first

mentoring roles at work to gain more experience in this part of the leadership mantle, and then they discussed the implications of that with their own mentors during this BCA-AHRI program.

5. **Seeing the benefit of undertaking small board directorships as an emerging young executive.** Most did this by seeking out a not-for-profit organisational board role, both to enhance their understanding of corporate and board governance and also to assist their senior promotional credentials through gaining practical experience of how a board operates.

'Mutual myth-busting' – was a major benefit of this program to both mentors and mentees – on certain 'mind barriers' to a woman's advancement within a senior team, and tips on how to test and separate them, (e.g. accessing men's lunches and golf days, or evaluating and testing better/or effective networking alternatives to them). This led to improved understanding and acceptance by these senior businesswomen that being different is 'OK', and moreover not to be feared. Some mentors have stated they gained new insights on former blind-spots they didn't appreciate they had. All mentees remarked upon the value of having constructive 'two-way–in my shoes' discussions of valuable strategies and actions that could be used by them with their colleagues at work, and in very many cases these were applied almost immediately, and with some significant successes noted. Areas covered in the discussions were quite diverse and led to the identification of new approaches by mentees for managing senior teams, choosing times to make an impact and speaking up more.

Another advantage that flowed to the younger leaders was the value potential that came from setting core priorities in their own careers, and not just deriving them from good work towards achieving their employer's mission, and trying to do 'everything under the latter heading that moves into your field of view or responsibility'. As one said:

> "I have learned more about the value of managing the 80/20 rather than the 99/1 as many women try and do. I now understand why I was getting buried and stressed out as well. This has been a major learning opportunity for me, and exploring my mentor's own experiences and career choices has been invaluable to me."
> Karyn Munsie, Former EGM Stockland.

Participants often discussed the low threshold for failure and rejection that many women have, and more positive approaches and strategies to overcome this psychology that the program had taught them. Many of the discussions focused on developing strategies for resilience to failures and setbacks, instead of suffering in silence and brooding alone with their shortcomings, as women in business are prone to do.

As part of designing new and better approaches to handle the administrative management load, and those around you, a particular priority became how to manage work-life-family balance. Sometimes direct language was the best means to deliver a message. As one mentor advised his mentee:

> "You need to be organised and there for your children. They're only teenagers once (sic)." Ralph Norris, former CEO, Commonwealth Bank.

Other positive learnings from the program were insights from the mentor on 'learning to manage the CEO'; reviewing the 'life of a different CEO' and discussing the strategies the mentor would have used in confronting the mentee's challenges.

> "I have a great CEO here, but I have also learned a lot from my mentor in this program on some of the challenges he faces in maintaining the balance and also in being able to keep his business and private lives separate." Lyn Cobley, then-Treasurer, Commonwealth Bank.

In today's globalised world of rapid transfers of information, and also hyper-competition in product markets, one of the biggest challenges confronting top leaders is a dynamic management of ethical dilemmas and conflicts of interest that emerge in the workplace. The content of discussions covered the issue of managing some of the typical and actual conflicts of interest that can arise at a very senior level. Mostly these discussions have involved reviews of third-party experiences or events that had been encountered by third-parties, but some exchanges were on conflicts being managed by the mentee currently.

Finally, many mentees commented that their senior executive life had been substantially with the same employer, and that they had really valued learning about an alternative industry environment and challenges faced by the mentor.

Benefits of the Program to the Mentors

One of the more surprising outcomes from this program was the benefit in learning that accrued to the mentors themselves. By stepping outside the confines of their own organisational boundaries, many of the mentors acknowledged different perspectives of a woman's challenges at work.

This has had a double benefit, as one mentor expressed:

> "I realised my mentee feels exactly the same as many senior women must feel within their own organisation, but you would never expect to hear of them because of concerns about negatively impacting their careers. However, having heard it from my own mentee has encouraged me to make some in-house changes to ensure similar fears aren't held here." **Michael Rose, Chief Executive Partner, Allens.**

Further, a number of mentors developed a broader appreciation of the value that women can bring to senior roles. As three mentors said:

> "My mentee has gained maturity and greater self-awareness on how she impacts others. Without that I doubt she would have made it. Now I believe she will." **Ralph Norris, former CEO, Commonwealth Bank.**

> "Mentoring women is generally a source of great satisfaction. The top ones are almost always well-organised, they work hard and always get the job done to great standards. And they are a pleasure to have around the workplace." **Michael Luscombe, former CEO, Woolworths.**

> "I realised the unconscious bias in my own organisation, as a result of listening to my mentee, and thinking to myself – gosh that sounds awfully familiar and that must be the feeling here too – amongst both our senior men and women. We don't give enough credit for women being able to undertake more challenging roles, when many clearly want to." **Tim Ebbeck, former CEO, SAP Australia and New Zealand.**

Reverse-mentoring occurred through exposure to alternative viewpoints and experiences of senior women from other corporate environments. A few mentors advised they developed new perspectives on potential changes within their companies. One remarked that this mentoring relationship was more transparent and valuable, because of its cross-organisational nature.

In a few instances, mentors developed some unique perceptions that were not available from their own in-house mentoring roles. As one mentor said:

> "I now realise the conflict that external mentors have to the organisation employing them. If the mentoring relationship is genuinely confidential and going to be of value, then you have to be prepared to confront critical issues with your mentee and advise them on what will maximise their career best interests, without prejudice. Sometimes that may not be the advice your employer would expect you to give in serving its own best interests. It's

probably in a scheme like this where the mentoring relationship can be completely genuine, and not constrained by the employer's needs and expectations." **Michael Rose, Chief Executive Partner, Allens.**

All mentors felt that the experience had been a rewarding pro bono contribution to a major business and community challenge, not only in Australia but also in our region.

Benefits to the Program Sponsor (BCA) and Organiser (AHRI)

Over its two year tenure, the existence and positive collateral emerging from the BCA–AHRI program has enabled both parties to maintain a position of public leadership over not only a critical issue affecting performance and equity in the workplace, but also over the best internal solution for managing senior executive skill shortages (i.e. by positive actions to arrest the attrition of senior women from top executive ranks around the ages of 38 to 45).

A program like this also can benefit the BCA through its access to critical issues emerging from discussions of these cross-organisational mentoring pairs, about the challenges and barriers to the development of women's careers.

The enthusiastic participation of mentees and mentors in this mentoring program also gives the sponsors a major and contemporary resource-base of ideas and perspectives that they can seek to manage and draw from in other ways. That resource base can provide information, policy and practice guidance notes and ideas that can be disseminated further into the business community.

The BCA–AHRI top executive women mentoring program was the first of its kind in Australia, but it ended after two years in 2012, as it closely paralleled the Chairmen's Mentoring Program of the Company Directors. Opportunities exist to replicate the BCA-AHRI program at a State and regional level. It is hoped that many other employer, employee and industry organisations will see fit not only to emulate this experience and so assist rectification of a major inequity in business life today, but also to use the sponsorship to gain real-life intelligence about the challenges and issues confronting a woman in her career.

In designing any new such program, the following learnings should be borne in mind:

- The calling for nominations should be led by the CEO of the sponsoring organisation, with a request for each organisation to nominate a mentor and up to two mentee candidates.
- Nominating organisations should provide a CV for each mentee candidate, and confirm them to be of significant executive potential.
- Matching criteria should include 'same city' residence for each pair, as a core priority.

There is significant value in a 'kick-off' conversation between the CEO sponsoring the mentee and the nominated mentor covering the candidate's career potential, the sponsor's specific expectations for the mentee from this program and protocols of confidentiality through the mentoring.

- The launch of any program should be treated as a cause for celebration and with positive spirit and expectations for the participants.
- A guidelines pack should be provided for any future course on principles set out in this book, plus difficulties that may arise, such as executive search activity, and case studies in handling prospective conflicts of interest.
- Extended diary-matching is highly recommended to all matched pairs at the beginning of any program, and for the full 12 months.

- A period of three months should be established to ensure compatibility of pairs by the end of the first one or two meetings, and that a reasonable schedule of meetings can be programmed for the next 12 months.
- Flexibility is desirable in the mentoring process.
- Provision should be established for quarterly mentee networking meetings.
- An alumni group should be established to assist future programs.
- Large-scale mentoring programs benefit from having someone independent of the parties do the matching, and then be available to resource, advise and inform the initial connections. Further, you may need someone to play facilitator, intermediary, honest broker and progress-mapper.

The Company Directors Chairmen's Program for Potential Women Directors

The BCA's CEO's mentoring scheme was designed to help higher potential female executives accede to the nation's top executive posts, and particularly our next generation CEOs. The move to a non-executive director role is another major step-change in a career, and like top executive roles, it is a terrain that has been dominated by males since the end of the Second World War. In the pipeline of career growth for a high potential businesswoman, the Australian Institute of Company Directors (Company Directors) moved to fill this gap with the establishment of the Company Directors Chairmen's Mentoring Program that commenced prior to the BCA CEO mentoring initiative. The experience of the Company Directors scheme encountered many women mentees who needed to further build on their executive careers, prior to targeting board positions, and also a number of mentors were being involved in both BCA and AICD schemes. Accordingly, the BCA chose to suspend its own program and practical support of its members flowed to the Company Directors scheme, which has flourished ever since.

The sponsor of this innovation by the Company Directors was its Chief Executive and Managing Director at the time, John Colvin, who says in his characteristically dry, self-effacing style:

> "I grew up in a family of very talented women and married one and we have a daughter who is growing up along the same lines. I have always struggled to keep up. I was just a year or so into this CEO role and the community debate was beginning to rage around only 8% of our top company directors being women. Like most fair-minded people, I felt this was wrong and that positive action to remedy it was needed. Part of my drive to take action reflected my own upbringing in my home town of Orange, NSW. My mother died from breast cancer when I was only six years old, but following her own diagnosis, she still made time to set up a cancer patient's assistance society (Can Assist) branch in Orange, and had a life of always trying to help others and raise us as best she could. My sisters Deeta and Christine were in the same mould of incredibly gifted women, even if they spent a lot of time beating males like me up with their very credible arguments about the challenges of a woman's life in a man's world."

John spoke with a number of high profile directors like David Gonski, Kevin McCann, John Story, Rick Lee, Belinda Hutchinson and Don Argus, to test out the idea and he received a spontaneously positive response. Then he phoned another 55 leading ASX chairmen about the proposal to set up a program for them to mentor women who had the potential to get on to top boards but hadn't or couldn't find the right pathway. All accepted John's invitation to be part of this initiative, and so it gained momentum very quickly. John asked those chairmen for their own nominations of potential mentees, as well as his state Company Director divisions, Company Directors' board, Elizabeth Broderick, Chief Executive Women, Women On Boards (see next section) and others. He requested CVs for candidates and he appointed a colleague within Company Directors, Anthea McIntyre, to run the program. They finally received 180 applications. The 56 nominating chairmen mentors were matched with 63 aspiring mentees, following a selection process overseen by a committee comprising a number of chairs including David Gonski, Rick Lee, and Kevin McCann, as well as Elizabeth Broderick and John and Anthea themselves. In 2011, the same process was repeated but primarily through a national promotion and management of expressions of interest via the Company Directors' membership. This time, 342 applications were received and 83 mentees were selected and matched with 80 mentors. In both 2010 and 2011 some mentors took on more than one mentee. In those two years, 124 appointments of women were made to ASX200 company boards, including many graduates from this program.

John is keen that this form of 'direct action' continues to demonstrate progress, and that Australia isn't tempted to legislate for gender quotas on our boards. John is concerned if we go in that direction:

> "Quotas would kill the merit process. Management would be attending the board table and addressing their comments to the independent directors who are there on merit, and then to those statutory directors who have been forced onto the company by virtue of legislation. We need to avoid that, but also we must show we can get to a better merit-based result from our own actions. One serves as a spur to achieve the other."

The objectives of the program were to introduce the mentees to chairmen and other experienced directors of ASX200 listed companies to assist them in developing connections with influential business leaders and to gain knowledge and skills to achieving director appointments. Other benefits would be in career development to increase their understanding of governance issues in listed companies and how listed company boards work in practice and gain valuable insight, advice and guidance on the process of selecting and appointing new directors.

The program was also designed to enhance the connections of chairmen and experienced directors of ASX200 listed companies with experienced and skilled women who may be suitable for director roles.

In the long-term, it is hoped that the program will assist in helping the mentees towards achieving their professional goals.

The Chairmen's Mentoring Program provides a simple two to three-page guide for mentees and mentors covering many of the same issues as the BCA initiative (e.g. recommended length of the program, frequency and duration of meetings; preferred informal mode of conduct; preparations for same; roles of participants; practical tips to get started; early objective-setting; group networking events and timetables; and feedback and evaluation processes. An examination of the views of mentor and mentee participants in the Chairmen's Mentoring Program provides a comparable, but also complementary, set of benefits to those experienced in the BCA scheme.

The list of the 80 chair mentors is a veritable who's who of corporate Australia and includes: Don Argus (formerly BHP Billiton), Graham Bradley (Stockland), Roger Corbett (Fairfax Media), Patricia Cross (Director of NAB and Qantas), Paula Dwyer (Tabcorp), Bob Every (Wesfarmers), David Gonski (Coca Cola), Nick Greiner (Infrastructure NSW), Jane Hemstritch (Director of CBA, Tabcorp, Lend Lease and Santos), Graham Kraehe (Brambles), Catherine Livingstone (Telstra), Peter Mason (AMP), Don Mercer (Newcrest Mining), John Morschel (ANZ), Elizabeth

Proust (Nestle and Bank of Melbourne), Kevin McCann (Macquarie and Origin), James Strong (Woolworths), Brian Schwartz (IAG) and Ziggy Switkowski (Suncorp).

Surveys by the Company Directors' program managers have shown the benefits to mentors as being:

- Access to a new directors gene pool – i.e. exposure to a new high-calibre group of aspiring female directors whom they may not otherwise have had contact with. Many have commented that nominations of women directors from executive search firms had become stale and predictable over the last few years.
- Gaining knowledge and skills that will assist this new and diverse group of mentees achieve director appointments, but also enhance their career development.
- Develop their own leadership skills with respect to managing board appointments, enhancing women candidatures and improving board composition.
- Acquiring a better understanding of the barriers faced by women aspiring to board roles, and also the nature and extent of the gender equity challenge at board level.
- Sharing their knowledge and expertise.
- Extending their own professional networks and public profile as a positive change-agent on diversity.

Both the Company Directors' management team, and the mentees themselves, have all commented very positively on how enthusiastic and accessible these high-profile mentors have been to ensure the success of the program. The mentors reciprocate this and have embraced the opportunity to give back and help solve a problem on which they share the community's concerns. The task has been challenging sometimes as many advise they have to spend time explaining why a director role is not another executive one.

Director attributes focus on a range of strategic, governance, IT, risk-management, marketing, investor representation, people management and leadership issues.

Taking their mentees through the challenges of director life, and encouraging them to look at what they have of relevance to that, is a basic but extremely important task in this mentoring program. Kevin McCann, Chairman of Macquarie states:

> "It is very difficult for qualified women who don't understand corporations law, stock exchange requirements or haven't worked with chairmen and CEOs to have a profile ...(they should) try to find a mentor in the business community who would be prepared to advise them on how to develop their directorial skills and raise their profile." **CD Sept 2010, P16.**

Further, John Schubert, the former chairman of CBA, says:

> "Boards look carefully at skills required to monitor and challenge management and to help develop policy and strategy for the organisation. They need to look at which of those skills are already covered." **CD May 2010, P17.**

The clear implication is that so should protégé female directors. It's not about what your last executive project was, it's about what you have to offer your prospective board colleagues that they don't already have.

Participants have stated the mentors have willingly embraced a discussion of their own irreconcilable challenges – and also failures – inclusive of the ways they chose to manage them, and shared within the confidentiality of the program's code of conduct. How to position oneself for boards, and ways to maximise value from selecting and managing networks is another commonly discussed topic.

Unless permission is given otherwise, the identity of the mentees in this program is maintained as confidential. Advice from

Company Director mentees who have been prepared to go public, nevertheless ratifies these points:

> "Think about what you can offer and make sure you articulate it effectively; read widely and keep aware of the key issues affecting business." **Rebecca Davies.**

> "See your point of difference in a positive light. Don't think of yourself as a woman who can't get a fair go, because the negative and cynical aura will come through" **Vanessa Guthrie.**

> "To be … ready for an ASX200 Board, you need to ensure your experience and education are in areas of value to the boards you aspire to be appointed to." **Louise Herron.**

> "Attributes of teamwork, listening and influencing are essential in a board environment, and having a personal relationship is very helpful when these attributes are being assessed."
> **Ilana Atlas, 2010.**

> "Female mentors can assist in sharing their experiences, but the males are usually in the majority when determining board appointments." **Jane Harvey.**

Mentee participants in the Chairmen's program also speak of improvements to their confidence as the BCA mentees did. Andrea Staines of QR National said:

> "The program also provided me with the self-confidence to remain patient, and focus on work and networking until the next right role came along." (P41) Company Directors advises it can take up to five years before someone might find the right position."

The program has also led to development of a small grey market in potential new board directors, that is provided amongst other chairs and directors on a freely-exchanged basis, much to the chagrin of some executive search firms. One of the challenges of this program has been whether to call it a mentoring or a sponsorship program. The decision has been to stay with the former, and for good reason. The American literature on mentoring often states the core role of a mentor is to sponsor the mentee (e.g. Hewlett, Marshall and Sherbin in *HBR* 2011). However, this practice comes from US mentoring programs generally being internal to an organisation, and for high potential young executives. So sponsoring is a more natural component of that. The Company Directors' program is more exploratory and cross-organisational in nature. Mentors have often concluded their assignments with advice that the mentee needs considerably more experience in executive roles to determine whether they will be board-ready or not. In this case the requirement or expectation to sponsor a protégé would be premature and misleading. In some instances the journey has revealed a moment of truth that 'board life is not for me', so sponsorship can't apply.

Appointments of women to Australia's top boards have shown more positive progress than to senior executive roles over the last two years. Currently, Australian women comprise 17% of CEO roles from which board directors are most commonly selected. Women constituted 30% of all board appointments in 2014, or 54 seats. The pipeline for future directors will come from experienced women in future senior management ranks, and corporations, professional and executive organisations could well take a leaf out of the Company Directors' book and adopt the equivalent of their much more comprehensive approach at board level. It's clearly a case where Australian board leaders have been outperforming management in the successful management of this critical priority.

Women on Boards

In the early 2000s, Ruth Medd began a fledgling group known as Women On Boards (WoB). Five years later it was incorporated as a private not-for-profit organisation by Claire Braund, who became its first CEO, and Ruth took the chair role. Since that time WoB has doubled its membership each year and today has nearly 14,000 affiliated members, 4,000 of whom are full financial participants in its programs and activities.

> "When I started my career, there was really no-one to help me develop my career potential through improved interpersonal skills and relationship management. A boss's job wasn't seen to require any career support for their people." **Ruth Medd, Chair, Women On Boards.**

WoB is effectively a giant informal mentoring association for women seeking a board role, or assisting someone who is. The company runs an online jobs board for vacant non-executive director roles, and WoB has assisted more than 1,000 women achieve a place at the board table. This group offers professional programs, assisted pathways (including CV preparation), advocacy and presentation training, and also profiling services to help prepare their members for board roles. It provides informal networking events and a formal mentoring program.

While Ruth and Claire have had limited numbers of mentors in their own lives, outside their families, they both strongly support the value of independent mentoring for women seeking to take the next step in a senior career.

Despite a mentor-free start to her own working life in the bureaucracy, Ruth gained significant experience with mentoring when she was appointed as Head of the Secretariat to merge Telecom Australia and OTC into what is now Telstra, a top-ten listed Australian company. Ruth said:

> "The chair and deputy chair of the new entity, David Hoare and Alex Morakoff taught me a lot about being a good director. For example, how to operate in an environment full of tensions between stakeholders, shareholders and other players with different

> viewpoints on your company and where it should be going. They also taught me how to listen; the use of silence to get a point across; how directors could co-operate beforehand to get an outcome for a complex issue; and finally how a chair should develop and execute strategies for complex boardroom issues. They also showed me the best advisers in the Sydney market, and how they could be used to achieve results when independent arguments and data were needed."

Since that time, Ruth has played a major mentoring role herself in programs across the professions designed to help women with careers in IT, finance and marketing. Now her contribution is through WoB, set up to capitalise the potential for that medium. Claire Braund says Ruth informally mentors hundreds of women each year, including Claire herself. Whilst WoB offers coaching and mentoring, it's the latter that members want.

The formal WoB mentoring program handles about 30 mentees a year, over a six-month period. They recommend five meetings with mentors of up to two-hours' duration.

Both Claire and Ruth acknowledged the mentees sometimes didn't appreciate how available and flexible mentors were prepared to be in arranging meetings and in the contributions they were willing and able to make to their assigned mentees.

Ruth believes the three major contributions from these arrangements have been:

1. Giving the mentees better influencing and self-promotion skills
2. A confidential environment to discuss interpersonal relationship challenges
3. The mentees acquiring a better understanding of themselves and their relationship to what the director's job actually is.

The mentors are fairly high-powered men and women. (An example is David Mortimer who has chaired Australia Post and Leighton Holdings and has advised Bronwyn Evans, a senior executive at Cochlear, and now a director of John Holland. Another mentor is Andrea Staines who was herself a successful mentee on the 2010 Company Directors' scheme.)

Interestingly, the WoB scheme splits mentees into three segments: those just getting started; those who are director-ready now; and those whose director experiences have enabled them to seek out bigger and more complex director roles. This distinction has also emerged in the practices of the Company Directors' scheme, as the needs of the mentees are quite different at each level.

Claire Braund states that the formal mentoring scheme is at present fairly small as WoB is itself a significant informal mentoring network, and most members find they can draw value from that informality, combined with the extensive scope of their networking opportunities. Claire and Ruth have also consulted on, and established, in-house mentoring schemes for large corporates, such as Caltex.

Reflecting their overall mentoring philosophy, Claire Braund states:

> "At WoB, our informal motto is to ask someone who knows more than you do."

Mentoring: An Effective Reconciler of Gender Diversity

1. Successful mentoring programs in the diversity field have started with the same objective: to develop 'win–win' outcomes across the definitive difference between the mentor and mentee groups, by engaging them first in an activity where there is a common

cross-cultural passion. For the BCA, Company Directors and WoB it is to find ways to make access to senior roles more gender neutral.

2. These programs have four core elements:
   - Recognition and respect for gender differences, and the impacts, attitudes and bias these can drive in the workplace
   - A common action program that is gender neutral
   - A companion program based on reconciling sources of diversity for women in business
   - Building of new and extensive networks that can be farmed patiently for actual opportunities and knowledge to better position yourself – e.g. Company Directors.
3. These programs pass through typical natural growth phases: pilot trials; establishment of core working principles and practices; and then a rollout of the core program to new regions, new annual intakes and a broader set of participants.
4. Most diversity mentoring programs encounter second generation challenges – e.g. how to expand the education philosophies to accommodate the natural learning philosophies of the diverse mentees (i.e. softer female leadership skills of women executives and aspiring Directors).
5. Some mentoring program organisers realise other tools and resources need to be put in place – not only to help build a pipeline of future applicants, but also to enhance mentoring participants to get most value from their program, before it's over (e.g. Company Directors' Board-Ready and Public Sector Mentoring Board programs, and the Tomorrow's Boards booklet).
6. The final challenge is to generalise these learnings more broadly in society, in a way that expands the reconciliation results to be well embedded in, and accepted as, 'second nature' within society itself.

12

HOW THE BEST GET BETTER: MENTORING PROGRAM EXCELLENCE

Whilst formalised mentoring programs are quite recent in their origins and development, the art of mentoring has been around for centuries. In the last five years, mentoring program excellence has shown itself to be quite dynamic. What worked superbly a few years ago may only be fair, average-practice today. The arrival of formal programs has introduced a sponsoring organisation's eagle eye, and most of them want to know after a year or two – "how successful have our efforts at mentoring actually been?"

The immediate answers are fairly straightforward in principle, but often very difficult to measure. Mentoring is expected to produce:

- Better leaders making higher quality decisions, and more sustainably managing complex relationships with their stakeholders
- A faster development path for potential leaders who have been mentored
- A lift in the organisation's staff engagement scores – reflecting the broader impact of a successfully mentored leadership cadre practising modern servant and ethical leadership

- A greater appetite for necessary change amongst mentored leaders, and higher enthusiasm to see those needed changes through to completion
- Evidence that ethical and moral dilemmas, innovation and sensible risk-taking are being pursued in a more enlightened and durable way.

In reviewing the progress of many of the mentoring programs identified and described in the first edition of this book, it has become clear that the best mentoring program sponsors are their own hardest taskmasters. Since 2011-12, the leading programs all questioned whether they have the right objectives, values, frameworks, processes and ultimately the right people driving and participating in them.

Beneficial progress is evident from the internal reviews and subsequent changes to eight quite different mentoring programs at the AFL, AHRI, ANZSOG, Centre of Ethical Leadership (CEL) at the University of Melbourne, Company Directors (AICD), FEI, Male Champions of Change (MCC), and Victoria Police (VicPol). These programs have been selected as examples of potential improvements that can take place when an open mind is taken about what mentoring progress looks like, and how best to arrange its key drivers. Rather than review each scheme separately, the approach taken below is to compare and contrast how different program sponsors have challenged themselves and introduced change and innovation within four comparable mentoring program elements:

- Purpose and objectives
- Key processes
- Mentor value and management
- Mentee value and management.

Fundamental Purpose and Objectives

Most program sponsors start any internal mentoring program review here, even if it's just for a brief sanity check.

In a review of the Male Champions of Change (MCC) program which began in April 2010, Federal Sex Discrimination Commissioner Liz Broderick convened a group of 25 current and former CEOs and chairs, who had publicly committed themselves to more action on gender equity, to serve as agents of change for that within their own companies and also mentor and sponsor women within their own organisations.

At their regular meetings, the MCC members had enhanced their core gender-equity objective through the following explicit roles that only evolved over the last two years:

- Listen deeply to the experiences of women
- Share learnings on what it means to be a good mentor
- Exchange views on what success looks like
- Lift the bar on gender reporting, and share relevant KPIs, and also best practices
- Openly share their journeys
- Sponsor their own public research report cards and recommendations, and extend their reach to international networking and partnerships.

These MCC mentors-in-chief have learned to appreciate what delivers the greatest positive impact within their institutions. The cross-learning benefits and adoption of better practices elsewhere have been considerable, as a result.

Victoria Police has also added to its objective set. The five-program objectives for 2011 were described on pages 44-45. VicPol states these five remain intact, but they also see value in the objective of simply exposing police to different leadership styles and philosophies, which they encourage mentees to adopt into their own capabilities. They also want active capture of reverse-mentoring benefits and knowledge to be evident to participants by the end of the program.

VicPol has pushed the edge of its mentoring objective framework by having it linked explicitly to the service's organisational development and talent strategy. Top management asks the Leaders Mentoring Program (LMP) manager to identify impacts from mentoring on individual growth through to improved organisational performance. That's a tough ask, but it seems to be bearing early fruit, and the next few years will enable a better assessment of those explicit connections. So objectives for each mentoring assignment are set within the framework of the senior officer's own tailored career development, and meant to be part of helping that person become a more successful senior executive in VicPol's sworn ranks. These objectives will often be qualitative and cultural, as mentors are used from outside the Police service, (i.e. from Rotary and business). This internalisation of mentoring objectives can work within the police and defence forces, as they are independent systems, compared to other professions, and mentoring is seen as hard-wired to developing better internal leadership. The outside-the-square stimulus comes from using non-Police mentors.

At the AFL Indigenous mentoring and development program, Jason Mifsud says:

> "Five years ago, we probably felt success of the mentoring program was producing another élite player like Cyril Rioli at Hawthorn. Now it's about two much broader sets of objectives: first, how do Aboriginal people (female footy is our fastest growing segment) access a playing career but also any of the later future senior executive, business, coaching, management, match official and other development roles related to the football industry. Second it's now about improving cultural health and understanding within football."

In terms of the first objective, Jason instanced a number of former élite players, such as Michael O'Loughlin of the Sydney Swans who now is head coach of its Academy, a role formerly held by Paul Roos who became the successful head coach after that. Prior to that, Michael was head football coach at the Australian Institute of Sport (AIS). Andrew McLeod, formerly of the Adelaide Crows, was thereafter transitioned through the AFL's Indigenous programs. He is now working to better understand the AFL system and decision-making machinery, and has decided to use that knowledge to set up his own business to work with and help develop young Aboriginal talent. Xavier Clarke from St Kilda has undertaken various coaching and people-management programs, and coaches the Northern Territory Thunder. Aaron Davey and Chris Johnson are undertaking the early stages of this post-élite career development program, to enable them to make the best quality career choices they can going forward.

On cultural health and education, Jason is sponsoring initiatives to help Indigenous athletes manage the dual sets of expectations and obligations from their Aboriginal and western cultures. Jason said:

> "Success is measured here by imparting skills and abilities for young Aboriginal men to meet the cultural obligations of both civilizations."

He has also taken a range of approaches to combat what he describes as "casual racism", through actions and programs leading to a better understanding of Indigenous community behaviours and experiences.

> "Apart from helping people understand the cultural obligations of Aboriginal men across the 320 nations within Australia which speak 500 different dialects, I have role-modelled the importance of the senior Indigenous community leaders in decision-making. If that Indigenous leader doesn't think a younger member is ready for

more responsibilities, they have to wait. In my own case, I have just received permission from my uncle to occupy a leadership role within my own nation as a representative of Native Title, but many years after I thought I was ready for that. You have to learn to be patient, until the relevant elder says you can do that."

Evolving Better Mentoring Processes

At the Centre of Ethical Leadership (CEL), the objective of the mentoring program is fairly straightforward – to engage mentors to work with the Vincent Fairfax Fellows after they graduate from the one-year program on ethical leadership, on an embedding project to improve ethics within the workplace they return to. That objective hasn't really changed substantially over the last five years.

As Peter Collins observed:

"The prime value of mentoring is that the mentee recognises the gift of having someone there, who is genuinely prepared to invest time and care in them on a disinterested basis, and to help with the transitional moments in their lives and careers. That's very hard to measure, but you know from feedback whether they have it, or not. In simple terms, mentoring is an apprenticeship model that works or it doesn't, and it's usually clear one way or the other".

Notwithstanding that, the processes of mentoring have changed significantly at the CEL. Its Director Bob Wood says:

"Mentoring is complex, and the contextual identification is important. Each pairing is unique, and we have strengthened basic processes to enable participants to find their own way. We are conscious from our experience of the last few years of what is known as the 'optimal clarity problem', where you can be too specific on means and ends, and so peg down too many inflexible objectives as to what participants have to do. Too early a focus on outcomes can get you badly off the track."

Instead, the CEL has changed the mentoring process from being a fairly flexible self-start affair to a proactive planned one, where participants are required to meet a number of times around 'themes for mentoring conversations'. CEL has identified that the issues to be discussed are a function of the person's values and relevant career point, and also that of the mentor (in terms of their ability to help), and the organisational context, leadership and decision-making structures and culture at the mentee's place of work need to be worked through up front.

> "Mentoring is only part of a complete set of structures that contribute to a mentee's performance, and so that overall context needs to be examined and understood, before specific expectations can emerge. We set processes to encourage the development of organised minds that set the right targets and solve the critical problems."

CEL has also eliminated all networking mentoring, or 'many-on-one' sessions. Mentoring is now clearly understood to be an individual and contextual process, and one that can't be usefully advanced in a group setting.

The Company Directors program also has simple objectives that remain largely unchanged – to better prepare senior female executives for top roles and board positions. But there has been significant change to how the Company Directors achieve that objective. The third annual program is nearly finishing, but there was a break of almost a year between the second and third programs, while a major review was undertaken.

> "We had 56 in the first program and then immediately increased the second to 86 mentees", John Colvin CEO of the AICD said. "We probably had too many in the second program and the quality of the experience declined as a result. Many of the mentees weren't anywhere near board-ready or likely to be soon, and we had also

> pushed the mentors so we ended up with a number of them being severely fatigued, and needing a rest from this pro bono activity. So in the third program we tightened up the selection criteria and dropped back to 56."

Sonya Price is the manager of what has become the largest and most successful gender quality mentoring program by company chairs in the world.

> "We had to work harder in both selection and matching to ensure greater quality control for the third program," Sonya said. "Induction was strengthened so, overall, we were getting the pairs off on the right foot."

Company Directors also worked hard to realign expectations. Their guidelines made it clear that participation in the program didn't guarantee board roles, as many had thought would occur. Like other reforming best-practice programs they strengthened the discipline of the process, and clarified the expectations around it. They encouraged peer-mentee networking only and that was seen to be valuable during the first two programs.

At the Australia and New Zealand School of Government (ANZSOG), a different set of learning experiences emerged. After a few years trialling a new mentoring approach, this School developed a comprehensive 24-page handbook and induction program for new participants, as from 2013. That handbook sets out a comprehensive set of mentoring principles and rationale, as well as the need to refine mentoring objectives, and formalise agreements between participants. As the objective is more about career knowledge transfer from experienced and senior public servants ('the mentors') to emerging leaders and ANZSOG students ('the mentees'), that formality in structure is more aligned with success of the program objectives. This contrasts with the more complex embedding of a specific ethical leadership change program in a workplace which the CEL participants pursue. Further, the ANZSOG mentoring handbook summarises case studies from public sector leaders such as John Howard, which were actually outlined in the first edition of this book. ANZSOG also includes continuous improvement opportunities within its mid-term and final surveys of participants, with the expectation it will continue to evolve and enhance future programs as a result.

The Australian Human Resources Institute (AHRI) mentoring program has also evolved its structures, rather than objectives – which very simply have been for a senior HR practitioner to assist a younger professional either to aspire to and achieve a promotion, or manage one or a major functional or geographic change that they have just taken on. Learning-curve benefits and changes have been driven from a few different sources. As the program is delivered through decentralised, state-based structures, the program manager, Anne-Marie Dolan, has used ideas and experiences from the best states to drive improvements elsewhere, and so lift the overall national performance of the scheme. Not a lot of the materials used in this program have changed over the years, but Anne-Marie is finding five years of progress has produced some excellent alumni experiences, and these graduates are being beneficially used within induction and briefing processes for current participants. Having 'been there and done that', the alumni experience and perspective is seen as very valuable by the scheme's newcomers, especially when these are recounted in a face-to-face environment. This program measures:

- Satisfaction rates with mentees, whereby over 80% agree or strongly agree objectives are being met
- Meeting frequencies which have improved, whereby over half meet 11 times a year, and 70% meet at least bi-monthly
- The value of induction materials and other core processes.

Extended use of webinars is now made to induct and network with remote participants or mentoring pairs. As Anne-Marie Dolan says:

> "For some participants outside capital cities in a 500-person national program, we just can't always meet face-to-face. So we use webinars for briefings that especially help those in remote connections. That's useful, and it allows us to host more social networking events for participants looking for that type of interaction in addition to the formal online sessions. Participants seem happy with this change to the program."

Furthermore, the data is rich enough that AHRI is able to identify and manage under-performing mentors. Fortunately this is rarely required.

At the Financial Executives International (FEI), Peter Day states that objectives are largely unchanged but that years of experience in the scheme, especially with patterns of behaviour amongst the participants, have honed the matching skills of mentor and mentee and that has improved the success prospects for the relationship. They also measure satisfaction rates which have averaged around 90% in the last five years, and also the frequency and duration of meetings, which drives FEI's advice on this aspect to future cohorts. A significant majority of mentees see value with networking amongst themselves, so that is facilitated by the FEI where possible.

Mentor Value and Management

A third major area of reform in the management of the top mentoring programs has been in the area of the mentors themselves. This is different to issues discussed in earlier chapters where the assumption was of a strong self-start approach by each mentor.

Most schemes reviewed have stated that not too much detailed prior knowledge should be assumed amongst either mentors or mentees. Good program managers understand the need to constantly remind mentors to be good listeners before they can become good mentors.

Within the MCC program, the prime customer is the mentee, but the CEO members have acknowledged they now understand more about what it takes to be a better mentor than when they started.

Nearly four years down the track, MCC convenor Liz Broderick acknowledges too that what can be expected now from the MCC group as mentors themselves is quite different to what was contemplated in 2011.

> "Initially, we had very general objectives and the MCC members saw their prime role as to facilitate and encourage change by others in their companies. Now it's much more about actively leading by example, examining what each member is doing, and the group is being more constructively critical within its own number, as to what success looks like, and what it takes to get there."

The MCC peer review process has been very important for one CEO mentor to pick another up on what they would otherwise continue to assume is sound practice.

In the MCC program, Liz Broderick sees the reverse-mentoring benefits to mentors as becoming the subject of significantly greater importance to participants. From her own experiences, Liz commented:

> "Mentees teach you a lot about courage, and help you to develop a greater willingness to take on taboo subjects, and the best ways how."

Many of these eight program managers report having to re-approach mentors who have completed mentoring training, but who have demonstrated that they are still falling into one of two traps:

- Talking at, rather than listening to, their mentee

- Seeing their role as to get actively involved in fixing the mentee's problems, or outlining specific tactics or solutions to be followed.

The CEL finds they need to watch these two problems as does the MCC. Bob Wood says:

> "Mentors often get sucked into collaborating on false expectations. By this we mean, they become drawn into solving the mentee's problem, rather than building the mentee's problem-solving skills."

In his cross-cultural environment at the AFL, Jason Mifsud is more engaged now at leveraging Indigenous and white members of the football industry to absorb reverse-mentoring lessons and focus on the substance of how to relate to each other's culture and to avoid the chronic past dilemma of a 'white man trying to solve an Aboriginal man's problems'. Mentoring to Jason is more now about 'informed influencing of a cross-cultural nature'.

Another technique Jason uses to enhance cross-cultural understandings of different approaches to being a mentor relates to his own conduct of some meetings within the AFL:

> "Within Indigenous culture, the power is often vested with a person sitting under a tree, who is located well away from a meeting circle of elders. No matter what those Aboriginal people discuss in the circle, nothing will change until the older person under the tree agrees. At the AFL in my own group, I will often start a discussion with my colleagues, and then leave them after ten minutes or so. They find that unsettling, as they want me to stay and be part of the conversations and agreements that flow out of that. Instead, I will give them that experience as an example of what processes Aboriginal people follow and why. It's a reverse-learning experience for them, that helps them better understand our culture and what a mentor is there for. You don't achieve true reconciliation by constantly trying to work out solutions from the same point on the compass."

Similarly at the CEL, Bob Wood continually encourages mentors to ensure they have the right organisational and contextual understanding before they move the conversation to constructive conflict and influencing of the mentee to devise a plan that fits his or her own organisation. They constantly reinforce in their mentors that the job is to support 'true capability' in the mentee.

Peter Collins astutely acknowledges the gains to being a good mentor are the acquisition of greater thought-leadership about the community and business environment in which they operate. The respect they receive as a leader usually rises as their reputation as a good mentor also grows.

At ANZSOG, Mentoring Director Michael Mintrom believes mentors who use stories of comparable experiences to a mentee's current challenges are particularly valuable:

> "When you have the stature of a respected senior leader discussing experiences from their own career, that's very compelling and powerful listening material to mentees."

VicPol began its mentoring program with police mentees having two mentors – one from Rotary for community learnings and issues and one from business to learn about their strategic and financial approaches. As the LMP has achieved successes over time, the reach of the program has extended down from Assistant Commissioner level to Senior Sergeant. Assistant Commissioner (AC) Kevin Casey, who took over leadership of the LMP from AC Kevin Scott, said that the duality of two mentors for each mentee needed a re-think.

> "We found that community perspectives were most valuable to Senior Sergeants with responsibilities at the local community level. At the senior levels of the organisation, amongst those with executive potential to assume the rank of Assistant Commissioner and above, they are already well versed on community engagement, but usually need an exposure to high-level, strategic,

enterprise and external stakeholder engagement – thinking that you can get from our top business mentors. So we realigned the program accordingly to have one mentor per mentee, based on this principle. It has now introduced major efficiencies and greater effectiveness to the overall LMP program," AC Casey said.

Mentee Value and Management

As cited elsewhere in this book, the mentee is the prime customer in the relationship, but it should not be assumed mentees have all the skills immediately to be a sophisticated customer to their own needs.

At the CEL, Bob Wood and Peter Collins press their mentees with the following questions:

- "Do you feel you are developing your capability?"
- "Is this useful to you?"
- "Do you feel you are growing and becoming more effective?"
- "Are the problems being solved just short-term, immediate issues, or are you acquiring skills and expertise to address longer-term challenges that will shape your career?"
- "What is your line of sight between the mentoring experience and all the other things that are necessary for you to solve your problems?"

Bob also says you need to be alert to the physical and mental position of the mentee. He says, "it's hard to solve a philosophical problem when you have a toothache." Conversations often need to go into the challenges around enhancing the self-confidence of the mentee, and not getting sucked into irrelevant tasks. Whilst some of that is the mentor's responsibility, the mentoring program manager also has an obligation to quality-assure the health of the mentoring connection amongst the participants.

Peter Collins says:

> "The best mentees are those who have some idea of what they want from the mentor before they start. When mentees don't have, or apply, the ability to obtain clarity, that's when you have problems – as they can't guide their own mentors in a useful way. Getting onto that quickly is a key skill for mentoring managers."

Michael Mintrom of ANZSOG says teaching its mentees how to acquire many mentors over their life, and how to both engage and disengage when the needs are met, is a critical skill.

> "It's not just who they get matched with in our EMPA degree at ANZSOG, it's how they apply those career skills of mentor acquisition throughout their professional life".

ANZSOG also measures mentee satisfaction and drivers of that, more systematically than it did at the scheme's inception.

At the FEI, Peter Day states that the mentees must have the energy and drive to pursue the value from their relationship, and also – as others have observed – to know what they want or what problems they have that need solving.

At the Company Directors, Sonya Price said:

> "We use this program to give women the licence to self-promote, and to ask. Women are reluctant to promote and push themselves in business. We didn't publish our lists but we did encourage our mentees to be quoted and interviewed about the program. Those who did this learned a great deal about those presentation and marketing skills as well. We encourage the 200 women who have been through the program to be accessible to the other 3,400 female members of the Company Directors."

The best mentoring programs don't sit still, as this analysis attests. Further, all of them expect to continue to learn and evolve as their successful tenure gains further traction and extends out into the future.

PART IV
LEARNING FROM
MY MENTORS

13

SIX MENTORS IN WORK AND LIFE

"Who were your mentors?", and "what have you learned from them?"

These are two classic questions to ask a group of mentors being inducted for a new program, or a 'one-on-one' mentoring experience that's about to commence. Having people focus on these two questions can give their mentoring a more compelling set of personal connections, especially at the inception of a new relationship. Mentoring can sometimes be a process of a continuous, but also diffuse, set of exposures to those who care about you and from whom you learn, and their identities can be a bit blurred without the challenge of asking yourself about these identities and lessons learned. In my case, a short reflection did enable a clear recollection of six people outside my family whose contributions were substantial to my own growth in career, life and learning. That number is eight if you include my parents, Les and Vera, and I do. It's also worth saying that my experiences with mentors gave me certain critical 'breakthrough' insights that have stayed with me throughout my work and life. It's not like a curriculum-build at school, where you add a little bit more each day you go to class.

Many mentees report this characteristic of their learning, which comes on top of who you are, your basic intelligence and professional skills and experiences.

The six major mentors external to my family were:

1. **Dr Jim Cairns**, who was a very controversial Federal politician in the 1960s and '70s and for a time Deputy Prime Minister in the Whitlam Labor Government
2. **Professor Peter Sheehan**, a famous Australian academic, economist, prolific researcher and author, and for a time, senior public servant
3. **Stan Wallis**, long term CEO of APM/Amcor and then Chairman of AMP, Coles Myer, Amcor, the 1997 Commonwealth Financial System Inquiry, Business Council of Australia, and more recently Sane Australia, a leading national mental health advocacy group
4. **Bob Santamaria**, now General Counsel at ANZ Banking Group, and before that Partner at Allens Arthur Robinson, a leading national corporate and commercial law partnership. Bob was a peer of mine from university and fitted the role of a peer mentor
5. **Lindsay Gaze**, famous Australian and Olympic basketball player, coach and administrator
6. **Dr Fons Trompenaars**, eminent author, academic, thinker, and world cross-cultural expert.

This chapter outlines what I have learned from my parents and the first four of the six external mentors listed above. All of them taught me an enormous amount about work and life challenges, and at the end of this chapter there is an integrated summary of those key learnings. The chapter thereafter is devoted to advice and lessons from my only mentor from the world of élite professional sports, Lindsay Gaze. The sixth great external mentor of mine,

Fons Trompenaars, is perhaps most memorable from encountering a set of circumstances on which I chose not to consult with him as they were happening. A later consultation with him revealed my folly at not having done so. Those events are outlined separately in Chapter 15, entitled 'Life and Death in Shanghai', and represent one of my biggest failures, which could have been avoided.

But first a short 'ode' to my parents, Lesley David Duncan Wilson and Vera Ethel Wilson.

Les and Vera were married after the Second World War in 1946 and were well into their thirties at that time. Compared to their peers, that was a very late stage to start both marriage and a family, but also quite understandable because the Great Depression and the World War took precedence during a prime 15 years of their young adult lives after 1930.

Lessons from my Father

My father Les was disabled during his twenties, a few years before the Great Depression hit in 1930. He had contracted tuberculosis in the radius bone of his right arm near the elbow, and it had to be removed by surgery. After the operation, his right arm was effectively fixed at a right angle with the ulnar and humerus bones hinged together in a way that gave him little flexibility from his reconstructed elbow. Before that my father had been a jack of all trades, but primarily a cattle drover on the Atherton Tableland in Queensland. After surgery on his arm, he had to give that career of active physical work away, and then retrain as a printer. In 1928, he returned to Victoria to begin work in a North Melbourne printing shop, which apparently went well for two years. When the 1930s Depression hit the world economy, Les lost that job in favour of the son of the printing shop proprietor, and he was then unemployed for nearly ten years – something I only learned about from my mother when I was in first year university.

He never seemed to get angry, or show regret or rancour over the consequences from the loss of his job to nepotism in 1930. In fact, on a few occasions he said to me that if he had been in his employer's situation he would have done the same thing.

That was in late 1969, when I had been selected to row internationally after my university crew won the national championships, and it meant training through the winter and being away in Tokyo for the championships during the month of August, and only a month or two from my first year final exams. My father and I had an enormous argument as he didn't want me to go for fear that I would fail those exams and get tossed out of university. According to my mother, his fears were that my life would become like his own after losing that printing job.

Due to his disabled state, my father was unable to compete for the few jobs that came up between 1930 and the start of the Second World War. During the war, he was also deemed unfit for military service but managed to put together some temporary employment roles to help with the domestic side of the war effort until 1945. He never spoke much about these 15 years, but it's fair to say he was greatly underutilised as a worker during that period, and also felt poorly valued as a person and as a man. So marriage and supporting another was out of the question for Les at that time.

I then understood more clearly my father's early advice to me on the need for patient application in life, whatever it offers to you; persistence to develop your skills, together with a spirit of perennial optimism; and the importance of both compassion and a good sense of humour. In fact, I probably owe this book to him. At primary school I was terrible at English, and writing in particular, so he would take me on walks and ask me to write what I had seen when we got back home. At first I resisted but with his patient encouragement I knuckled down and then got to enjoy doing it, and so acquire my own motivation to persist.

Earlier in 1958, when Les was 50 (and I was seven) years old, he was working as a storeman for Coles in Port Melbourne. One day a stack of boxes and crates toppled over and pinned him to the ground and a wall for a very long time. Fortunately that accident didn't crush or seriously injure him initially, but the stress at not being found for some time caused him to have a bad heart attack. He recovered from that, but thereafter he was invalided out of employment with Coles. No radius, poor ticker, not a good look for any employer. My dad often said "I had no radius but could always find my circumference, so what the hell, I can work with that". He had a marvellous sense of humour that left you in no doubt as to what he was thinking. For example, one day after we had both been listening to a political broadcast, he turned and said to me "Bullshit comes in all shapes and sizes, but the smell is pretty much the same."

Over the next 25 years from that first heart attack, he had a number of serious illnesses and diseases – gall stones, kidney stones, bladder operations, shingles, another heart attack, a stroke, and finally pancreatic cancer that proved fatal. Throughout all this time, he always appeared to suffer in silence, because he never ever complained about any pain. He had a stoic philosophy and kept as high a level of mental and physical fitness as he could throughout. I often thought the Grim Reaper found him just too tough to tackle and best left alone until the very end. My learnings from him of patience, self-discipline and finding your own internal strength were considerable. Optimism and resilience also drove him, when many others would have given up in despair.

Lessons from my Mother

My mother Vera was born on a dairy farm near Drouin in South Gippsland, and with her other sisters she assumed some of the maternal roles in the family household, when her mother left Vera's father for another man. Mum believed the marriage break-up and the new quasi maternal roles forced upon her as a result, had unfairly stolen a large part of her adolescence. Vera came to dislike the hard life of farming and keeping the family household going as well, and looked for an option to get away from that, after she and the family had both gained greater independence. Towards the mid-1930s, at the age of 18, Vera left the farm and began training as a nurse. She was later employed as a Ward Sister in Charge at the Albury Base Hospital from 1940-45. Vera learned the horror of the aftermath of war through nursing the struggles, impaired recoveries and disablements of many wounded returning soldiers. When that role ended, she returned to nursing in Melbourne, and soon after met my father. There seems little doubt that, in addition to their love for each other, my mother's understanding and empathy for men carrying long-term disabilities bonded her and my father together the more so. After their marriage, they had two sons – the elder was my brother Tim, and then I was born in Richmond. My parents then moved us to a large house in Middle Park which my mother converted into a boarding house for a time, after which they purchased our first home in Bentleigh. This was about the time my father took the warehouse role with Coles and my mother took up home duties with her two sons. But Mum's business skills led to the construction of a large sun room out into the backyard, which became the scene for a local kindergarten she ran commercially five mornings a week. Couldn't stop that woman starting up a business from home (twice in a row)!

Working for Themselves

After my father's heart attack and his invalided retirement from Coles, the game of work and life in the Wilson family had to completely change. Thereafter, my mother and father decided they had to combine their skills and buy into self-employment as small business owners and operators – through two florist shops in

Murrumbeena and Bentleigh, and a share of a flower and plant nursery east of Warrigal Road, in Melbourne's outer eastern suburbs at that time. From this period, came my strong sense of the importance of gender equity. Mum and Dad shared the home and business responsibilities based on merit and need. Gender was not of any relevance to that part of our lives. My mother ran the retail and decorative side with weddings and funerals and Dad ran the supply chain to both florist shops, and the back office – accounting, tax and debts.

My job was to help out wherever I could. Most memorable for me were the trips I made alongside my father on his debt collection duties, typically on Saturday afternoons after the two florist shops had closed for the week. You learn a lot about life from debt collection and I observed a broad inverse correlation between the size of the family home and the apparent wealth of its occupants, on the one hand, and the willingness to repay a simple debt to a flower shop on the other. In this business, you had to arrange the delivery of many products, such as wreaths for a funeral in two days' time, ahead of a grieving person's ability to pay for the service. One Saturday afternoon, my father and I pulled up outside a very large home in the wealthy suburb of Toorak. I remained in the car as my father walked up to the veranda and knocked on the front door. My view of my father and his surrounds was perfectly clear, as a man appeared at the door and behaved very irately towards my father. Then he returned back inside and slammed the door. My father waited there and about five minutes later the man returned and immediately threw a handful of loose coins at him, with most of them spilling around the front veranda. Dad said something to this man, which seemed to take him aback, before he uttered a few final words and then retreated inside, slamming the front door yet again. My father knelt down and carefully collected all the coins he could find with the hand on his good arm and then returned to the car. On the drive home, I asked my father what he said to this irate customer after he had thrown the money at him. My father smiled, "I said to him 'I could see you were excited to see me, but I didn't realise you were saving up for this moment. Thank you and good day.'" The customer's retort was neither dignified nor worth repeating. Then I asked my father "did you get all the money?" He replied, "no, but it's close enough and there's no need for us to go back there, ever again."

Notwithstanding my father's skills as a debt collector, if both my parents were alive today and discussing their business experiences, I am sure my father would probably say Mum was the better business person. She was very skilful at the creative side of floral work and did the flowers for many high-profile society weddings. She was irrepressibly courteous to the customer, even the most infuriatingly demanding 'all about me' types. I learned the power of brand management, quality control and the importance of customer service from my mother. Being more emotional than Dad, she would often burst into the kitchen, in part of the building where we lived behind the shop, to let off steam about some ridiculous customer 'who believed all our flowers on display were flawed and should be made available free of charge'. I actually quite enjoyed these steam-outlet moments because I never saw them from my Dad. (Apparently I have these moments myself sometimes.)

My mother was also extremely quick to assess a difficult and threatening situation. One day we had pulled into a service station on the way home to get a tank of petrol. We were both sitting on the front seat when, out of the service garage in front of us, a man in overalls appeared running and screaming with flames covering half his body. Quick as a flash, mum rocketed out of her seat and around to the boot of our car from which she retrieved a blanket. Then she headed straight at the mechanic and took him down, wrapping him up in the blanket with a tackle that would have impressed John Eales. When they hit the ground, Mum ensured the blanket smothered and arrested all the flames. As I got out of the car I could hear her intermixing soothing words to the burns victim who was in a state of shock and also shouting to the garage proprietor to call an ambulance. The mechanic had been servicing a car on his back, atop a set of sliding wheels underneath the chassis. That was unexceptional activity for a motor mechanic, except he was smoking at the same time and his wheels were on top of a large oil and petrol slick which his cigarette ash surely ignited. After the police and ambulance came, my mother spoke to me and asked if I was alright to walk home alone, as she wanted to accompany the burns patient in the ambulance to the hospital. Later that night she reappeared at home, and we talked about the experience and also others from her nursing days during the war years. I realised the trauma I had witnessed that day was nothing to what she had experienced, or had had to manage. She said to me, "It won't be the last time you are confronted by threats to the health and wellness of another human being and, while it's good to have some basic training, sometimes it's best just to let your instincts take over."

My mother's instinctive judgement was quite compelling for me, on that day she seemed to assume the speed of the Lithgow Flash, Olympic Gold Medallist Marjorie Jackson! Soon after, my mother arranged for me to do some basic first aid training, after which she asked if it had covered responding to burns victims. When I said it hadn't, she replied "Well I guess we have got that covered now anyway." A spare blanket is a regular feature of my car boot, just near the jack.

The Ties that Bind

Inevitably, you collect political values from your parents. Mine were from opposite sides of the spectrum, so life was very confusing at the start. Dad was a loyal Printers Union member and Labor man, due to his concerns at the causes of the Great Depression and the consequential loss of so many thousands of jobs. He could never get over seeing hundreds of wool bales tipped off Station Pier into the water at Port Melbourne during 1930 because there was no market for them. He almost became a Communist, but never quite reconciled with all of their beliefs.

Vera on the other hand was a firm Liberal and National Party supporter. She loved Elvis Presley, and also Liberal Prime Minister Bob Menzies, but not necessarily in that order. So the home dinner table conversation on politics was always an interesting one. It vested me firmly in the centre of the political spectrum, and my vote has been captured at various times by governments of the left and right, but I have probably become more conservative since my forties. Nevertheless, a peaceful co-existence of different political views in a democracy was something I learned about at home, as being a 'good thing'.

The ties that bind us are more important than those which separate us. On some issues, I learned that perceptions and relative values will differ but that's also to be respected. My father used to challenge me with infuriating political dilemmas like, "Why can't we have a single world government where every elected member exercises his or her vote, according to conscience, and on the merits of the issue?" That was a nice way to explore the subjects of power, relative values, ambition and self-interest, and we surely did. Unsurprisingly perhaps, the first half of my career was in the Federal and State bureaucracies working mainly in the Treasury portfolios which inevitably went to Ministers from the centre of each mainstream political party. I always enjoyed working for those from the mainstream centre of political life, which is the advisory position I occupy most comfortably. The one exception was Jim Cairns, Federal Treasurer for a time, who was very much from the political left. Nevertheless, that working relationship was close but also different, as Jim had been a very early mentor of mine long before I worked for him as a Treasury official.

Eventually the business instincts developed from my mother took over and I moved my career out of the public service to become part of the business economy after 1990. My later mentors influenced that career transition too, as well as what happened to it thereafter.

Dr James Ford ("Jim") Cairns, My First Encouraging Mentor

My father lived and moved around the Collingwood-Fitzroy area in Melbourne during the Depression and war years. At that time, he came to know a member of the police force, Jim Cairns, who was then a young detective gaining notoriety through his role with a special surveillance team known as "the dogs" shadowing squad where he was involved in a number of dramatic high-profile arrests. Jim also completed an economics degree at the University of Melbourne, and was the first Victorian policeman to hold a tertiary degree.

Towards the end of the war, Jim Cairns left the police and was employed as a lecturer in the army and then as a senior lecturer in economic history at the University of Melbourne. He was also a committed socialist, but had an application rejected to join the Communist Party in 1946.Cairns later joined the Labor Party and became active in its socialist left wing. Inevitably, he became a leading opponent of the Roman Catholic 'Groupers' who had infiltrated the Victorian Labor Party to arrest what they saw as its communist influences, and with much encouragement from the late and famous Archbishop Daniel Mannix and B.A. (Bartholomew) Santamaria.

After the major split in the Labor Party over Catholic 'Grouper' influence in its affairs during 1955, Cairns sided with Dr H.V. ("Bert") Evatt and stood at the 1955 election for the Federal House of Representatives in the working class seat of Yarra which was held by the leading Grouper, Stan Keon. Jim Cairns defeated Stan Keon after what he described as "an intense and vigorous campaign".

Thanks to my father, I met Jim Cairns in 1962 and I both knew and encountered him at various times throughout the rest of his life. In the early 1960s, there was much discussion about the space race between USA and Russia. Space exploration was well known to cost a lot of money, and about a year after both countries had put up manned spacecraft into the stratosphere to circle around the globe, I was given an essay topic at school to "Discuss the space race – is it worth the money invested?" I had the whole term of ten weeks to complete a 350-word essay on the topic, but had absolutely no idea where to start. So I asked my father, who had strong views on the value and relative priorities of public expenditure, about what to do. Dad said, "I know an ex-copper who is a Doctor of Economics and is now in Federal Parliament. Jim Cairns is his name and he would know about this, so why don't we write to him and ask what he thinks?" That seemed a good idea, even though I had never heard of any human disease called economics, but I did think parliament must be a cool place to work, because they all just sat around and talked to each other each day. And so we cleared the table one night after dinner and wrote that letter to Dr Jim.

About two weeks later, a brown paper package arrived at home from Jim Cairns with a hand-written note on his letterhead, together with three books from his personal library. In the note he thanked me for my interest in the topic, shared some excellent viewpoints, and marked passages in these books with some slips of paper which he thought would be relevant to my research. Needless to say, they were and I used them all! Much later I submitted the essay and was pleased those contrarian viewpoints didn't excite my conservative mainstream teacher too much. Then I wrote a thank-you note to my first ever mentor and Dad arranged for us to go and meet Jim in his office in order to deliver it personally.

I remember seeing him the first time and being in great awe. Jim reminded me of both Keith Miller, the swashbuckling Australian cricket all-rounder, and there was also a touch of the American actor, John Wayne, about him. Later in life, I realised the looks might have been similar but their political views could not have been further apart from his! At our meeting, I triumphantly reported to Dr Cairns I had received 8 out of 10 for my excellent work (mostly on 'his' ideas), and he commended that result with a big smile, hearty congratulations and strong handshake. That meant a lot to this little boy, I can tell you. And yes – I gave him his three books back. Needless to say, neither his advice nor my essay had any immediate impact on those Russian and American space people, until the Vietnam War started to compete with that style of use for public funds. Then those views did start to have somewhat of an impact, but of course that was much more about the coming of Jim Cairns' own time in Australian political history.

After graduating from secondary school, I began a commerce degree at Melbourne University where Jim Cairns had taught and he was still an occasional visitor and lecturer at the faculty. It was about the time of the 1970 Vietnam Moratorium, and I encountered him one day after a lecture. Jim remembered me and my father and invited me to come and listen at a rally for the Moratorium where he spoke. It was powerful oratory, and as we walked back to the faculty building, he turned and asked me what I thought, and "whether you are going to march with us?" My answer was unmistakably affirmative. "That's good. Our democracy needs bright young men like yourself prepared to stand up and be counted on important moral issues like this. Thank you", he said again to me when I was the one who needed to thank him for the interest he had shown in me. In a few weeks, I joined the 100,000 people who marched down the full length of Bourke Street, Melbourne on 8 May 1970. At that stage, my university rowing coach, Harvey Nicholson, was appalled at my decision to go on the march, as I was in the Melbourne University senior eight and the national rowing championships were only three weeks away, following six months of extensive and onerous preparations and training. Harvey was concerned that I would be arrested and be lost to that cause of winning the championship boat race. There was general tension and uncertainty about the Moratorium across Australia at the time. The Queensland and New South Wales governments were known to be very intolerant of any public demonstrations about the Vietnam War and encouraged very heavy-handed treatment of demonstrators by the police. Victoria was a bit more permissive as the then-Premier of Victoria, Henry Bolte said just before the Moratorium that "they can march until they are bloody well footsore". In fact, it was a very peaceful relaxed march and we all got to sit down on the road in the middle of Bourke Street and listen to Dr Jim once again. I concluded my participation in this event with my feet in very good shape for that night's rowing training, and not having to rest them up on a prison bench. Three weeks later, Coach Harvey and I were both happy, as my eight had just won the national rowing championships in Canberra and we received our gold medals from Sir Paul Hasluck, then-Governor-General of Australia. I wondered at the time whether I should ask him if he had marched too, but thought better of it, especially when he was handing me the gold.

After graduation, I commenced work in the Federal Treasury in Canberra, just after the Whitlam Labor Government won in 1972. Dr Jim Cairns was initially responsible for the trade and industry portfolios. Two years later, he became the Deputy Prime Minister and Federal Treasurer. As a young economist in Treasury, I got to take memoranda and letters across to the Treasurer's office for signing in what is now known as the Old Parliament House. Those times were very relaxed and little security existed outside the PM's office. You could quite literally walk up through the entrance and down the corridor to the Treasurer's office. On these occasions, I met Jim in his office a number of times, and he usually had time for a chat. One of my jobs at Treasury was to fix the daily exchange rate between the Australian and US dollars that had to be advised by telephone to the Reserve Bank which published it at 11am. So at the time in my career, I was a legal price-fixer on international financial markets. Jim often asked how my work was going and what I was up to. One afternoon I confessed that my exchange rate price-fixing had gone awry that morning. (This was actually after a hard night partying with some mates, which I chose not to confess to him. However, I think he seemed to work out what I had been doing the previous evening from the look of me and what he said to me after that.) In my foggy-headed state that morning, I had determined a rate for the Australian dollar that was quite a few decimal points stronger than it should have been, on a day that our wool exporters had been bringing significant amounts of US dollar denominated revenue into the country to swap into our home currency. I must have cost them some tens of thousands of dollars that day. When I told Jim this he said, "Oh well, don't worry about that too much. They can probably afford it. But you will need to be more careful in future, won't you? And don't do those important things when you are not feeling your best". I gave him another affirmative answer, which I was also determined to keep. And did.

I did not see Jim for many years after that, by which time his political career was over due to his involvement with Junie Morosi, his Chief of Staff who became his lover, and also his involvement in the Connor/Khemlani Loans Affair, which he actually succeeded in stopping, only then to issue a similar mandate to a dentist-turned-businessman, and former Carlton Football Club President, George Harris. After leaving parliament, he became involved with the counterculture movement, and the Down to Earth festival, but that ended badly for him too. In the last years of his life, he used to sell his books from a small fold-out table at the Prahran and South Melbourne markets, where I did stop and chat with him from time to time. One day in the 1990s, I asked him how he felt about the way his political career and life in general had gone. He looked at me and said, "That's just who I am. I have been to the edge of the abyss in life and looked down into it, but was able to step back. And that's OK."

Those words marked the last time I saw and spoke with him. Jim Cairns died in October 2003. Whilst he was an enigma to many, and a socialist demon to some, he was neither to me. Thanks to my father, Jim Cairns was the first adult outside my family who showed any real interest in me as a mentor and who genuinely wanted to help. Over time, he openly shared some of his own life experiences with me, in the expectation that they would be of some help in shaping my own.

His various advices over the years are as clear to me now as when he first spoke those words.

Professor Peter Sheehan – Mastering the Bureaucracy

Whilst it is generally true your current boss is unlikely to be a career and life mentor until you have left that direct reporting relationship you share, there are some exceptional bosses who are natural and gifted mentors as well. Elsewhere in this book it has been stated that current bosses don't usually make good mentors because the objective of acting in the organisation's best interests can serve as a conflict when also trying to serve the best interests of the individual. That perceived conflict might for example inhibit a mentor advising a mentee to take a decision to leave that organisation, when the latter individual is also a highly valued employee, and a subordinate too. When relieved of this perceived conflict, many former bosses do become good mentors to help their protégés' future careers elsewhere.

For me, Peter Sheehan was a person who held both roles of boss and mentor at the one time. We worked together for nearly eight years, at the end of which time he strongly advocated that I take a promotion to be the head of another Department in the Victorian public service in my career best interests, and at a time when his own Department was coming under enormous pressure for higher performance, given the failing state of the economy and also deteriorating relationships with some of its political masters. In this situation, many would have just sought to hold onto all of their best talent for as long as they could. But not Peter Sheehan, when the combined case for the individual and the bigger picture ran the other way to that of communal self-interest.

Peter was the boss everyone would want to have at that critical development time in their career, when they move from being a manager to an executive leader. He was very intelligent, generous, open, inclusive, and very strategic in not only what he did, but also how he went about it. He pushed you to achieve objectives you wouldn't have regarded as possible, but he did so in all of the nicest, subtlest, and when needed, in the most direct of ways too. He showed a concern for you the professional, and as a person with family interests and individual needs. He worked us hard but usually allowed our conscience and values to be the hardest taskmasters of all, including decisions about when not to be there when we needed to be with our families.

Peter is a Science and Arts graduate from the University of Melbourne, and then went to Oxford University where he obtained his DPhil in Philosophy. After his return from Oxford, he took up successive roles as Research Fellow, Senior Research Fellow and Principal Research Fellow, at the Institute of Applied Economic and Social Research at the University of Melbourne, under its then internationally renowned Director, Professor Ronald Henderson, from December 1972 until May 1982. During that period he was also Editor of *Australian Economic Review* from 1975-1978.

I worked for Peter when he was Director General, Department of Management and Budget, Victorian Government, from October 1982 to April 1990. During this period he was also Special Adviser to the Australian Prime Minister Bob Hawke from March to April 1983, just after the Hawke government came to power.

Professor Peter Sheehan was Founding Director of Centre of Strategic Economic Studies (CSES) at Victoria University from 1993 to 2011, and is now its Research Director. He has made a substantial contribution to the field of studies of the global knowledge economy, and of its Australian and international ramifications, since 1994. He has also contributed to both the analysis of new technologies and their application in Australia, and to policy and commercial developments related to the commercialisation of such technologies in Australia, over two decades in roles as chairman or director in companies like AMRAD Ltd (Australian Medical Research and Development Consortium) that became listed on the ASX, as well as Vistel and ACCI Ltd. In August 2003, he was elected to the position of Academic Co-Chair, APEC Life Sciences Innovation Forum (LSIF), chaired by the Deputy Prime Minister of Thailand.

Professor Sheehan has published ten books, including *Crisis in Abundance*, Penguin Books, 1980 and *Hidden Unemployment: The Australian Experience* (with Peter Stricker), in 1981, and over 40 articles covering a wide range of academic and policy topics. His most recent publication is *China's Future in the Knowledge Economy: Engaging the New World* (Victoria University and Tsinghua University Press 2002).

With this considerable research and academic background before his nine-year stint as Head of the Victorian State Treasurers department, there was a considerable degree of scepticism in 1982 as to whether he possessed the wherewithal to become a successful senior public servant and departmental CEO. A year or so into the job, and after being seconded to Canberra to assist Australia's newest Prime Minister, those sceptics were all silenced.

The first major learning I acquired from Peter was that the shape of our society and public administration can both be changed beneficially through a focus on the institutions we have (or need to establish), and also their culture and behaviours. My career was an immediate beneficiary of that approach. Peter arrived in 1982 as the Director-General designate of the new Cain Labor Government's Treasury portfolio and department, under Treasurer Rob Jolly. During the state election that year, a key platform was that Victoria's economic and financial policies and strategies were outdated and in need of substantial reform. So rather than immediately take over the Treasury as it was then known, Peter chose to set up and lead a separate task force of younger economists and leaders from inside and outside the Victorian Public Service, including yours truly, and won the confidence and co-operation of the then-Treasury head Ian Baker, for the latter to continue managing the state's finances whilst a new platform for strategic economic and financial management was put in place over the next nine months. Thereafter, the task force and the Treasury were merged into the new department and Ian Baker became Peter's deputy. My role was to head the new economic policy and planning division for six years and then I became Peter's deputy for another two years.

That approach of parallel-running two institutions bound for ultimate merger, with one of those driving a reshaping of the overall culture, was a role-model for seeking and securing needed institutional change. Its inclusive and transparent approach and process won support all round.

Secondly, Peter taught me the importance of securing support for change in a political environment. Apart from being left or right in their political alignment and belief on the value and extent of intervention in markets, professional economists probably sort themselves into one of the following three groups:

- The pure (or perhaps rarified) analysts, who spend time with the data in the company of other economists and become frustrated when the recommendations they make aren't implemented totally and without qualification. The independent research think-tanks are sometimes an example of this group. I started my working life in this camp.
- There are also applied economists who make qualified assessments and judgments based on both qualitative and quantitative data, but live under the discipline of having to couch their recommendations to be of practical relevance to their employers. Economists attached to a bank's foreign exchange dealing room are an example of this group – i.e. those who have to make predictions on interest rates, exchange rates and economic growth rates, that immediately underpin the setting of asset portfolio decisions and thence buy or sell decisions by the foreign exchange traders. Other examples are applied economists who are expert on a certain industry, the automotive and resources industries are two examples. I moved into this camp a few years before I worked for Peter Sheehan.
- Senior policy economists, whose value is putting all of the above skills together but within a close understanding of how

political processes work; how to assess the current political climate, in terms of what will work or not. They also have the skill and courage to argue against the status quo and know how to manage the politics to enable the greatest chance of success for acceptance of their viewpoints and proposals, and when to exercise that judgment to push against the established grain. Peter Sheehan drafted me into this group, which I found to be the most professionally satisfying of all.

Peter nurtured these practical analysis and implementation skills through his mentoring of me in seven areas, all of which drove his own thinking on public sector leadership:

1. **Understanding and engaging with critical political processes** – Peter shifted my thinking from relying solely on an applied economist's 'inside out' approach – i.e. viewing the world from that profession's analytical lens, to also adopt a political 'outside in' perspective. He got us to ask and consider, "What did governments and the Parliament want, and how could both sets of perspectives be reconciled to what change the bureaucracy believes is needed?"
2. **Shadowing** – Peter actively involved me in high-level, political discussions with ministers and ministerial/political staff so I could come to understand what they were thinking and why; this enabled me to better couch our analysis and recommendations.
3. **Setting strategic goals** – Peter was a classic believer of the 'light on the hill' approach. That meant you start by surveying the relevant parties and stakeholders to assess their material views on any subject and then draft a strategic template that could assist all involved not only to lift their sights towards a future end-game, but also to set out how that would enable us to achieve a new mode of operation and overall performance, whilst achieving as many of the

individual objectives held as possible. Simple but yet very powerful in its engagement and results.

4. **Publishing strategic economic templates** – Peter believed that once the necessary stakeholders had been engaged and reconciled on a new set of objectives or plans, the public sector had an obligation to set this out in detail for all to see. That could be in the form of detailed economic papers and reasonings behind the Annual Budget, or a separate document on a field of government economic policy that the public and all relevant stakeholders could work through and understand. In this last aspect, Peter taught me a lot about complex analysis but also the equal importance of subsequent clear and simplified public communication.
5. **Pre- and post-meeting briefs** – Nothing we did happened by accident. Peter was a stickler for analysing the agenda and issues, as well as the special interests of the parties before and after any meeting, whether that was on hospital funding and meetings with their CEOs; with trade union officials over any changes to industrial laws and workplace health legislation; or medical research experts and leaders on how to commercialise more of our science within Australia.
6. **Public-private sector interface** – Peter believed in a public sector that was not faceless but one that needed to spend time networking and trying to understand where and how it impacted on society and/or business. He believed in co-operation and transparency and would spend time seeking out stakeholders and decision-makers outside the public sector whom he believed we needed to engage for greater or maximum impact.
7. **Managing blockers and obstructionists** – Peter shared a range of techniques with me to flush out the special interest groups who were endeavouring to obstruct or delay. The

most obvious tactic he used was to analyse the situation with and without the elements they favoured and allow the greater transparency of the superior case or position to mobilise other forces to push that opposition over.

The other major characteristic I learned from Peter was that of servant leadership – long before the term become popularised in American business text books. He personified the approach of leading as the first among equals, based on acceptable ethics and values. Peter believed leadership positions were best won and sustained by open and honest intellectual debate and respect, and to garner support by sharing the directions overall and the implications for individual parties, as something that your co-workers would want to buy into, rather than be directed towards or coerced into.

Whilst these approaches, style and tools helped my career in the public sector advance to enable me to head up departments reporting to a Minister in my own right, I found most of them were also applicable to a career in the private sector, especially with large listed entities which are also political creatures (albeit with some definingly different characteristics). Corporations are political beasts too, as they are governed by people and their power structures which are subject to regular election by either shareholders or constituent members, as opposed to voters who install governments and ministers who then hire and fire public servants.

Analagous processes and similar behaviours, but for me – one mentor who helped me connect all the dots.

Stan Wallis AC – Ethical Business Leadership

Most executives aspire to be mentored by one of the great leaders of modern corporate life. I have been very fortunate to have one such person take a close interest in me and serve as a mentor to my career. Stan Wallis AC, has a commerce degree from Melbourne

University, and holds an honorary Doctorate of Laws from Monash University. Stan's experience as a chair and leader in industrial and financial services spans 40-plus years, and he is still a very active 75-year old in a range of activities including his role as Chairman of SANE Australia and Deputy Chairman of Rubicon Water. During his career, Stan served as the Managing Director (for 18 years) and chairman (for four years) of Amcor Limited, and was the President of the Business Council of Australia. Stan was a former chairman of the 1996-97 Committee of Inquiry into the Australian Financial System commissioned by the Howard Government. He has also served as chairman of Santos Limited, Coles Myer Limited and AMP Limited, and as a director of Walter and Eliza Hall Institute of Medical Research and the Melbourne Business School.

Like many of his generation, he valued the contributions of mentors to his own career, but noted:

> "During my career and life, mentoring was not as explicit and high profile as it is now. I had mentors at school like Jack Kroger, (Michael and Andrew's father), and also Charles Montagnat – at APM both a great friend but also a demanding and challenging business associate. I have also been fortunate for nearly 60 years to have a group of friends from university remain peer mentors over my life."

Stan instilled in me the importance of being mentally tough, which he had learned from his own mentor Charles Montagnat, but also emphasised an important distinction in making that happen. He said many leaders can fail to understand this distinction and erroneously see that characteristic of mental toughness as something to justify intimidation of others at work, which is not OK.

Stan advised me:

> "The importance of being tough-minded doesn't mean being tough on other people. Rather, it's about mental toughness for yourself – to pursue the right answer rather than a short term compromise.

> This distinction gives you focus. It distils the core issues that enable you to do something about the challenges you are facing."

On a related note he said to me that:

> "One of the biggest problems in business is those who get stuck in their comfort zones. Part of your own tough-mindedness is to push to the edge of what you can do yourself. And then 'What we all can do'. It's amazing what your group can achieve if you do."

Stan was one of the earliest leaders in Australian corporate life to practise what is now known as servant leadership or ethical leadership. For Stan that means four things. First:

> "Business is like a family and you need a moral compass for that, as the famous CEO of GE, Jack Welch once said, 'The people that will almost certainly fail as leaders and often wreck a good company are those without a moral compass'."

His second principle follows the first.

> "That's the importance of identifying, describing, discussing, sharing, and finally codifying the proven principles important to you and the business. Early in my life at APM, we also adopted some critical ethical principles that could be applied to complex problems encountered – the company wrote those down and we discussed and updated them at management and board level every year. That enabled you to align your own to those of the company and for both to develop as a result."

Following on from these two principles, and with experience as a leading chief executive for nearly 20 years, Stan surprised me when he said that:

> "As CEO, there are relatively few decisions you confront that are make or break decisions for the business. You need to get these right, and often the right and tough decision is to say no. Careers and companies (large and small) are often destroyed by the wrong

> decision to proceed on a matter which should have been avoided. There is always a solution."

Third, Stan believes (and I saw him practise many times) the importance of spending time on people.

> "You need to think about how you communicate because of the value of having to intellectualise with others in ways they can best understand what objectives or issues you are driving at – you have to adjust and think about what you say to the person you are facing. Everyone has their own unique way of absorbing data, needs and implications. Alignment comes from being a good and thoughtful communicator."

Fourth, Stan's humility comes out with his further belief:

> "I am always trying to learn from others. Staying open to where and how you can learn is also very important."

In recent times I have sought his advice on how to relate to people at the very top of leadership in business, politics and society. They can appear quite intimidating. Stan's views on that are very clear:

> "People at top of business and politics are still human beings. Relate to them as you do anyone else and don't get overawed by their position or reputation. Speak to them like you would to your neighbour because they are probably much the same as you and you need to have belief and confidence to succeed, and to be able to show that to others in how you relate to them."

Perhaps the following words aren't often heard publicly, but they would probably resonate with all of us:

> "It's hard to trust politicians, because you don't always know what's driving them or where they are coming from or whether conflict exists. But if they ask for your help – always try and give it. They have a vital job, and are essential to our well-working society."

A few years ago, I transitioned to roles as a non-executive director and chairman but gravitated back to Stan for his advice on what isn't written down about jobs such as these.

Stan said that:

> "As a Chair, you are the first amongst equals. It's a great honour to have that role in the group. But the obligations are to work the members of the board inside and outside meetings to ensure everyone can contribute to their best, but also that you know and understand their hopes and fears. With your CEO you are confidential counsellor but also responsible for assurance by him on all strategic and operational matters that are agreed by the board. You can be friendly in your professional relationships with the CEO but you are ultimately responsible to the company's shareholders or members and that vests the right to hire and fire the CEO, which is the chair's job to monitor and lead on, when needed."

In my own experience as chair, one of the toughest jobs I encountered on three different occasions was how best to confront and resolve the presence of an intransigent director. Stan's advice on this was very clear. If you can't resolve the matter on a one to one basis then you need to marshall the support of your fellow directors. If you can't obtain substantial and majority support from the board, then if the issue is sufficiently important to you and the company, you may have to put your own position on the line and accept the outcome. In the final analysis it is the shareholders who elect directors and they should always have the final say.

During the last few years my mentor Stan Wallis, who was himself a former Amcor Chairman and CEO, asked me what it had been like in the company during that period after the discovery of the Amcor–Visy Box price cartel in 2004, some years after he had left the company. I replied that it was a fairly horrendous experience and that during that time I had seen the best and the worst of formerly close colleagues, but it was a great learning experience.

Bob Santamaria – Great Peer Mentor in a Crisis

In looking back on the second half of my career as a senior executive in business, I am deeply appreciative of having made a number of friends at university who pursued different professions to my own studies of economics, mathematics and accounting. Most of these remained in contact with me over the years and I was able to draw on their different professional expertise when needed. Probably the most prominent of these in the field of law was Bob Santamaria, who was a solicitor and partner at one of Australia's top law firms, Allens Arthur Robinson (now known as 'Allens'). Inevitably, a career in business takes you into commercial and corporate law matters and sometimes litigation. Bob and I were friends at university in the 1970s and I was pleased to find that both my major employers in the private sector, ANZ and Amcor, had dealings with Allens professionally and that Bob was part of that. At Amcor we became quite close as Bob was the client engagement partner at Allens for the company. From time to time, I was able to speak with Bob about various legal issues and I was always impressed with his work ethic and ability to distil sometimes complex commercial issues into concepts and language that were easy to comprehend. Not all lawyers possess these skills. Further, Bob's analysis and assessments were always an astute combination of commercial sense and legal reality. He probably got some of his powers of clear explanation and advocacy from his father, B.A. Santamaria, who was one of the key players in the split of the Australian Labor Party during the 1950s that I talked about in the section on Jim Cairns, earlier in the chapter. Bob always seemed to have a steady hand in a crisis, a characteristic his late father had certainly portrayed in the arena of public debate.

There was one critical occasion when the discovery of certain work-related events confronted my psyche and sentiments on some extraordinary challenges in my job. I was fortunate to be able to confront them with the support of Bob as a colleague and peer-mentor who helped me to work them through, and move inexorably towards an ultimate but very expensive set of conclusions.

The year was 2004, and the circumstances encountered did evolve into one of the most contentious and significant falls from grace for two of Australia's leading CEOs at the time, Russell Jones and Richard Pratt, as well as significantly tarnishing the reputations of their two great companies, Amcor and Visy respectively. At the time, I was the Group Executive in charge of Human Resources & Operating Risk at Amcor, based in Melbourne. My role was located in the company's small corporate head office, and I reported to the Group Chief Executive, Russell Jones, who was ranked in surveys by investors and market analysts as one of the most highly regarded and respected CEOs of ASX-listed companies in Australia.

Early in 2004, the new Managing Director for Australia came to me after a few months in the job, and advised that he wished to undertake a restructure and compress the number of divisions and senior staff reporting to himself, as a response to requests from our head office to find cost-savings and other efficiencies. As part of that he wanted to merge the folding cartons and corrugated box businesses into one and take the opportunity to put some fresh blood into the senior management ranks within the new combined division, which would still be dominated by the cardboard box business. He sought my help to negotiate with the then-head of the box business, Jim Hodgson, to agree not only a transition with Jim and to effect a replacement executive in his role, but also to terminate his contract which had nearly two years to run before its expiry. All began well but then it became clear Hodgson was losing amicability towards the process and was seeking nearly a year's more pay than we could afford under either the terms of his employment contract or executive termination policies set by the board of directors. At that stage, I enlisted Bob Santamaria's help to engage one of Allens' top employment law partners, Julian Reikert, to assist us as the negotiations seemed headed for a formal breakdown and possible litigation. Hodgson asked for a meeting with Russell Jones alone, which I agreed to, but before the two of them met, and on advice from Bob, I went to see Russell to give him some background on the offer and said the following to him at the end of that conversation:

> "What we have offered to Jim is as far as we can go. It's important that you don't offer him anything more at the meeting or we would first need to revert to the board for approval as it would be outside our delegations. But it's also unlikely to be approved there, given board sentiment on these matters".

After his subsequent meeting with Hodgson, Russell told me that he did not offer any more money to Hodgson and encouraged him to take the package on offer. He also said this meeting with Hodgson was inconclusive as he had not been able to persuade him to accept our last offer.

On the same day of the Hodgson and Jones meeting, four of Jim's most senior team resigned. This group subsequently became known as the "Amcor Five". However, each of these four colleagues actually used the same 'form' resignation letter with their respective names and signatures inserted by handwriting. The letters contained common advice that they were intending to set themselves up together as manufacturing consultants. The following day, Amcor served a notice of retrenchment on Hodgson with a requirement that he serve out his notice period on a year's gardening leave and not infringe Amcor's intellectual or any other property over that time, or work for a competitor. Hodgson subsequently took an unfair dismissal action to the Supreme Court of Victoria, which took nearly eight years to resolve.

Because of the apparent action in concert of Hodgson and his four senior team members who had resigned in unison, I initiated a forensic accounting and IT audit by the Deloitte firm of all their IT devices and offices in the corrugated box business. I did inform my CEO Russell Jones later that I was doing this as part of my job but hadn't sought his permission to initiate that. This forensic audit found significant anomalies around the management of Amcor's property, including customer and plant information. In discussion with Bob, he recommended we seek an Anton Piller order from the Federal Court, which would empower us to conduct a more extensive search for any of Amcor's property and assets, located in the homes and private property owned or leased by the Amcor Five.

Anton Piller orders

An Anton Piller order is a somewhat extraordinary form of legal power granted in favour of an applicant to search the premises of an accused third-party, the respondent. Because such an order is essentially quite invasive to the accused parties and their privacy, Anton Piller directions are only issued exceptionally and according to the three-step test set out by Ormrod LJ in the UK Anton Piller case in 1976:

1. There is an extremely strong prima facie case against the respondent
2. The damage, potential or actual, must be very serious for the applicant; and
3. There must be clear evidence that the respondents have in their possession relevant documents or things and that there is a real possibility that they may destroy such material before a public application can be made.

Before that week I had never heard of this order and at first blush it seemed to be a right more befitting a Stalinist political system than it did a healthy and well-working democracy like Australia. But English common law grants us this power and in the new globalised world of rapid information transfers and hyper-competition it is likely to be used much more frequently in future. Bob explained to me that this order was used in cases where, for example, contraband was suspected of being on a ship and the owner of that property would seek a private order from the court for that ship to be searched, without anyone getting wind that this might happen and thence being able to sail away into international waters before that search took place. In cases like this, Bob advised that an application for an Anton Piller order made commercial sense and that we had information relevant to the precedents for an application to succeed.

The Anton Piller order was duly obtained from the court and executed early in November 2004 at the homes of Hodgson and the others in the Amcor Five. As a result of findings from the searches granted by the court under the Anton Piller orders, we learned that copies of confidential Amcor documents had been retained personally by these five now former executives of the Australian box business. Surprisingly to both of us, evidence also first emerged of the existence of an Amcor–Visy box price cartel. In fact, Bob Santamaria was the first to see this material on 19 November and he then telephoned both Russell Jones and myself to advise us what he had found. Because of the prospective seriousness of this discovery, Bob also reached out to involve two colleagues and peer mentors of his own. The were partners at Allens and experts in competition law – Pat Ryan, who had earlier been General Counsel at the Australian Competition and Consumer Commission (ACCC), and litigation expert Paul Meadows, who is now General Counsel at Wesfarmers. Following consultation with Pat and Paul, and on Bob's advice, I convened two meetings in my office for as many board and senior executives as possible to review this data, including Russell Jones who was referred to in this newly-discovered material as an active participant and at the top of the cartel command chain within Amcor.

All boxed up and nowhere to go

After that meeting, and on the evening of Sunday 21 November, Bob Santamaria and I arranged to meet alone with Russell Jones in his ornate Tuscan-designed home in leafy Canterbury, in order to agree with him that there was only one option available to us – to advise the chairman and the board to assemble and declare the material to the ACCC, and seek immunity from prosecution as the first party in a cartel to do so. For that evening meeting, Bob had prepared a hand-written speech to provide to Russell following consultation with his own mentors beforehand. Bob laid out the speech notes in front of himself on Russell's dining room table, which he nervously read through verbatim to Russell with me as the independent witness, whilst the three of us were seated there together. I remember sitting next to Bob and across the table from my then-CEO, watching the blood drain out of the Russell's face with delivery of that message. At the end of Bob's statement, he looked at Russell and also said to him:

> "I hope we can remain friends but that may be too difficult for you given the advice I must give to the board."

Russell clearly knew there was no way either of us could be dissuaded from this course and he added his agreement to it.

Immediately after the meeting, Bob and I stopped in the street outside this house to discuss the situation and Russell's sombre attitude and reluctant response. I recall Bob saying to me:

> "You know what this means, Peter. If Russell is actually implicated in this cartel – that's the end in this business for him. Nor will there be any major board roles offered after he finishes here.
>
> "He and his family will face enormous public scrutiny and intense criticism and his friends in corporate life will disown him.

> And then there are likely to be extended court cases and class actions by customers. That's because, very simply, managing a cartel is stealing. You are making customers pay more for their goods than they should have to. It's like putting your hand in their wallet. Theft is a criminal offence here, although cartel conduct isn't – but it is in other countries, and that's likely to change here too."

All of Bob's very severe predictions ultimately became true and Russell did suffer all those personal and professional consequences. Sometimes you need a mentor to give you a good reality check about where serious and complicated matters may be headed. Bob certainly did that with me that evening. When friends go through an experience like this one that Bob and I went through, the mutual support and two-way learnings from such a peer mentoring relationship make those bonds of friendship stronger and ones which last for a lifetime. That said, neither of us would wish to go through anything like that ever again. But we did and we survived it. Mentoring among peers can be that valuable at times of crisis in your career.

After rigorous reviews supervised by the board of Amcor, our lawyers and the ACCC, the cartel chain of command was determined to have comprised nine people: Russell Jones, the two heads of the Australian business, the Amcor Five and one other senior officer. Independent reviews determined none of the company's other 15 international and domestic packaging businesses were found to have had any competition law irregularities, and no businesses at all were affected prior to the year 2000 when Stan Wallis had been the company's chair and before that its CEO.

When the case against Visy finally concluded, the Federal Court awarded fines against Visy and Pratt of $36 million. But that wasn't the end of it. Due to discrepancies between the sworn testimony of Russell Jones and Richard Pratt amongst other matters, the ACCC subsequently pursued four other charges with possible criminal conviction implications against Richard Pratt. The Federal Director of Public Prosecutions dropped these charges against the latter a couple of days before Richard died. Class actions by customers were pursued against Amcor and Visy and then finally settled by both companies for hundreds of millions of dollars.

The then-Federal Treasurer Peter Costello committed to the introduction of criminal penalties for those officers and directors directly responsible for cartel conduct as a result of this case and it is now the law of the land. That is a most appropriate course as a cartel is an unconscionable and underhanded way of stealing money from customers and preventing other competitors from earning their own keep fairly. Theft should have criminal consequences, especially in corporations where the public can reasonably expect high standards of conduct due to responsibilities held by leaders in business life, as well as the education and skills of the relevant corporate office-holders. In future, for this type of offence, there will be no more get-out-of-gaol-free cards. As a wake-up call to Australian business on this point, and subsequent to the Amcor-Visy cartel becoming public here, a former Qantas executive was convicted in the US of organising a cartel for air freight in late 2010. He served a prison sentence there for his involvement.

These circumstances comprise an all-too common dilemma encountered by business executives who discover something within their responsibilities that is either irregular, unethical or quite illegal (as in this case). On discussion with others in your own company, you can become confused or unsure as to what to do or how it should best be managed. In this type of instance, mentors are invaluable to have as a confidential resource to consult with. For those who find themselves having discovered an illegal commercial arrangement at their place of work, the best course is to immediately speak with your mentor and/or to approach an external legal counsel to clarify the implications and consequences, and then to approach an appropriate member of the board of directors above the management chain, such as the audit and risk chair. This both protects you as the discoverer of any wrongdoing and elevates the problem to where it can be solved. If the board were implicated, then you have at least given yourself a privileged protection under the common law, by taking advice from an external legal source.

I was very fortunate to have Bob Santamania as my fellow traveller during this horrendous professional episode; a person who was a personal, long-term friend, peer-mentor and external legal counsel.

In business, I have learned to keep your friends close, your enemies closer and your mentors closest of all – particularly your long-term peers who know the modern laws of the land, and especially when events around you suddenly become extraordinarily complex.

Key Learnings from my Work and Life Mentors

1. The best leaders always have a strong moral compass and use that to test and help an organisation's own values set to evolve and develop.
2. Great leaders show patience, resilience, compassion and a genuine care for others they work with. They exhibit mental toughness for themselves as part of their own mantle of leadership. But they are conscious not to see that as an excuse to bully or intimidate others.

3. They demonstrate respect and consideration for others who do not share the same values or beliefs as themselves and are very good 'inside-out' and 'outside-in' communicators who not only think about interpersonal differences but also develop their own strategies and approaches to impart their messages and receive feedback with that in mind.
4. These mentors all possess a belief that their own roles held can be transitory and show a concern that their primary legacy is what they leave behind in terms of how their people and organisations perform after they have gone, not that they are remembered as great and unique leaders themselves.
5. Their leadership has an active mentoring component. They all saw a significant part of their role as a leader as being to help others be better leaders, and that mentoring is the main channel by which this connection occurs.
6. At times of crisis and monumentally different or extreme choices, they all give themselves time to think and, where necessary, to consult a trusted mentor, or to act in ways that reflect years of not only training but also practical experience. Either way, they all showed a preparedness to confront the uncomfortable realities of their challenges and the implications of those for their work and life itself.
7. They exercise considerable humility in how they go about their roles, and both possess and use humour as not only an ice-breaker in dealing with others, but also as a way to self-efface their own significance and contributions (not always successfully, and rightly so).
8. My mentors have all thought hard about the institutional structures surrounding their work and life, and have seen their own challenges as constituting not only achieving success against what needs to get done, but also where, how and through whom are features to that legacy, of comparable importance.

14

MY MENTOR FROM PROFESSIONAL SPORTS: LINDSAY GAZE

Professional sports is a business where the participating élite athletes and their coaching and support staff are admired for their athletic excellence, dedication and 'peak of career' performances that amaze us. Australians in particular love their sports and all Aussie sports-watchers seem to draw part of their interest from also having played some game or sporting activity, somewhere, sometime. Many of us continue this participation well into old age, as the high level of participation in the Masters Games competitions attests, for example.

The world of professional sports is also very scary. We are made aware of many of the personal disasters that emanate from it – career-ending injuries, bankruptcy, marriage breakdowns, assault charges (and sometimes murder), incarceration, substance abuse, physical and mental harassment in public places, acute mental health illnesses, and failure of the participants to cope with life generally after their élite career is finished. The following quotation from *Sports Illustrated* denotes how life can change for top professionals after they exit the arena for the last time:

> "Many professional athletes who have made millions are often broke three years into retirement. ... Sixty per cent of the NBA's (National Basketball Association) often extremely well-paid players are virtually penniless within five years of retiring, according to a recent *Sports Illustrated* report. The numbers are just as bad, if not worse for the NFL (National Football League), the magazine says, with 78 per cent in financial duress two years into retirement." **Torre, P.S. (2009). "How (and Why) Athletes Go Broke".** ***Sports Illustrated*****, 110, Issue 12, March 23, 2009.**

A career in professional sports can also have a short life and is usually accompanied by an environment of high stress, with pressure on every next performance. The career options after the period of élite performance for an athlete has concluded can be uncertain and sometimes cruel.

Best-practice club and league administrators consider the career development for the élite competitor very seriously, both during and after their life of peak performance on the national or world stages. At about the age of 40, I had the privilege to be able to access the inside of professional basketball – a sport that I love probably more than any other – and obtain insights that not only helped explain some of its mystique but also proved to have enormous relevance to my own work and life outside of professional sports. I entered this sports administration arena hoping to learn a lot about how it all worked and also the importance of mentoring within that. I left that world of the sports back-office a few years ago but also with a personal connection to one of the best mentors I have ever encountered, and whose advice I still seek.

The professional sport of basketball is hardwired by mentoring. Lindsay Gaze possesses this philosophy of mentoring in his whole approach to the game and life itself. He is one of the most accomplished and decorated basketball personalities in this country and he impresses you with his knowledge but also his self-effacing humility that is both genuine and very engaging. However, that should never be mistaken either for lack of commitment, competitive drive or mental toughness, all of which he possesses in spades.

Lindsay represented Australia in seven Olympic Games from 1960 to 1984, both as an élite basketball player and then national coach. He was followed by son Andrew who debuted his Olympic career under his father's coaching in 1984 and retired from international competition at the end of the Sydney Olympics campaign in 2000.

I came to meet Lindsay when I played in the business houses competition at Albert Park Basketball Stadium in Melbourne during the 1970s, at which time he was the Australian Olympic basketball coach. He also managed the Albert Park Stadium, together with his wife Margaret who looked after the stadium shop and player admissions. A strong sinewy man, a little over six feet tall, I came to appreciate from that time how tough he could be. One night during a game on an adjacent court, two opposing players, who had arrived by car but who both appeared to be well over the legal limit for alcohol consumption, began niggling each other during their game. Soon a fight broke out between them. Like the marvel comic-strip character, 'The Phantom' (also known as "the ghost who walks"), Lindsay appeared from the shadows and disarmed both protagonists very, very quickly. The next image I had was like watching a zookeeper deal with two misbehaving and heavily inebriated koalas, as he picked them each up by the scruff of the singlet to frog march them out of the stadium. There were bewildered looks on their faces, bemused ones on ours, and also a very disapproving stare from gatekeeper Margaret Gaze. No way those guys were ever getting past the Gaze factor and back into this stadium!

Some years later in the late 1980s, I saw Lindsay arrive at my work and go in to see my boss and also one of my mentors, Peter Sheehan. Peter's son Mark played for the Melbourne Tigers Junior team and Peter came to know Lindsay as one of the players' parents. At the time, the Melbourne Tigers were running last in the National Basketball League (NBL). Notwithstanding that, the team had two decided advantages –Lindsay was its coach, and it had a young Olympic player at point guard who was the league-leading scorer and often put up over 40 points a game – Lindsay's son, Andrew. The Melbourne Tigers had entered the NBL a few years earlier but didn't have the resources of the other teams. Lindsay was at my work to meet with my boss and discuss ways to make the organisation more professional with a board of directors, and by attracting some major sponsors so the team could upgrade its playing roster around Andrew Gaze.

Lindsay said to me of that meeting:

> "When Peter approached me asking what we needed to compete successfully in the NBL my first response was, 'We need to establish a good board'."

Soon after that concept came to life a new board was constituted comprising four current and former Olympic players and coaches: Lindsay and Andrew Gaze; Ray Tomlinson; and John Maddock (who later became Chairman of Basketball Australia); and five others with business and management experience: former Victorian Treasurer and Cabinet Secretary Rob Jolly; Neil Walker who had been CEO of the TAB (now the listed company, Tabcorp); Gary Purchase; Peter Sheehan and myself. That board was well supported by its CEO, Bruce Ward, who had also been a successful businessman. Over the next 15 years of my involvement as a director and subsequently as a part-owner of the Tigers, the team went from bottom of the ladder to eight championship grand final series, winning four of them. Lindsay coached the first two of those championship teams in 1993 and 1997 and his successor as coach (and former long-term assistant coach) Alan Westover, coached the last two championship seasons for the Tigers in 2006 and 2008.

Through my exposure to Lindsay and the club, I came to realise that mentors were very important to Lindsay, to his own role in the development of the Melbourne Tigers club and also through their assistance in helping to mould his own career. Lindsay's own mentors were a group of professional coaches in the USA which he referred to as a coaching 'rat pack'. The main character for him was Stu Inman who coached in the US College system and ultimately became the General Manager of the Portland Trail Blazers in the internationally-renowned National Basketball Association (NBA).

Lindsay regarded Stu as a most exceptional evaluator and general profiler of personality and character in basketball players and teams, and he was capable of making very insightful assessments about players just by watching them play and train from the sidelines. Inman's judgment was recognised as exceptional by many in the industry.

Stu is well known for a life's contribution to the sport, but also for passing over Michael Jordan from the NBA draft in 1984, with the Chicago Bulls selecting him later. Lindsay explained the background:

> "Portland needed a big man and Sam Bowie (from the University of Kentucky) was recognised as the star they needed. Two years previously he was clearly the number one choice but he suffered a knee injury and missed a season. He returned to top condition for his senior year in college but there was still a cloud over his long-term prospects. Stu said they did so much research on Bowie they knew more about him than his parents did. Michael Jordan took a season or two to become the superstar as he is now recognised to be."

The wisdom of hindsight can apply in the case of not selecting Michael Jordan but the analysis at the time was as rigorous as it could have been without the benefit of perfect foresight!

Notwithstanding that episode, Lindsay learned enormously from Stu Inman and a broader cadre of élite US coaches. Lindsay said to me he learned from his mentors that there are two types of coaches – those who are all about themselves and the other group were 'mentor coaches' who practised psychology on their players all the time; showed concerns about the growth of the individual person who was also a player in their team and also a member of the world basketball family; and finally as someone who needed to be developed to have a later life. I came to appreciate that this distinction by Lindsay applied more generally in the world of business leadership, and particularly with CEOs and chairmen. I tried to model these behaviours into my own later career in each of these roles when I had the opportunity to take them on.

Lindsay told me any coach must develop individual and team skills, strategies and moves, but that is never enough. He said his continuous role in developing élite athletes is to work closely with them to ensure they can overcome their fear of failure – something emphasised from the positive psychology literature discussed earlier and also practised by all successful mentors interviewed for this book.

Other components of Lindsay's mentoring approach surprised me initially, but then made great sense as I thought more about it. He said:

> "You have to teach athletes that they will never reach the finishing line. Life in sport, and in fact for all of us, is a never-ending continuum. The morning after a championship is won there is training. It's a mindset that's critical to the long-term survival and growth of a professional athlete, and their life afterwards. All careers in playing sport end. Unless you drum into them that they need to keep going in their life, big problems will be encountered".

This is the same in the world of business. Lindsay's advice was that "it's never over until both your career and life itself are finished".

We need to keep going every day we are on this earth. Highlights are certainly to be celebrated but they never mark an end in itself. If they do – you will surely fail with later challenges.

On the issue of competition and the importance of winning, Lindsay also went on to say:

> "In fact, there are only two things in life where winning is important – that's surgery and war".

And he very strongly believes that. That cannot be mistaken to mean he doesn't care about striving to win on the basketball court nor that he is as disappointed as anyone to lose a critical game or championship. Anyone who knows him and his record will understand that he is extremely competitive and wants to compete well with the clear aim of his team winning. But he represents, lives and imparts this broader philosophical response towards professional sports and life. His winning quotation underpins the relationship in life that is shared with his players. As this type of mentor, it's not surprising that many former players still seek him out for advice on challenges in their lives and post-playing careers.

After one of the most high-scoring games in NBL history between the West Sydney Razorbacks and Melbourne Tigers (which the Tigers lost), Lindsay was asked at the press conference why he had been smiling as he walked out of the stadium after the game. His response attested his philosophy:

> "I realised we had just been part of one of the greatest spectacles our game is ever likely to offer, and it was a privilege to be part of that, even though we didn't win. That game had everything you are ever likely to see, or would want to, in a top professional basketball contest."

Mixed with his grounded philosophy about winning is a marvellous sense of humour. I found this out one memorable day when I was able to sit next to him on the coaches' bench during an Australian

National Basketball League match involving the Melbourne Tigers and the Sydney Kings – two great traditional rivals. It was a very tense match and I had been placed under strict instructions by the Tigers Operations Manager Nigel Purchase before the game that 'I could sit on the bench as long as I did not try and talk to the coach during the game. The strength and value of such an unreasonably restrictive edict clearly diminishes progressively with the passage of any very exciting game. In fact, this commitment had completely evaporated for me when a timeout was called some two minutes before the end of regulation time in the last quarter. The Tigers were 7 points up and I felt inspired to impart a somewhat uninformed remark to the coach, just as the huddle broke up and the players were walking back onto the court to finish their business for the evening. After checking that Nigel was facing in another direction, I turned to Lindsay and said that he must feel like he had this one in the bag. Lindsay turned to me with a resigned expression on his face, smiled knowingly, and went on to say:

> "We can be very inventive at finding ways to lose from a position such as this."

So much for the extreme game tension on coach Gaze's uncompromising desire to win! As always, Lindsay's judgement and intuition in matters basketball is infinitely superior to mine. The Tigers nearly made a meal of it in those last two minutes of play, but hung on almost despite themselves to win by the slimmest of margins after an Andrew Gaze three-pointer went down with two seconds left in the game. Another knowing smile came my way as we walked off the court and yet another learning episode for me that 'it's never over until it's over'.

Lindsay Gaze is also a great defender of the essence and integrity of the game and uses humour as part of that. In Malcolm Speed's book *Sticky Wicket*, he talks of Lindsay's defence of the game against the critics who say you only need to watch the last two minutes of play to get what's happening in the game. Lindsay replied (P 225):

> "You could say the same about sex. If you were to have sex for 40 minutes (the duration of a basketball match), the last minute would be the best. If you understand what you are doing, you can enjoy the whole 40 minutes".

Mentoring is an open and active part of professional basketball. Team strategies and capabilities are well understood and often coaches spend time discussing the character of their team and particular players in it. There is a parallel with American business approaches to talent management in an organisation. CEOs and also sports coaches in the best-practice group normally believe that you can rank a player by their values and their performance capabilities. Because of the pressures that exist, a very high value is put on a player's intelligence and character. So much so that a player who can perform to a high level will often be cut from a roster because of weaknesses in values or character. That is why so much effort is put into protégés or project players to build character and to develop their resilience to fear of failure.

Another key feature I learned from Lindsay's mentoring is the need for a person to understand their limits both as a professional performer and as a human being. He taught me there are three limits a player may encounter sequentially during any peak performance as a professional athlete as follows:

> "**Psychological limit** – the mental fatigue that occurs when the mind starts to tell you that you need to stop or do something else; that loss of concentration can cost you in a game and again a player will need to practise and develop skills to push through that barrier in their performance.
>
> **Physical limit** – every player will experience physical pain and

> fatigue, reach a point where they start to stagger and have to encourage their mental toughness and physical development to know that and when and how to push through.
>
> **Survival limit** – sometimes a professional athlete can confront a level of mental and physical exhaustion where their life is threatened. I saw that point reached by Ron Clarke at the Mexico Olympics, that was well known for its high altitude impact on the health of competing athletes. Clarke pushed himself to a point where he literally collapsed and technically died. Pushing limits like that in sport is not OK".

Lindsay believed that getting the most out of your players required a constant reinforcement of positive characteristics to enable belief and to develop the right attitude. He also said that the way you spoke to individual players needed to be different as they all were quite different people. Whilst extreme in nature, it became clear these three limits are stages all of us can face under intense challenges in our lifetimes – or ones we can see close colleagues or friends and family members encounter. The case of my mother and the petrol station mechanic discussed in the previous chapter is an example.

> "Sometimes as well as managing them through or out of these three stages you need to shake them up too," Lindsay said.

I experienced an unusual case of this one night as I was arriving for a Tigers board meeting. It was the week after a loss to an NBL team well below us on the ladder and the Tigers had played woefully to add salt to the results wound. At the first training session the week after, practice had clearly been physically harrowing and demanding and finished just before a Tigers board meeting was due to start. I encountered one of the players Ray Gordon on the way out to the car park to drive home. He looked exhausted and disconsolate and I asked if everything was OK. He replied all would be well by tomorrow's training session by which time he would have changed his name by deed poll to "dumb bastard". I guess the eliminating the negatives and accentuating the positives takes many forms. We are all human after all and tough love from the mentor coach can come with a range of emotional tactics and expressions. It's also the case with leadership in business life.

The father-and-son Gaze duo is a fascinating one. Both have been recognised separately as Victorian Father of the Year – Lindsay in 1992 and Andrew in 2004. When I asked Lindsay about the complications or conflicts inherent or experienced in coaching his son for such a long period at the élite level his answer was insightful:

> "In the early days at the club and long before I was married I played in the senior team, helped around with club administration and coached our junior teams. This often meant driving all over Melbourne and picking young team members up from their homes, getting to know the parents and players and spending long periods with them driving around in the car to playing venues. They became like family to me and I felt very much as if they were my own children. So when I did marry Margaret and we had our own children, Andrew and Janet, coaching them was already a fairly normal experience for me, as well as being their father."

When asked whether there were any particular protocols he put around the relationship to inhibit a sense of favouritism or nepotism, he said the following:

> "I ensured we never had an awards protocol. We never had a formal captain, apart from what had to be put down on the referee's scoresheet, but only because it was required that you do. Leadership roles were spread around the club for offense, defense, team management and the social schedule. Everyone had a role – no one more important than the other."

In Andrew Gaze's own words about his father:

> "If the Man from Mars had landed at our practice facility in North Melbourne to watch us train and play for a full season, and was then asked which player was the son of the coach, he would have great trouble making his final selection. Dad treated me like any other player. Neither of us wanted it any other way."

The key learnings from these episodes apply to careers in business which have many similarities to professional sports. Surveys of workplace engagement later confirmed exactly what Lindsay taught me – your co-workers like to be respected by their leaders, they prefer a workplace which is somewhat like a family where you are cared for as a person and interest is shown in your circumstances, what's going on in your life, and also realising your own potential. Lindsay believes it's an obligation of leadership that is best passed between the generations by explicit mentoring. That influence and perspective has had an indelible mark on me.

Svetlana, Aphrodite

On a few occasions, my mentoring lessons related to the development of my own worldly education about professional basketball, and life, especially about what was going on in other countries.

The Melbourne Tigers had a senior team in the National Basketball League (NBL) for men and the Women's National Basketball League (WNBL). The NBL allowed up to two imported players and the WNBL permitted one import. At one Tigers board meeting between seasons, we were discussing the prospects of recruiting a woman player from Russia, by the name of Svetlana. On that day Lindsay Gaze began inquiring of the Tigers WNBL coach, Ray Tomlinson, as to progress with Svetlana's recruitment. Ray was himself an ex-Olympian and also a successful coach of the Australian gold-medal-winning women's under 20 team from the 1992 World Championships. The discussion went something like this:

> "So Ray, have you been able to learn any more about Svetlana?" Lindsay asked.
>
> "I have made a few inquiries but it's still a bit unclear", said Ray.
>
> "Have you been able to talk to anyone who knows her well?" Lindsay further enquired.
>
> "I have but that they weren't prepared to say too much", Ray said in reply.

I remember thinking about this riddle of language and then interposing myself into the conversation to say that:

> "This is a bit strange, as she has played in the top European leagues, so someone must have her game statistics and at least one of the coaching staff or a former player would tell you what she was like off the court and in the locker room. So what's the problem about finding out how good she is as a player, with all the experience she has?"

Lindsay turned towards me with a look as if I had just appeared from outer space and said to me empathetically that:

> "We are trying to find out whether she is actually a woman."

After a short pause, I said:

> "Well I am just a simple chap who grew up in Bentleigh where a woman was a woman, a bloke was a bloke, and you could generally pick the difference at twenty paces."

Their cautious intuitive approach proved to be warranted. Further research confirmed it was not Svetlana Aphrodite. Rather it was Svetlana Hermaphrodite. So we left her to continue playing in Europe – although I am not sure in which league. In this and other ways my education was enhanced through instructions and advice from my élite professional sports colleague, who was also mentor to my naivety in this arena. I was a willing mentee for sure, but a babe in the woods on some matters.

A Family Ferocious Logo

I learned a lot from my involvement with professional basketball about brand, image, marketing and public presentation of a product. On one occasion, the Tigers board decided its logo was looking decidedly old school, somewhat tired and that it needed freshening up. An enthusiastic club member, who was also a graphic designer by the name of Michael, offered his services free of charge to the club to help our efforts in designing a new logo. He clearly anticipated the job was going to be a short, sharp, positive experience with much later collateral gain to himself and his business. How wrong can a man be? Michael was game enough to offer a design service in infinite supply at no cost. We readily took him up on the generous offer and Lindsay was clearly determined to use it to the fullest extent practicable to ensure delivery of the right outcome.

We started deliberations over a range of alternative logos. At the outset, Lindsay set the criteria for our brand logo:

- The Tigers, with its long established senior and junior élite programs for young men, boys, girls and women, was the family club and that's how we looked and should be represented.
- The image of any tiger on the logo had to be consistent with that positioning, and the tiger should not be depicted with any lustful or vengeful aggression, or any other form of threatening behaviour that would scare small children and prevent them and their parents sleeping well at night-time.
- The tiger image chosen should depict a 'don't mess with me' attitude, proudly protecting the ball, and having a look of quiet determination (that could not be mistaken for aggression), with eyes that did not spontaneously threaten but also said 'don't enter my space or else'.

- The desired image was similar to that of a kitten playing with a ball of wool – claws and open mouth gripping the surface. For kitten, substitute tiger; for ball of wool, a basketball.

Sounds simple enough, doesn't it? The graphic designer began to question his own self-confidence after what felt like the first 100 or so drawings. We screened images of some tigers that looked like they would have killed the crowds, eaten the ball, and probably the stadium as well.

In the case of one cartoon character, which I happened to like, we had the image of one real bad-assed dude who probably would have completed all of the above and used my car axle as a tooth pick after finishing his tea. When I asked Lindsay if the letters of T-I-G-E-R allowed us to have both a 'G' rated and an 'R' rated logo, I got one of those withering looks that would have vaporised all the blue ribbon winners at the Melbourne Flower Show. I took the hint, resumed my serious exterior demeanour and refocused on my participation in our long game of logo selection.

We also received presentations with pictures of some of the 'woosiest' pusses you were ever likely to see. Without a doubt, most 95-year old great grandmothers would have had some of these sad cats put down mercifully but quickly. One had a look on his face like he was about to fall backwards out of a skydiving plane with no parachute. I was surprised the ball he was clinging to still had air in it. There was 'angry tiger', 'soft and brooding tiger' and the 'cowardly tiger' who looked ready to take over from his cousin Lion in the 'Wizard of Oz'. By the umpteenth meeting of sifting through the tea-leaves for the right tiger logo, I was heartily sick of tigers logos, but Lindsay was determined that the search must go on until the right image crystallised the dream – and so it did. Eventually.

Finally, we remarked upon one not so bad-assed tiger who seemed to have a bit of attitude but also with eyes that looked like it was undergoing a colonoscopy without an anaesthetic. By this time, I had learned to keep my initial views to myself. Lindsay our mentor coach said, "that's close, Michael, but the eyes aren't quite right". There was a mixture of knowing looks and furious nodding from others in the room. No guess as to which group included myself. "Have another go – but only change the eyes. Leave the rest as it is", said Lindsay. After some acute ophthalmic surgery on his computer, Michael returned with four new ocular options. Option A had a touch of a frustrated Sylvester chasing after Tweety Pie. Option B looked more like Wil.E.Coyote after he had been hit on the head by the anvil meant for Roadrunner, and for the umpteenth time. Option C ... got there for me. I sat quietly assuming my best United Nations General Assembly expression. "Hmmm," said Lindsay "I think Option C looks the best". "Yes", we all agreed and I was silently high-fiving inside. Lindsay is the man for this club after all and the keeper of its cultural source code which comes from nurturing it for half a century.

The key lessons for me here were to choose your brand very carefully after you have set out all the key principles for it to satisfy; defining its image points; and engaging with extensive consultation of your key stakeholders; and finally to have respect for the most experienced person in the room with often the greatest equity in the final selection.

The new family ferocious logo lived on for another eight years, and saw two more championships come the way of the Tigers, so he wasn't all that bad a cat after all. Certainly not a big cat to be messed with, but nor did he frighten young children.

"Even Michael Jordan got dropped from his ..."

The Tigers family always embraced and supported its own, especially when needed. My time came in the period after I had left my employer in somewhat brutal circumstances, following the arrival of a new CEO from Great Britain, a country that has caused

Australia more torment and grief in its history than any other. This new corporate sheriff arrived in Melbourne and seemed determined to tip out half the top senior team and so change a company culture he understood little about. This is an all-too frequent situation in large companies these days, when a rush of blood to the heads of its board of directors forces them to ignore their own robust succession-planning maps and head overseas or elsewhere for a new superstar CEO, who often just proves to be a flop with the local audiences. The sword fell into the back of my neck about one year into his new reign. I understand very well why "Game of Thrones" is such a popular TV series.

Lindsay and another fellow director Peter Sheehan reached out in my new and uncertain professional state and asked me if I was prepared to become chairman of the Tigers. When I accepted this generous and most appreciated offer, they were pleased to give me a shared office with coach Lindsay and assistant coach, Al Westover. I remember my first day on the job. In what looked like office accommodation for submariners, I clambered past Al and Lindsay sitting and talking at one desk amidst huge sausage bags full of basketballs, liniments, assorted player uniforms, player codes and moves and junior clinic schedules – in order to take command of my pre-war laminated desktop combined with a very wobbly and rusty swivel chair that looked like it had been retrieved from 'The Bismarck'. For a long time, I sat there blinking at business statements and reports which I could have been holding upside down for all that I was able to absorb from them. I was still in a state of mild shock from becoming the latest piece of collateral damage after some brutal corporate politics.

After a while, Lindsay included me in the conversation and began talking about some players on the roster who had potential but were at risk of being cut at the end of the season, and he said further:

> "You know Peter, everyone gets dropped at some stage in their lives. Even Michael Jordan got dropped from his high school basketball team. That's not the issue. It's what you do about it afterwards that counts."

Lindsay knew what he was saying, and to whom, and I valued that advice enormously at the time. I still do, and I have used the anecdote with others at similar points during their careers.

In my role as chairman of the Tigers club, I was able to probe Lindsay on elements of his approach to making this professional sports team function well. Once I asked him what other sport basketball is most like. He responded without hesitation:

> "It's most like chess. In two ways – you are always trying to move your opponent around to expose their key weakness, whereby you have an opportunity to score and you also want to stay three moves ahead of your opponent. Basketball and chess – a bit like life itself."

I asked: "What about intimate relationships – how many moves ahead then?"

He said, "Ten, but that's impossible so don't even try." I must say at this juncture that I haven't always followed Lindsay's advice, but I am still alive, apparently sane, and able to write about it.

Lindsay also taught me that:

> "Basketball can be like international diplomacy. When travelling on an overseas basketball trip, it's a problem if you win or lose by more than 20 points. If you do, you won't get invited back. You can't bury your international friends, nor embarrass them with a bad showing. An international trip isn't about a championship. It's about building relationships, and all of the players on the tour team roster gaining experience."

It was also important to Lindsay for the game to be professional but also entertaining. He said:

> "The Tigers were the first in the League to do behind the back passing and between the legs dribbling, and the alley-oop pass. We are extremely professional and competitive on the floor, but understand that the fans come to be entertained too. Many of those entertaining moves are high risk, so it means we have to practise execution the more so to avoid being turned over and made to look stupid. We want our fans to come back for the next game because they have had an enjoyable experience at the last one, especially if that was a game we lost! Also it needs to be fun for the players too so they can enjoy their sports career. Sometimes, before a tense game is about to start, I will say to them 'to go out there and have some fun too'. It can ease the pressure on them, especially before a really big game."

This last theme of having fun and being entertaining is one philosophy I have worked hard at with the AHRI. We contract some of the best workplace and people researchers and practitioners around the globe to come out and speak to our national convention that attracts many thousands of delegates, and I always say to my colleagues on the selection committee:

> "We need to select speakers who are 50% content, 50% entertainment, and who use real stories to deliver their message. If those stories have the right content, they will be remembered because of that. If our delegates attending are entertained as well, they will remember the content and the experience the more so, and will want to come again."

When it came to managing players, Lindsay looked first for desire and then for IQ. Superior athleticism was not the prime selection-driver.

> "It's no good to have a very athletic player, who makes bad decisions in a tight finish. You need them to use their brain and make good choices. Sometimes that's for a game, later it's about where they go next..."

Lindsay and Andrew both retired as coach and player of the Melbourne Tigers on the same day in May 2005. On that occasion, Lindsay spoke in mentor's language at the press conference with his characteristic humility to mark their departure from élite competition.

> "Of course, I mean we're just a small asterisk in the grand scheme of things in the sport. As the sport has grown so much there's been many, many outstanding administrators who've devoted their lives to the game at all levels. So, without the support that they give, particularly for the junior basketball, then there wouldn't be the feed coming through to the top."

But Lindsay is still actively involved in the grassroots of the game in other ways – as mentors to others beginning their playing and coaching careers. Andrew is still a mentee coach with his father always there and available to provide advice, when needed.

As Lindsay said to me a number of times:

> "You must understand you never reach the finishing line. The game for you always goes on".

So it does for us all.

Key Learnings from Mentor Coach Lindsay Gaze

1. The professional sports community and team is like a giant family, and how that family functions and co-operates reflects the pastoral spirit, attitudes and behaviours of its leaders. A coach (or CEO/chair) is both the senior leader, mentor and father figure to others in that work community.
2. It's most important to compete well. Winning is only critical in two contexts – surgery and war.

3. His greatest mentor passed over Michael Jordan in the 1984 NBA Draft. Jordan's high school basketball coach dropped him from the team. All of us make mistakes. All of us get dropped. The critical issue is how you handle that, not that it will or does happen to you. Don't fear failure itself.
4. No game or contest is over until it's completely over. Don't get ahead of yourself prematurely, or you will pay the price. No single job or peak experience will define you. After the championship contest is over, there is training. After your élite career is over, the game of life always goes on. You need to think that way and always prepare yourself for whatever you need to do next.
5. Professional sports, work and life are all like chess. We all need to think and try and stay three moves ahead if we can, but also not to overanalyse ourselves or others in the attempt to be so far ahead it ends up making no sense.
6. Like a professional athlete, each of us has three limits – psychological, physical and survival. We all need to be prepared to encounter and manage those limits within ourselves, and also to help with others around us who are part of our pastoral and fiduciary responsibilities as leaders and mentors.
7. Most athletes and workers like to work hard and have fun along the way, and so enjoy the total experience. Leaders need to work that much harder to ensure that happens for others.
8. One of the most difficult challenges any business person can have is the selection of an image or brand, whether for a company or a product. Setting out the principles for that first is mandatory, but the subsequent passage to the actual image selection can be extensive and painstaking, and it's an area where humour can help guide you through to the best possible result.
9. In a globalised world of few boundaries, inclusive of what people can do to, or treat themselves with, it sometimes requires more patience to ensure we confirm that 'life is what it seems'. This is no more so than in professional sports and business.

15

LIFE AND DEATH IN SHANGHAI

(If Only I'd asked my Mentor!)

To round off this book's exploration of mentoring and its value throughout your career, I want to share with you an incident from my own career. Here I am acting as a mentor to the reader, and being honest about one of my own career failures. The sharing of one of my own critical misjudgements may help the reader confront and overcome some of their challenges as a future mentee. The most important lesson I learned from this experience was never to forget to call upon my mentor, especially when you don't think you have a sensible solution, or one that makes much sense at all.

Doing Business in China

For any western born and bred citizen from a country like Australia, life as an international business executive with responsibilities in Asia can be tough. The challenges are significant but then again so are the rewards. Australian businesspeople do well there and the experience can lift many a fledgling executive career. However, the challenges of such a role test and stretch your patience and skills. Many participating business executives are seriously confronted by what they have to negotiate under the heading of 'Doing Business in China'. These were certainly my sentiments during the 1990s when I had the role as Managing Director for the Asia-Pacific division for the ANZ Bank. That assignment gave me responsibility for ANZ's operations across 22 countries of the Asia-Pacific region: eight in the South Pacific, with Fiji as the largest business there; ten countries in South-East Asia, and Japan, China and Korea in North Asia; and finally Sri Lanka in South Asia. All exciting stuff. During that time I met the late King Tupou V of Tonga in his beachside weatherboard castle, Premier Zhu Rong Zhi of China, President Fidel Ramos of The Philippines, and Phan Van Khai the Prime Minister of Vietnam.

Because of the different cultural issues this role entailed, I developed a mentoring relationship with one of the world's leading authorities on cross-cultural issues in business, a Dutchman by the name of Fons Trompenaars (who I talked about earlier in the book). I completed a series of executive education programs with Fons and also with his close colleague at Oxford University, Charles Hampden-Turner. Together they had co-authored the world business bestseller, *Riding the Waves of Culture*, that sold well over 100,000 copies. This was based on Fons' doctoral dissertation during the late 1970s at the Wharton Business School, University of Pennsylvania, where I had also studied. Fons and I developed a close personal relationship that continues to this day. His regular guidance on the cross-cultural implications of the globalisation of business is something that I value highly. It is of no surprise that he is listed in the World's Top 50 Thinkers in business. In his chosen field, he is without peer.

To recount this true story is also somewhat embarrassing. Fons was my main cross-cultural mentor at that time, but due to a mixture of the business pressure and stress on me, I failed to consult him on the events in Shanghai that I am about to recount below. I did eventually consult with him but only well after this tragic saga had unfolded and concluded. Had I consulted him during those events, there is absolutely no doubt my mentor's advice would have enabled a superior win–win solution, and certainly one much better than that which my other expatriate colleagues operating in China and I had been able to devise and execute.

This story began when I received a telephone call one Saturday morning in 1995 from my Shanghai branch manager, who was an Australian expatriate. He advised me of his belief that just under US$30,000 had gone missing from the branch's cash takings from the previous afternoon. It was suspected that the money had disappeared from the tellers' area, and that it had been taken out of the considerable expatriate and embassy deposits that were lodged that Friday. This was always a time when significant monies were transferred from private safes in the Shanghai business district to be lodged with our branch before the weekend.

The ANZ Shanghai branch was located in a prominent high-rise commercial building well above street level. The tellers' area had three booths facing the lift-well area where customers would arrive to make their transactions. Each of the teller booths was manned by a locally-engaged, ethnic Chinese staff member. That Friday, three women – all in their mid-twenties – had been on teller duty. Apart from the branch manager and one other, all the staff there were locally-engaged and relatively young Chinese professionals – a few years out of university in most cases.

Our branch manager advised that he and the branch controller – a New Zealand expatriate – would continue to do the reconciliations in the hope that the money would be accounted for, but added he was not hopeful about that, based on the work they had already done.

In *China Daily*, ten minutes to the firing squad

The next day I flew from Australia to Shanghai, via Hong Kong. On the last flight leg from Hong Kong, I picked up a copy of the main English language paper, the *China Daily*, which is well known to all foreign business people who travel to China. On the front page of that day's edition was a picture of a young Chinese business woman being both flanked and frog-marched out of a Chinese criminal court in Beijing by two solemn-faced officers from the People's Liberation Army. The storyline stated that this woman had just been found guilty of stealing money from her expatriate employer, a well-known French multinational corporation. Theft from a foreign company was a capital offence in China. Within ten minutes of this photo being taken, the woman in the picture had been dragged around to the back of the courthouse where she was tied up and summarily executed by a firing squad that included her two escorts in the picture. This was one of the most graphically-violent, real-life photos I had seen for some time. My stomach churned at the sight of it. The terror and anguish on that woman's face stayed with me for a long time and certainly lived with me during the rest of that particular visit to China.

I had been travelling to China on business since 1982, about three years after Premier Deng Xiao Ping declared the beginning of a new era of 'openness' to world trade and commerce for China. As part of my regular travels since then there were lots of matters that I observed but which took time to be explained. For example, I learned that aircraft crashes by Chinese airlines were only reported if there were foreigners on board. Otherwise, why would the outside world need to know? Such was the perception of the local totalitarian officialdom. On another occasion, I was waiting to catch a flight home in the business lounge of the Shanghai airport when it was shut down inexplicably for over nine hours. Through the auspices of a fellow ethnic Chinese business traveller, we wandered around the airport until he discovered a trainee pilot had been practising landings in a Soviet-built Tupolov airplane, but had forgotten to bring the undercarriage down on his latest, and surely last ever, training approach to the runway. The airport was closed until the mess from this aeronautical belly flop could be cleaned up. Tarpaulins were placed over the fuselage and assorted broken bits on the tarmac, and that runway was closed away from public view. Taxiing pathways were later made very circuitous to try and ensure the tarpaulin-draped mess was excluded from the line of sight for foreign eyes. These days Twitter would have sprung this 'super snafu' very quickly onto the world's nightly news. But it showed the mindset of the new Chinese statism – if the world doesn't know, there is no way we Chinese will be telling them, and that way we can all be better off. Openness is for trade and not for information that may harm China's reputation abroad.

Of more significance to this story from my gallery of Chinese social peculiarity were the giant signboards or hoardings that sat on one prominent corner in Beijing and another in Shanghai. On these hoardings there were only Chinese handwritings marked up on plain cardboard postings that often weathered and peeled off at the edges. They weren't meant to be there for very long and were regularly replaced by similar pieces of signage in Chinese handwriting. Local people generally hovered around them, squinting up at the writings and never looked happy. I asked about these signboards for years and finally a Chinese-speaking expatriate told me that these were the execution billboards of the Chinese government. The writings on them were the names of people who were listed for the death penalty, or the disgraced names of the ones who had just been executed. He said they were meant to serve as a deterrent to local Chinese citizenry and especially those who worked with foreign employers. As noted earlier, stealing from foreign employers was a capital offence under the basic law that

Deng Xiao Ping and his politburo chiefs had written as a requirement of China's 'openness' dating from 1979. Years later these signboards became far too controversial and like a lot of things in China they just disappeared from view one day.

With this background I disembarked at Shanghai airport and was met outside the customs hall by my branch manager, who regrettably advised me that their further reconciliations had confirmed the loss of the money, almost certainly by staff theft.

Mexican Stand-off in Shanghai

Over the next few days we conducted staff group meetings and then 'one-on-one' interviews with all of the 30 locally-engaged staff, and then several more one-on-one meetings with the three tellers.

Our initial position was to appeal to their decency and to seek an immediate return of the money. The code of silence was very tight and no response was forthcoming. It was curiously a Mexican stand-off in Shanghai and the communication connections between the western and Chinese groups of the branch felt like ships in the night. We were definitely on separate passages with different value systems.

Finally we engaged in another three round robins on a team and then on an individual basis, offering consecutively:

- Immunity if the money were returned (which proved unsuccessful); then
- A small reward for anyone nominating the thief (also unsuccessful); then
- A general and final appeal to all staff that if the money were returned we would grant an amnesty to the culprit – if ever we found out who it was (equally unsuccessful).

Long story short, our good old Anglo Saxon efforts failed to deliver a return of the money. Six pass throughs between the Chinese locals and their western bosses, but absolutely no progress to show for it. Then to our considerable regret later, we decided we had no option now but to call in the local Chinese police. I will never forget the sergeant of police who arrived the next day. He looked like a supporting cast member from a John Woo Hong Kong action film. Sergeant Wu (I kid you not) had a large, round, broken face that looked like he had encountered some form of violent Humpty Dumpty experience along his own career journey, and it was one that I quickly decided I did not need to know much more about. His form of remedial plastic surgery would have led to both litigation and medical de-registration in many other countries. Sergeant Wu's overall looks and demeanour told me it was time for business, and nothing else. That suited me fine.

His tactics weren't much different to ours, except for his 'super bully' tone and also that he used the Chinese language to deliver his message. It quickly became apparent that nothing was going to be lost in translation with our staff along the way. I didn't attend any of his meetings with our staff – at his request. Of course, they were his countrymen and women. Nevertheless, I had no difficulty hearing his screeching and screaming in the room next door quite clearly. Sergeant Wu basically reprised his form of the group and one-on-one interview processes in Chinese. There is no doubt he was deliberately intimidating and threatening the local staff, especially the three women tellers.

At the end of a day and a half of these innovative Wu-style interviews later, he said he had some suspicions and some possible leads and that he would go away and investigate them all and get back to us by the weekend. I journeyed up to Beijing for the rest of the week on other business. When I returned to check progress in Shanghai, the branch manager reported he had heard no more from one of Shanghai police's finest.

Sergeant Wu to the Rescue

By mid the following week, there had still not been a peep from Sergeant Wu and so we decided to ring him at the Chinese police station. He seemed aggravated that we had come back to him (probably at all), but nevertheless he agreed to visit with us at the branch that afternoon.

Upon his arrival at our premises, he sat down, looked me squarely but impassively in the eyes and said the following words that I will remember very clearly for the rest of my life:

> "We have done our investigations and have not been able to find any firm evidence or come to any conclusions. So YOU have two options. YOU can let the matter rest, and then we will be on our way, or YOU can ask us to continue – in which case we will find the guilty party."

I was shocked and dumbfounded, and we adjourned to consider our position. It was very clear that the second option would inevitably lead to the arrest, trial, conviction with no right of appeal, and then immediate execution of a person we guessed to be one of the three tellers – another page-one story and picture for the *China Daily*. In fact, we were pretty clear which one he was likely to pick out. Of these three tellers one in particular seemed extremely nervous and it had been alleged she had a boyfriend who was involved in the local drug trade and who may have put pressure on her to steal the money. But that was basically all rumour and innuendo, and there was no clear evidence one way or the other. So the responsibility for one young worker's life was now sitting squarely in my hands.

What to do?

"Death Becomes her" – A Business Option

As well as the ethical and moral issues we were confronting, the local business market for foreign firms provided little help. The

Chinese employment market was 'red hot' at the time. It was extremely difficult to find and retain good staff; any dismissals or resignations usually had little impact as the individuals concerned were able to find other suitable work within days – if indeed it took that long! Local Chinese hires were often organised through a company called FESCO – the Foreign Employers Service Company – a sort of compulsory government-controlled employment agency. There was often suspicion amongst the foreign banks operating there as to which employees placed with you by FESCO were the government-planted spooks. These ghost spies were planted to keep up with what we banks were doing with our foreign exchange, profits and possible transfer-pricing strategies, but also Big Brother wanted to know what their own local citizens may be getting up to.

ANZ knew some foreign firms were taking a tough line on staff fraud and any other misbehaviours; companies seen to be going soft on local staff were held in poor regard amongst their peers and were the subject of negative formal or informal reports back to their global head office. There were few secrets amongst the expatriate community – fuelled mainly by a very effective ethnic Chinese grapevine working across all foreign firms.

So we outlined our objectives and possible solutions:

- We wanted a return of the money – but that objective now looked pretty hopeless whichever way we decided to go
- We knew if we did nothing, the risk of another staff defalcation was significant, and we would be seen amongst the local staff and their colleagues as foreign employer pushovers
- We did not want to pass the buck to Sergeant Wu. The Wu way would mean certain death for someone, and for an offence that had its equivalent in a minimal custodial sentence in our home jurisdiction. And there was no substantive evidence, so natural justice could not be served through

further engagement of Sergeant Wu's services, nor according to our own values

- If we took any action – by way of dismissal or forced redundancy – the morale of the branch was likely to disappear down the gurgler, probably along with our best staff, given the readiness of other employers to take on any of our top people.

We decided this was a nice LOSE–LOSE–LOSE–LOSE line up. But we had to do something.

The first action was to wave Sergeant Wu goodbye for the day (and for a lifetime I was hoping), and ensure he had no matters from us to exercise his mind about on his way home.

Secondly, we decided to terminate the employment of the three tellers, but with a letter acknowledging their service with our company. As expected in the red-hot market for labour, all of them had jobs within a fortnight. Then we did the normal western business thing of tightening up procedures around security for cash collection and preventing any private bags being taken into the teller area to sit at the feet of young Chinese tellers. Banks are renowned for sending in lots of their own internal helpers when things go wrong. So we had our inevitably painful prudential risk and audit reviews that produced lots of the usual bureaucratic cackling but not much in the way of any productive laying of eggs (that we hadn't already thought of). And then we had the forelock-tugging ritual of appearing before the Audit Committee of the Board, and the inevitable squeeze back in that year's bonus outcome. Phew, finally it was all over. But not really. The memory of what happened continued to bug me for a long time afterwards. A few months later, I did what any good mentee should have done the day after I got off the plane into Shanghai. I took the opportunity to contact my mentor, Fons Trompenaars. His wisdom was succinct but very powerful, and he shared with me a brilliant solution that I wish that I had capitalised upon much earlier.

Lateral Thinking – Cross-Cultural Style

Fons said the dilemma that we faced reflected a clash of basic cultural values between west and east. In the west we are driven by our principles of natural justice; the rights of the individual for fair treatment under the law; to find the guilty party and retrieve the stolen money, and then to bring the villain to justice in our courts for the appropriate custodial sentence. These principles are driven into us in many ways and for years as children and young adults, from our education, the way news bulletins are structured, to our most popular TV crime shows. In the east, and particularly China, the value systems at work are almost entirely opposite to this. The prime value system is Confucian, based on the 11th century philosopher Confucius. The important core of one's life in China are the relationships that you have with other people. The most central relationships are those with members of your own immediate family. Next in importance are your neighbours, then there are your friends in the local village, then other Chinese with the same name as yourself, followed by the remainder of your Chinese compatriots. These relationships are more central to your life than western principles of natural justice and the court system. The relationships that are valued the least are those that Chinese people have with foreigners, or Gwai-Loes ("Round-Eyes"). When a Chinese person sees a member of either the police or the People's Liberation Army coming towards them, they are inclined to think that person is probably corrupt, and they think the same about a judge at the local court house. These people aren't to be trusted. They are Chinese of course, but they are members of institutions set up by Deng Xiao Ping to protect the interests of foreigners that we value least in life. So they are to be respected but also to be avoided at all costs.

Fons further advised that to resolve this dilemma required us to give up trying to find the guilty party because after a short time it's clear you never will. The Chinese will bend over backwards to protect their local Chinese relationships above all else, as these are the things that nurture them through their lives. He said we should have spoken with the informal Chinese leader in the branch staff and offered to the other local staff, through him, to do the following:

- Ask that the money be returned, but confirm no action would be taken against the party who had stolen it
- Promise to set up a five-year benevolent trust fund for the local Chinese staff funded by the returned monies, and managed by the ANZ as sole trustee under written agreement with the Chinese branch staff
- Offer to add $5,000 per annum to that fund for five years
- The trust fund would be paid out in equal shares to all staff present today, who were still employed with the branch at the end of those five years
- The trust fund monies would only be paid out on the absolute condition that no further theft of money by staff occur from the branch over that time; otherwise these monies would be forfeited to ANZ.

This solution was very likely to work said Fons because it delivered an outcome to the Chinese community whereby the actions of the thief were standing in the way of their communal good. That would change the problem to be one where they had the incentive to solve it amongst themselves. The ANZ would also have some significant insurance against any further staff defalcations, and also there was now a great incentive for the retention of key employees during a time when there was rapid turnover amongst locally-engaged staff in China. And morale at the branch was likely to improve, as well as productivity, because ANZ was an employer that showed it cared, and also understood where Chinese values could integrate with those of the west. Yes the ANZ audit-heads might have been unhappy as we wouldn't have got immediate title to the money back, but we weren't going to anyway, were we? A fact we all knew, because no reasonable western attempt to do that had worked, with or without Chinese constabulary assistance.

I wished I had tried my mentor's solution. It was far better than mine and it probably would have worked. What's more I checked it informally later with the CEO of ANZ and he felt the board would have accepted it, especially considering where we had ended up – without the money and with no-one in either country feeling much good about the whole damn thing.

This story illustrates that within the 50/30/20 sourcing for career and workplace learnings that was discussed in the introduction to this book, it is likely that knowledge and experiences coming from mentoring will include some of the most significant insights you are ever likely to encounter in your lifetime. So always seek advice from your mentor and listen to it, no matter how great your experience or wide your responsibilities. Remember to discuss critical challenges with him or her when they are a 'work in progress', and preferably well before the point of no return is reached.

Western zero-sum game logic doesn't usually work that well in China.

Mentoring and the Value of a Human Life Abroad

1. Across cultures and societies of the east and west, there is enormous variation in the value placed on a human life and the varying national laws under which it can be taken away. The greatest cross-cultural differences exist between western democratic societies like the USA, Canada and Australia on the one hand, and the statism of China, the feudalism of the Arab world, the strength of tribalism in parts of Africa, and even parts of a more modern and democratic East Asia. Globalisation has pushed different national value systems together into single workplaces, and in a way that sometimes defies the logic of our traditional mono-cultural teachings. Mentors with international understanding and experiences are a prime way for this knowledge and experience gap to be closed by a young professional worker.
2. Sometimes the clash of two cultural value systems can have life and death implications, as it did in the Shanghai branch case. These prospects can produce an amygdala attack in the mind of a mentee, who is untrained to analyse, assess and remedy what he or she is being confronted with. In fact, even finding ways to cope will provide a major challenge. Contact with your mentor is a recommended solution. More than likely that person will have encountered similar experiences in their own life, or know someone within their own network to whom you can go, in order to try and make some sense of it all.
3. Cross-cultural skills are dynamic and cannot be rote-learned. For most international organisations, there will need to be a readily accessible or resident elder or mentor available to discuss the common ethical and moral dilemmas emerging for people drawn from one culture, and who find themselves working for extensive periods with another.

4. Some of these dilemmas may easily become life and death choices, as they did in the Shanghai branch case. The nature of such dilemmas will often be vested in two or more cultural systems and practices. It is here that utilisation of a mentor with a different cultural training context to yourself can be of inestimable value as the world of business continues to globalise and integrate across national boundaries.
5. Despite the sometimes extreme nature of these challenges, the option for achieving a 'win-win' solution is almost always there and available to be taken. To understand that opportunity, a person may need not only to look at the competing cultural issues through a different lens and focus, but also to let go some of their own traditional notions, e.g. to find the 'guilty party', when the evidence is that the continued application of one's own value system and practices won't succeed in doing that.
6. In large and complex business organisations, having access to a world cross-cultural expert to act as your adviser and mentor is becoming mandatory. However, you also need to remember to call on your mentor at times of extreme need, and not to rely on the Lone Ranger approach.

16

MENTORING WRAP

It would be nice to think that a working career will proceed with no real problems, reputational risks, or life and death challenges along the way. Possible – but these days that's very unlikely. It's the same with life itself for most of us, excluding perhaps those lucky ones in life, but there really aren't too many of those around today. In my experience, mentors can hold the key to both confirming initial sound judgments or to pinpointing a superior outcome (as in the Shanghai branch case). We are all like Telemachus after all – young at heart, hopeful in spirit and in need of strong nurturing and conditioning for what lies ahead. At these times in our life, we can feel besieged by matters that seem too big for us. We all need help and a mentor can provide that – if we can find him or her, and then use that experience well.

The good news is that mentoring has been rediscovered for its fundamental benefit and the inevitable quest for truth and peace in our ever-more complex lives. Something old is indeed new again.

Positive mentors aren't just 'nice to haves' in your career. They are now an essential tool of trade, in this ever-more globalised world of commerce where ethics and ethical dilemmas are getting stretched out around us every day we go to work.

But how best to go about that? Does one-size mentoring fit all? Whilst there are some core universal elements to all forms of mentoring, there are also differences – especially with the circumstances whereby you will find the greatest value.

First of all, mentoring is a proactive bespoke art that confers rights but also places obligations on both mentor and mentee. As a relatively new rediscovery in human learning, many participants rock up for their first day with this new found experience having relatively little idea about what they are supposed to do, or how to go about it. Tentative starts and embarrassing moments at the get-go are common experiences amongst new mentors and mentees. Hopefully this book gives a strong supply of techniques and approaches that have worked in a wide array of places and career development points to avoid these.

It's worth remembering any mentoring experience will generally have four simple phases.

First, it will be all about the two parties taking the time necessary to get to know each other. That can take a while, but it also needs an adequate allocation of time to be spent together for this purpose alone. Impatience, and an early push into substantive matters before the parties get to know each other well enough, is a common mis-starting point in mentoring relationships. Progressive disclosure of each party to the other is necessary, as mutual trust and confidence needs to build into a deep and sincere relationship. It should be remembered that about 10% to 15% of these relationships probably won't work or will be seen to have insufficient potential, due to inadequate chemistry between the participants. So maturity is needed in these instances to cease discussions, and then to move forward with good grace in order to seek progress elsewhere.

Second, it's about getting the right maps, GPS and compasses out. The journey can and should be documented with either clear formal or informal agreements that cover the objectives and the preferred pathways ahead. Like any change program, these may need to be adjusted when necessary – especially as and when a crisis point is encountered by the mentee. A GPS in the sky is useless without a map down below, and vice versa. Taking the career overview at a current point in time is critical, but only if both parties have established where they are on the mentee's journey. Professor Bob Wood's 'me and you; here and there; now and then' is a dependable way to set all this up when you encounter problems starting out.

Third, most significant value generally comes in the second half of the mentoring journey. In this period, there has been sufficient hard work completed by both to take them to their 'ah ha' discoveries, and then finally to the much sought after 'moments of truth'. This is the ultimate test in the value of a mentoring association. Some go the full distance of their unrealised potential identified at the outset. Even those who only get part of the way are usually valuable enough in themselves. As mentors and mentees, don't be too hard on yourselves when the glass is left partly empty. Recognise and celebrate the progress you have been able to make together. No mentoring pair with good chemistry and solid purposeful habits has failed to make significant progress in my experience and review of a wide range of schemes and individual scorecards.

Fourth, it's about being able to say goodbye at the right time – but an 'au revoir, pas adieu'. 'Until we meet again' is the right note to hit. Mentors are only human too. Their ability to help a mentee intensively on a set of career challenges, at a point in time, will be finite. That doesn't stop the mentor and mentee remaining friends and keeping up on an informal and less frequent basis. But it's a different need to that of the intensive journey which the formal mentoring stage may have been.

The most desirable and productive patterns of behaviour for mentees and mentors have been extensively covered in this book. They are summarised below.

The key issues and objectives for mentees to remember are:

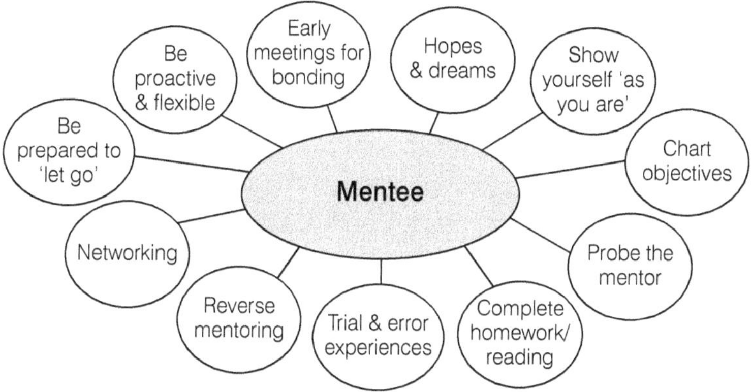

Key issues for mentors are:

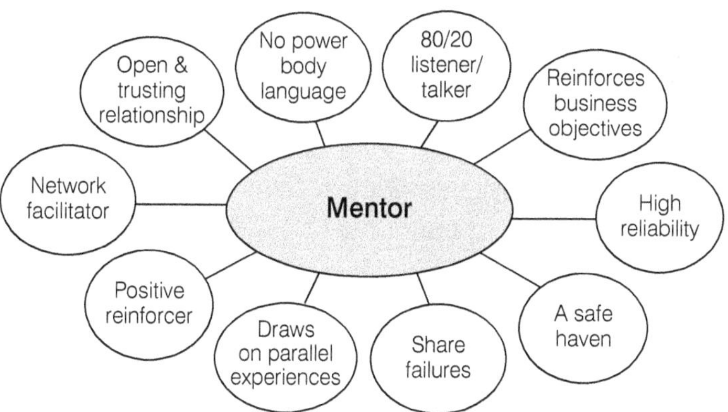

Moreover, the different applications for mentoring now cover an extensive canvas and go well beyond the needs of a specific employer. As well as people in business and government, mentoring is being savoured by the professions, both leaders and cadets in policing, newly-arrived immigrants, asylum-seekers and refugees, kids without parents, Indigenous people, students and élite sportsmen and women living through their own hi-performance cocoon, only later to emerge from their sporting chrysalis and endeavour to take on an equally productive post-élite life.

Within this mentoring panorama, the current generation has put in place more formal mentoring schemes to do the matching, briefing, hustling and hassling for more action where there is none or when it's too slow, and the inevitable progress reviews and reports needed to keep the sponsoring officialdom happy. Not that there is anything wrong with any of this. From an immediate post-war era where mentoring was a casual and informal game of pick up, it has now been recognised for its business fundamentals, and also its organisational and personal value to both participants and sponsors alike. Many schemes well display the necessary fundamentals of being a robust and well-structured process for business and organisational learning, with bespoke tailoring, as necessary for the personal growth needs of the individual. Moreover, it's a process for continual innovation and reshaping as the experiences of the participants yield more knowledge-based enhancements to what's gone on with the latest episodes of mentoring, and what the next generation might benefit from. In this vein, the Company Directors and the Victoria Police Leadership Mentoring Program are two examples of the best schemes around today. But the competition is catching up fast, and innovations in mentoring are beginning to bloom. What's best today will merely become tomorrow's sound operating practice.

Where to Find a Good Mentor

The other key issue is where is the best place to find a good mentor? The evidence from reviewing all the schemes in this book is that the best mentors are usually external to where a person is employed.

There is one critical exception to this rule – those professions operating in harm's way – the police and the armed forces. In all other business and political environments, there is a competitive aspect to life with your subordinates, peers and bosses that is highly likely to inhibit that trust and confidence necessary to establish a full and intimate mentoring relationship, whereby the mentee's genuine career interests can be discussed and enhanced. In the American literature on mentoring, the default case for mentoring is usually for it to be conducted internally within an organisation, and it's often part of either organisational performance imperative, or acts of succession-planning for the senior levels of a company. The dilemma with internal mentoring schemes in business and politics – resourced with local mentors – is that the underlying relationships are often too competitive to allow the process of mentoring to work well, robustly and fairly. As former Federal Minister Lindsay Tanner said, in a career where it's "all versus all", true mentoring won't work with internal mentors. True mentoring is now moving to be about finding the right zone for a mentee's career, and that may mean the mentee giving up on an unsustainable ambition, or moving elsewhere to work. As Michael Rose, CEO of Allens, described in an earlier chapter, being a good mentor may mean advising your mentee about what is in his or her best interests that may not be aligned with those of his employer. Recent evidence has shown many mentors still need to be wary of two traps that they have been trained to avoid – talking at their mentees too much, and reaching in to fix their immediate problems, that just creates a moral hazard that inhibits the necessary skill transfer.

Unsurprisingly, those mentoring schemes built around a professional life, community integration, reconciliation, as well as surviving together against a common enemy, are the environments where mentoring works best.

Mentoring will also fail in situations where torturous triangles are encountered. In these situations the mentee's candour is compromised because the internal mentor is a close colleague of a mentee's nemesis, whether that be the latter's boss or another key relationship on the job. The torture of such triangles is hardly ever encountered when the mentor is sourced externally, or if they are later found to exist. They can then be declared and dealt with in a more straightforward fashion as existing relationships in the workplace are unlikely to be a source of collateral damage.

Mentoring Towards Leadership

At its heart, mentoring is also about 'life leadership'. It's about becoming a leader in your own life with a little help from someone who has already shown it in their own, and whose chemistry matches well with you. At the top end, the leaders interviewed for this book have all had mentors, or have become mentors in their own lives. They have six characteristics in common, and these provide a foundation for their own learnings and the journeys taken through their chosen careers. At the end of the day, they are people who are much the same as the rest of us. Their own experiences with learning from mentors is now being picked up on a much broader front as many seek to be better at who they are and what they do with 'a little help from their own friends'. The six common features of great leaders and mentors are:

- A strong set of core personal and work-based values
- Humility – they see their colleagues and associates as paramount in a life of service to others
- Patience – unflappable seekers of energy and resolve from within; calm on the outside but paddling madly below water's surface like most high-energy ducks
- Vision – there is always a light on their hill; something to be

kept in view even on those totally distracting days at hand

- Mental toughness and resilience – all of us get knocked down, but it's how we bounce back up afterwards that counts
- They work incredibly hard at who they are in their careers, what they do, and how they go about it.

There are some similarities in the above to what Jim Collins described in his internationally-acclaimed book *Good to Great*. But also there is one very significant difference. Collins describes Level 5 Leadership as leaders who are humble but driven to do what's best for the company. These days the core of leadership has moved to the relationship between a leader and doing the best by his fellow man and neighbour in the workplace. Such is the pace of life these days, there is sometimes no escape from the right answer being the one for our chapter of mankind, whatever the organisational circumstances are that we find ourselves in. Fortunately, today's best-practice employers get this difference. There is no point having employees in their midst who are up against the grain of trying to be someone who they are not, or never will be. Sometimes a mentor acting in the best interests of the individual will not also be in the best interests of the organisation that employs the mentee.

Finding one's true north will often come with the help of a mentor's compass, even if it ultimately takes you onto a different career map. Goodwill and being a compassionate employer is something that's blogged and Tweeted about on a daily basis. Those companies that make the right calls on their colleagues will become known as employers of choice. Having or supporting a mentoring program, with external mentors who encourage an individual to make the right decision in the next step for their career, is the best option for all. The collateral damage from the loss of a critical employee for the right reason will be more than compensated by the reputation gains from being known of as a place where there is a genuine interest in, and care for, the people who work there.

An independent and widely-respected mentoring culture has become an essential part of achieving that in business. The trick is to establish one with the necessary integrity that comes from allowing a genuine and independent external perspective to be brought to bear on a mentee's career, and also an appetite for the risks that flow from showing the courage to do that. Today, the competition for top talent demands it. More importantly, the best people understand that, and demand it happen for them too. But that's pretty much all of us, isn't it?

The Mentoring Essence

1. Mentoring is about developing your leadership towards its fuller potential, through the careful and trusted intervention of a wise elder, who has been there and done something similar in their own lives already.
2. Mentoring relationships need to go through four interrelated stages: (1) building upon the foundations of common value sets between the participants; (2) finding the right maps, compasses and GPS; (3) reaching breakthrough points together; and (4) respectfully transitioning out of the relationship.
3. Mentoring skills and practices need care, forethought and attention on both sides.
4. Modern mentoring schemes have emerged in many walks of life and business, and the best have the minimum required number of core components, but also a way of ensuring that there is sufficient bespoke tailoring for the needs of the individual. Both attributes are essential to success.

5. Great leaders and great mentors both display the same six characteristics: (1) strong core values; (2) patience; (3) humility; (4) clear vision; (5) mental toughness and resilience; and (6) an absolute determination through their underlying work ethic.
6. The obligation in mentoring to the individual mentee surpasses the needs of any one organisation or employer. In business and politics, your best mentor is highly likely to be someone who is independent of your present employer, and by definition has your best interests at heart.
7. Mentoring is nevertheless a hallmark of organisational brand and reputation which is forgotten or trivialised at its own peril.
8. The core of mentoring nurtures a most fundamental human need for all of us. At times of crisis and challenge we need someone trusted we can talk to who cares about us with an open heart but also a caring and questioning mind.

EPILOGUE: 'IF' AND 'UNLESS'

Mentoring is a mantle that has now passed to this career mentee.

Like many later in life, my thoughts are to try and help those coming through the next generation of work and life. Energy and passion are positive characteristics that many young adults have, as they must. Sometimes that can take a positive pathway, sometimes it can err into unproductive behaviours and combative episodes. Perhaps too often I find myself confronted by a mentee in anger, and obsessed by a desire to win a battle with a colleague at all costs, or to overcome what they see as deep-seated intransigence on the part of others. There is nothing new in that. Usually I empathise with these feelings as how all executives feel from time to time, and which were indeed similar to some of my own past thoughts.

Often I end up providing my mentee with one or both of the following – Rudyard Kipling's poem 'If', or my own contribution entitled 'Unless', as a means to keeping it all in perspective

If

If you can keep your head when all about you
Are losing theirs and blaming it on you;
If you can trust yourself when all men doubt you,
But make allowance for their doubting too;
If you can wait and not be tired by waiting,
Or, being lied about, don't deal in lies,
Or, being hated, don't give way to hating,
And yet don't look too good, nor talk too wise;
If you can talk with crowds and keep your virtue,

Or walk with kings – nor lose the common touch;
If neither foes nor loving friends can hurt you;
If all men count with you, but none too much;
If you can fill the unforgiving minute
With sixty seconds' worth of distance run –
Yours is the Earth and everything that's in it,
And – which is more – you'll be a Man my son!

A few years ago I wrote a postcard entitled 'Unless'. At the time I had been sailing in the North Atlantic with a close friend. After a heavy-weather sailing episode, we had moored off the coast of northern France, when I put the following reflection into writing for close friends and family. The poem is included opposite.

Unless

It was a hot sweltering summer night as we bobbed around our French coastal mooring
After hours of sleepless tossing, I went atop the main deck for some fresh air relief
Everyone was asleep, and all was still – just as the dawn's early light began to break
From my vantage I could see the shore and a line of sand from tidemark to green hills

By instinct alone, I chose to lower the dinghy and myself into it, casting off towards shore
"Clip… Clip… Clip," as the crisp blade work pushed me to the edge of the tide line
The crimson rays of a breaking dawn burst and filtered the low clouds in the east
The sharpening light was enough to see the low rising cliffs and grainy watermarks

And so I started to wonder – where was I … really??

The lines of sand exposed by the tide were low, flat, smooth and slowly rising
A good safe sort of place to let children swim – or so I thought
And they had been there the previous day – as their sandcastles bore testament
These fortresses themselves were ornate but futile embattlements against the high tide
Soon they would go the same way of all castles in the sand from children's play

The sun was up now but eery – a fiery red centre edged by a golden hue shimmering
It looked warm, but I felt really cold. There was more to this place than met the eye
I reached the low foothills and there it was – an old concrete war bunker
A fixed asphalt cup in the sand, with a hinged lid to keep the heads clear of fire

But something bizarre – no rear entrance. From the front, only one way in and one way out
Here death was certain for young battle men – either you kept away an approaching enemy
Or they entered your coffin to perform the last cruel ritual of a military combatant's life
Hitler had no compassion for his own – no plan 'B' retreat from this cold grey foxhole
'Deutschland uber alles, oder nein' was how they probably felt squatting inside

Beyond the bunker the green foothills rose like rolling steps
No retreat from the bunker but plenty of retreat lines elsewhere
For the open troops falling back, bombs and shrapnel would pave escape's avenue
At least they had a chance! Smarter ones would have avoided retreats to bunkers, I thought

Near the top was a sign in French 'Overlord. L'assaut' …'Overlord – the invasion'
The code name for that monumental D-Day operation launched nearly 63 years ago
But where exactly was I? Then it came – around the corner, another sign: 'Omaha Beach'
The bloodiest killing field immortalised in Saving Private Ryan's merciless opening minutes

I finally stopped and sat quietly atop the hill looking out whence I had come
The sun matured to a bright clear golden circle, proud and rinsed of its early crimson
Sixty-three years before the sand ran red with all men's blood post a likely same dawn
Brothers ran, crawled and shot their way to shore for someone else's greater glory
Soldiers died both sides of those heartless bunkers, whilst others felt trepidation and fled

Very many would never return to see that shore again, or any other
Here was I, the blind-sided intruder and one relatively ignorant witness
To what was and also to what might have been then, and many more times again.
But who among us today would ever really know? ... Unless.

Peter S. Wilson, The Beaches of Normandy, France, September, 2007

Happy Mentoring. Remember – choose your counterpart carefully. Work hard on the basics of who you are and where you want to go, and you will do well. The history of human development and learning guarantees your success in ways you haven't yet contemplated.

And you should have quite a bit of fun along the way, too.

REFERENCES AND BIBLIOGRAPHY

Allen, T., Eby, L.T., & Lentz, E, 2006, "The Relationship between Formal Mentoring Program Characteristics and Perceived Program Effectiveness", *Journal of Personnel Psychology*, 59, 125-153

Argyris, C. 1991, "Teaching Smart People How to Learn", *Harvard Business Review*, May-June 1991

Bell, C. 2002, *Managers as Mentors: Building Partnerships for Learning*, Berret-Koehler, San Francisco

Boudreau, J. & Ramstad, P. 2007, *Beyond HR: The New Science of Human Capital*, Harvard Business School Press, Boston

Brenchley, F. 2003, *Allan Fels, Portrait of Power*, John Wiley & Sons Australia Limited

Brounstein, M. 2000, *Coaching and Mentoring for Dummies*, Wiley Publishing, New Jersey

Brown, A. J. 2011, *Michael Kirby, Paradoxes I Principles*, The Federation Press, NSW

Cascio, W. F. & Boudreau J. 2008, *Investing in People: Financial Impact of Human Resource Initiatives*, Pearson Education, New Jersey

Clutterbuck, D. & Megginson, D. 1999, *Mentoring Executives & Directors*, Elsevier Butterworth Heinemann, Oxford

Collins, J. 2009, *How the Mighty Fall: And Why Some Companies Never Give In*, HarperCollins

Collins, J. 2001, *Good to Great: Why Some Companies Make the Leap... and Others Don't*, HarperCollins

Collins, J. & Porras, J.I. 2002, *Built to Last*, HarperCollins

D'Alpuget, B. 1982, *Hawke The Early Years*, Pan MacMillan, Australia

D'Alpuget, B. 2010, *Hawke The Prime Minister*, Melbourne University Publishing, Victoria

Drucker, P.F. 2005, "Managing Oneself" *Harvard Business Review* article (HBR Classic)

Dychtwald, K., Erickson, T.J. & Morison, R. 2006, *Workforce Crisis: How to Beat the Coming Shortage of Skills and Talent*, Harvard Business School Press

Eales, J. 2006, *Learning from Legends – Sport*, Fairfax Media Publications, NSW

Eales, J. 2008, *Learning from Legends – Business*, Fairfax Media Publications, NSW

Erikson, E. 1980, *Identity and the Life Cycle*, W.W. Norton & Company Inc., New York

Erickson, E. with Erickson J. 1997, *The Life Cycle Completed*, W.W. Norton & Company Inc., New York

Friedman, T.J. 2005, *The World is Flat,* Farrar, Straus & Giroux

Fritts, P.J. 1998, *The New Managerial Mentor, Becoming a Learning Leader to Build Communities of Purpose*, Davies Black Publishing, California

Fischer, T.A. 2011, *Trains Unlimited, in the 21st Century,* ABC Books, Harper Collins Publishers, Sydney

George, B. & Sims, P. 2007, *True North: Discover Your Authentic Leadership*, John Wiley, New Jersey

George, B. 2003, *Authentic Leadership: Rediscovering the Secrets to Creating Lasting Value*, John Wiley, New Jersey

Goleman, D. 2001, *The Emotionally Intelligent Workplace*, Jossey-Bass, San Francisco

Goleman, D., Boyatzis, R.E. & McKee, A. 2002, *Primal Leadership: Realizing the Power of Emotional Intelligence*, Harvard Business School Press, Boston

Goleman, D. 1998, *Working with Emotional Intelligence*, Bantam Books, London

Greenleaf, R.K. 2003, *The Servant-Leader Within: a Transformative Path*, Paulist Press, New York

Hamel, G. & Breen, B. 2007, *The Future of Management*, Harvard Business School Press, Boston

Hamel, G. 2000, *Leading the Revolution*, Harvard Business School Press, Boston

Harvard Business Review (HBR) 2004, *Coaching and Mentoring, How to Develop Top Talent and Achieve Stronger Performance*, Harvard Business Essentials, Harvard Business Publishing, Boston

Harvard Business Review (HBR) 2011, *Guide to Getting the Mentoring You Need*, Harvard Business Review Guide series, Product # 10470, Harvard Business Publishing, Boston

Harvard Business Review (HBR) 2011a, *Leadership Lessons from the Military, Spotlight Collection*, Harvard Business Review Guide series, Product # 11169, Harvard Business Publishing, Boston

Hay Group Ltd published "World's Most Admired Companies" in *Fortune Magazine* annually since late 1990s

Hewlett, S.A. with Peraino, K., Sherbin, L., & Sumberg, K. 2010, *The Sponsor Effect: Breaking through the Glass Ceiling, Center for Work–Life Policy*, Harvard Business Review Research Report, Product # 10428, Harvard Business Publishing, Boston

Howard, J. 2011, *Lazarus Rising*, HarperCollins, Sydney

Isaacson, W. 2012, "The Real Leadership Lessons of Steve Jobs" *Harvard Business Review*

Jaques, E. 2007, *Requisite Organization: Total System for Effective Managerial Organization and Managerial Leadership for the 21st Century*, Gower, London

Johnson, B.J. & Ridley, C.R. 2008, *The Elements of Mentoring*, Palgrave Macmillan, New York

Karoly, L.A. & Panis, C.W.A. 2004, *The 21st Century at Work, Forces Shaping the Future Workforce and Workplace in the United States*, Rand Corporation

Kirby, M. 2011 *Michael Kirby – A Private Life*, Allen & Unwin, Sydney

Klasen, N. with Clutterbuck, D. 2002, *Implementing Mentoring Schemes, A Practical Guide to Successful Programs*, Butterworth Heinemann, Massachusetts

Levinson, D. with Darrow, C.N., Klein, E.B., Levinson, M. & McKee, B. 1978, *The Seasons of a Man's Life*, Ballantine Books, Random House, New York

Maitland, A. & Thompson, P. 2011, *Future Work*, Palgrave MacMillan, UK

Maxwell, J. 2005, *Ethics 101*, Jossey-Bass, John Wiley & Co, New York

McIntyre, A. 2011, *New Corporate Governance Recommendations on Diversity, Tips for Getting Started*, Australian Institute of Company Directors, Sydney

McIntyre, A. 2011, *New Corporate Governance Recommendations on Diversity*, Early Adopter Case Studies, Australian Institute of Company Directors, Sydney

McLennan, K. 2007, *The NeuroScience of Leadership and Culture*, Mettle Group, Sydney

Nicholson, J. & Nairn, A. 1995, *2020 Vision: The Manager of the 21st Century*, The Boston Consulting Group

Nixon, C. with Chandler J. 2011, *Fair Cop*, Melbourne University Publishing Limited, Victoria

Prahalad, C.K. & Krishnan, M.S. 2008, *New Age of Innovation: Driving Co-created Value Through Global Networks*, McGraw Hill

PricewaterhouseCoopers study 2008, "Managing Tomorrow's People: The Future of Work to 2020"

PricewaterhouseCoopers study 2009, "Managing Tomorrow's People: Millennials at Work – Perspectives from a New Generation"

Robb, A. 2011, *Black Dog Daze*, Melbourne University Publishing Limited, Victoria

Robinson, K. & Aronica, L. 2009, *The Element: How Finding your Passion Changes Everything*, Allen Lane, London

Robinson, K. 2001, *Out of Our Minds: Learning to Be Creative*, Capstone Publishing Limited, West Sussex

Schwartz, P. 1999, *When Good Companies Do Bad Things*, Wiley, New Jersey

Schwartz, P. 2001, *China's Futures*, Jossey-Bass, San Francisco

Seligman, M. 2002, *Authentic Happiness: Using the New Positive Psychology to Realize Your Potential for Lasting Fulfillment*, New York: Free Press

Seligman, Martin E. P. 2011, *Flourish: A Visionary New Understanding of Happiness and Wellbeing*, New York: Free Press

Skills Australia 2010, "Australian Workforce Futures: A National Workforce Development Strategy"

Speed, M. 2011, *Sticky Wicket, Inside Ten Turbulent Years at the Top of World Cricket*, Harper Sports, Harper Collins Publishers, Sydney

Society for Knowledge Economics (2009), "Workplaces of the Future", prepared on behalf of the Department of Education, Employment and Workplace Relations, for the Workplaces of the Future Forum, Melbourne

Strack, R., Francoeur, F., Dyer, A., Ang, D., Caye, J.M., Bohm, H., Minto, A., McDonnell & Leicht, M. 2008, *Creating People Advantage – How to Address HR Challenges Worldwide through to 2015*, The Boston Consulting Group (BCG), World Federation of Personnel Management Associations

Sun Tsu, *The Art of War – Second Century BC* – translated by Lionel Giles (2005) – Special Edition, El Paso Norte Press

Sweetman, K., Ulrich D. & Smallwood E. 2012, "Results Based Learning", *Chief Learning Officer Magazine*, Mediatec Publishing, Chicago

Tanner, L. 2011, *Sideshow*, Scribe Publications Pty Ltd, Victoria

Taylor, F.W. 1911, *The Principles of Scientific Management*

Trompenaars, F. & Hampden-Turner, C.M. 2002, *21 Leaders for the 21st Century*, McGraw Hill, New York

Trompenaars, F. & Hampden-Turner, C.M. 2000, *Building Cross-Cultural Competence: How to Create Wealth from Conflicting Values*, Yale University Press

Trompenaars, F. & Hampden-Turner, C.M. 2004, *Managing People across Cultures*, McGraw Hill, New York

Trompenaars, F. & Hampden-Turner, C.M. 1997, *Riding the Waves of Culture: Understanding Diversity in Global Business*, McGraw Hill, New York

Ulrich, D. 2011, "Australian Human Resources Institute MasterClass" Session Notes, Sydney 9-10 June, 2011

Ulrich, D. & Ulrich, W. 2010, *The Why of Work: How Great Leaders Build Abundant Organizations that Win*, Harvard Business School Press, Boston, Massachusetts

Ulrich, D. 2010 "People Transformation: The Path to Turn Down the Downturn" Asia Pacific HR Congress 2010, Plenary Presentation, Bangkok, Thailand, 23 February 2010, Centara Grand & Bangkok Convention Center

Ulrich, D., Losey, M. & Meisinger, S. 2005, *Future of Human Resource Management: 64 Thought Leaders Explore the Critical HR Issues of Today and Tomorrow*, Harvard Business School Press, Boston

Ulrich, D. & Smallwood, N. 2003, *Why the Bottom Line Isn't: How to Build Value Through People and Organization*, Harvard Business School Press, Boston

Ulrich, D., Carter, L. & Goldsmith, M. 2004, *Best Practices in Leadership Development and Organization Change: How the Best Companies Ensure Meaningful Change and Sustainable Leadership*, Harvard Business School Press, Boston

Ulrich, D., Smallwood, N. & Zenger, J. 2000, *Results Based Leadership: How Leaders Build the Business and Improve the Bottom Line*, Harvard Business School Press, Boston

Ulrich, D. 1997, *Human Resource Champions: The Next Agenda for Adding Value and Delivering Results*, Harvard Business School Press, Boston

Ulrich, D., Ashkenas, R., Kerr, S. & Jick, T. 1995, *The Boundaryless Organization: Breaking the Chains of Organization Structure*, Harvard Business School Press, Boston

Vogt, E.E., Brown, J. & Isaacs, D. 2003, *The Art of Powerful Questions*, Whole Systems Associates, California

Welch, J. & Welch, S. 2005, *Winning*, HarperCollins, New York

Welch, J. & Welch, S. 2006, *Winning: The Answers*, HarperCollins, New York

Welch, J. & Byrne, J. 2001, Jack: *Straight from the Gut*, Warner Books, New York

Wilson, P.S. 2010, "people@work/2020: The Future of Work and the Changing Workplace, Challenges and issues for HR Practitioners", Australian Human Resources Institute Publishing

Wilson, P.S. 2010b, "Ethics repositioned front and centre", *Australian Financial Review*, 6 March 2010

Wilson, P.S. 2009, "Time's up for closed-shop on Australian boards", *Australian Financial Review*, 23 October 2009

Wilson, P.S 2014 "Australia in a Globally Competitive Workplace – Challenges and Opportunities" The Twenty Second Kingsley Laffer Memorial lecture, Sydney Business School, University of Sydney, 26th November 2014

Zachary, L.J. 2000, *The Mentor's Guide, Facilitating Effective Learning Relationships*, Jossey-Bass, John Wiley & Sons, San Francisco

Zachary, L.J. 2005, *Creating a Mentoring Culture*, Jossey-Bass, John Wiley & Sons, San Francisco

Zachary, L.J. with Fischler L.A. 2009, *The Mentee's Guide*, Jossey-Bass, John Wiley & Sons, San Francisco

INDEX OF MENTORING PROGRAMS

INDEX

www.ingramcontent.com/pod-product-compliance
Lightning Source LLC
Chambersburg PA
CBHW060355200326
41518CB00009B/1150

9780987542991